THE TROUBLE WITH LITERATURE

CLARENDON LECTURES IN ENGLISH

The Trouble with Literature

VICTORIA KAHN

OXFORD
UNIVERSITY PRESS

Great Clarendon Street, Oxford, OX2 6DP,
United Kingdom

Oxford University Press is a department of the University of Oxford.
It furthers the University's objective of excellence in research, scholarship,
and education by publishing worldwide. Oxford is a registered trade mark of
Oxford University Press in the UK and in certain other countries

© Victoria Kahn 2020

The moral rights of the author have been asserted

First Edition published in 2020

All rights reserved. No part of this publication may be reproduced, stored in
a retrieval system, or transmitted, in any form or by any means, without the
prior permission in writing of Oxford University Press, or as expressly permitted
by law, by licence or under terms agreed with the appropriate reprographics
rights organization. Enquiries concerning reproduction outside the scope of the
above should be sent to the Rights Department, Oxford University Press, at the
address above

You must not circulate this work in any other form
and you must impose this same condition on any acquirer

Published in the United States of America by Oxford University Press
198 Madison Avenue, New York, NY 10016, United States of America

British Library Cataloguing in Publication Data

Data available

Library of Congress Control Number: 2019946477

ISBN 978-0-19-880874-9

DOI: 10.1093/oso/9780198808749.001.0001

The manufacturer's authorised representative in the EU for product safety is
Oxford University Press España S.A., Parque Empresarial San Fernando de Henares,
Avenida de Castilla, 2 – 28830 Madrid (www.oup.es/en).

Links to third party websites are provided by Oxford in good faith and
for information only. Oxford disclaims any responsibility for the materials
contained in any third party website referenced in this work.

Preface

This book consists of the Clarendon Lectures in English Literature, which I gave at Oxford in the fall of 2017. I am grateful to the English Faculty at Oxford for the invitation, and to Lorna Hutson and Ros Ballaster for their hospitality during my visit. I have preserved the lecture format as much as possible, including its brevity and informality, and I have tried to keep quarrels with other scholars at a minimum. I took my brief to be to ask the most important question I could about the discipline—what makes something literary?—and to reflect on this question in my capacity as a scholar of the English Renaissance. I don't pretend to have answered this question to my entire satisfaction. In fact, it's a premise of these lectures that the question is permanently troublesome. But the lectures will have succeeded if they prompt others to test some of my hypotheses on other texts of the early modern period, and of other periods as well.

In writing these lectures, I have been mindful of the bemused objection of a colleague in History that literary scholars are in the habit of making large claims about epochal historical shifts with reference to a handful of literary texts. This is undoubtedly the case here as well. In some places, the argument I make proceeds by synecdoche, as when Sidney, Shakespeare, and Jonson stand for the secular literary production of the English Renaissance. In other cases—for example, those of Hobbes and Milton—my goal is to show what it was possible to think in the mid-seventeenth century, and the startling conclusions it was possible to draw from the confluence of Renaissance humanism and Reformation theology. Hobbes and Milton are the fulcrum between the earlier literary culture of the sixteenth century and the rise of aesthetics in the eighteenth century. This is the case not because they are representative of their time—to the contrary, they are quite exceptional. But their very exceptionality helps us understand in a quasi-allegorical fashion what it means to move from a culture in which religious belief is a gift of God to one in which it becomes possible to imagine such belief as an artifact of human making, a made thing. In both cases, I argue, this reimagining of belief was aided and abetted by the literary and rhetorical culture of Renaissance humanism. The last lecture takes up the topic of literariness after the Renaissance, and focuses on what will strike many as an odd trio—Kant, Kierkegaard, and J. M. Coetzee. Here too the figures function synecdochically for three different views of the relationship between literary making and believing: Kant for the German idealist tradition of aesthetics, Kierkegaard for the relevance of the literary for rethinking belief in the bright light of German idealism, and Coetzee for the fate of the belief in literature in our own time.

Writing these lectures has been a great pleasure, not least of all because of my conversations with the many friends who helped to make them better. I am particularly grateful to Lorna Hutson, who divined the heart of the argument and helped me stick to it. I owe an immense debt to Annabel Patterson, who went over the lectures with a fine-toothed comb, helped me to see what they were really about, and urged me to address a wider public. I have stolen many of her good ideas and tried to live up to her high rhetorical standards. I am profoundly grateful as well to Dori Hale, who read all the lectures with care and gave me comments that were detailed, exacting, and extraordinarily generous; and to Jeffrey Knapp, for his encouragement and probing criticism. At a late stage of revision, Rachel Eisendrath intervened with surgical precision to help me clarify my argument and to challenge some of its assumptions. To all these friends, I am happily indebted.

For comments on individual chapters, I thank Alan Tansman, Ethan Shagan, David Marno, David Bates, Kinch Hoekstra, Jonathan Sheehan, Joshua Scodel, David Quint, Jane Tylus, James Martel, James Turner, Dora Zhang, and Charles Altieri. Alex Walton was a research assistant of remarkable resourcefulness and lightning speed, whose labors greatly facilitated the process of editing and revision. I am grateful to Kathy Eden for her friendship, her work, and a helpful discussion of Quintilian on argumentum; to Louise George Clubb for her interest and encouragement; to Hannah Ginsborg for several conversations about Kant; to Maura Nolan for her knowledge of medieval literature; to Eric Naiman, for an exchange about Russian formalism; to Dori Hale, again, for conversations about fiction and the novel; to George Starr for a spirited email exchange about belief and knowledge; to my editors at OUP, Jacqueline Norton and Eleanor Collins, for their support; and, especially, to Marsha Silverberg, whose unplanned transatlantic flight literally made the lectures possible. To Helene Silverberg, who deserves her own sentence, I owe everything else.

Contents

List of illustrations   xi

1. Literature and Literariness   1
2. Hobbes and Maker's Knowledge   33
3. Milton and the Problem of Belief   62
4. Modern Literariness: Kant, Kierkegaard, and Coetzee   95

Notes   123
List of Works Cited   173
Index   191

List of illustrations

1.1	Title page of Ben Jonson's *Workes*. Royal Collection Trust. © Her Majesty Queen Elizabeth II 2018.	23
1.2	Lorenzo Ghiberti, doors to the Baptistery of San Giovanni, Florence; image of Adam and Eve. © age fotostock.	26
2.1	Frontispiece to Hobbes's *Leviathan*. © The Trustees of the British Museum. All rights reserved.	44
3.1	Frontispiece to [King Charles I], *Eikon Basilike*. © The Trustees of the British Museum. All rights reserved.	66
4.1	Image of Kierkegaard, courtesy of the Danish Museum. The Museum of National History, Frederiksborg Castle. Photo: The Museum of National History.	102
4.2	Rembrandt van Rijn, *Sacrifice of Isaac*. The State Hermitage Museum, St. Petersburg. © The State Hermitage Museum. Photo: Vladimir Terebenin.	106
4.3	Caravaggio, *Sacrifice of Isaac*. Galleria delle Statue e delle Pitture degli Uffizi, Inv. 1890 n. 4659.	116

1
Literature and Literariness

I want to begin with an anecdote that is telling about the discipline of literary study—or at least was for me when I was first starting out. When I was a first-year graduate student at Yale in the 1970s, it was an affectation of the more advanced students to perform their intellectual seriousness by saying that they were troubled by some aspect of a literary text. The moment I'm thinking of occurred in a seminar on Romanticism led by the late Geoffrey Hartman. We were reading Coleridge's mysterious poem, *The Rime of the Ancient Mariner*, which is brooded over by a great white bird, the albatross. I still remember hearing a student say at the time that he was troubled by Coleridge's use of the figure of the albatross. And I still vividly remember thinking, "Really? You're *troubled* by that? You've got to be kidding. You must have had a very easy life."

I never did get the hang of being troubled in this way. But, with hindsight, I've come to understand this scene as a kind of allegory of our profession, in two ways. I can see that the affectation of being troubled was a symptom of the anxiety felt by advanced graduate students, and a pose of existential seriousness about one's chosen career. But it could also be read as staging the trouble with literature more generally, the trouble of how to think about it, where to locate it, the kinds of trouble that (at least in the Western tradition) seem, almost uniquely, to be associated with literary texts as artifacts, made things that stand in a vexed relation to questions of belief and believability, and of which Coleridge's albatross—I now see—is an almost perfect example. It's this kind of trouble with literature that I want to focus on in these lectures, with particular attention to what the literature of the English Reformation can tell us about our discipline.

Specifically, I want to trace the shifting conceptions of the essence of literature by looking at the relationship between poetic making and believing from the Reformation to the present. I begin with the Reformation because of the uniquely vexed relation between literature and belief in this period. In the usual account, literature was vexed during the Reformation because belief itself was newly vexed. After Henry VIII's break with the Catholic Church, one could no longer simply accept the mediation of the priest in spiritual matters. Instead, as Luther had argued, one had to work out one's own salvation through a direct encounter with God's word. This injunction, along with the Renaissance recovery of ancient texts, brought literature to the fore in new ways. Some Reformers worried about the seductions of imaginative literature, and the intensity of their attacks provoked new defenses of poetry and fiction-making. Other Reformers argued that the Bible was itself a compendium of literary forms that encouraged imitation. For both these reasons, it's often argued, the Reformation contributed to or was even largely responsible for the remarkable flowering of English literature in this period.

I think there is a lot of truth to this claim, but the argument I want to make in these lectures is different and in some ways the mirror image of this more familiar account. Instead of looking at the effects of the Reformation on English literature, I want to look at the effects of literature on the long-term legacy of the Reformation. Instead of arguing that the Reformation fostered English literature, I will argue that literature helped undo the Reformation, with implications for both poetry and belief. Specifically, literature, in the broad Renaissance sense of a poetic and rhetorical technology for producing belief, shook the foundations of the Reformation understanding of belief as a divine gift or sign of grace. Ultimately, I claim, literature in this period is one vehicle by which religious belief was itself transformed into a human artifact, whether we understand this as a poetic artifact or a mental fiction. This transformation created the conditions for later and, in some important respects, contrary views, such as the eighteenth-century discipline of aesthetics, with its emphasis on our experience of non-cognitive pleasure in the work of art, and the modern formalist definition of literature, according to which—in Derek Attridge's words—"literature solves no problems and saves no souls."[1] This modern definition of literature, in short, has a history;

this history is intertwined with the problem of belief, and by returning to the fraught years of the late sixteenth and seventeenth centuries in England, we can come to a new understanding of how the trouble with literature has shaped our discipline.

The dialectic between making and believing in Renaissance England also points us to a new understanding of the trouble with literature in the Western tradition. It helps us to see that this trouble did not begin with the twentieth century. Nor, as is sometimes argued, did it first appear with Kant. Historically, literature has always been troubling in the Western tradition, beginning with Socrates' objections in *The Republic*, if not before. But what has been less often recognized is that, historically, this trouble has had less to do with the formal essence of literature and more with its practice and its effects, more to do with literature as an art of construction and the powerful beliefs and actions such constructions can give rise to. To put this trouble in epigrammatic form, we can say that from our very earliest records, literature has been uncomfortably situated—at least for its critics—at the vexed intersection of making and believing. From Plato onward, philosophy has defined itself over against literature's troubling power to solicit false belief. For Socrates in *The Republic*, poetry was essentially a kind of rhetoric, a knack of persuasion that involved no real knowledge. In response, Aristotle defined poetry as an art, with its own canon of technical expertise. Against Plato's condemnation of the poet's false beliefs, Aristotle emphasized instead the poet's skill at making. Not belief, but believability was the poet's goal. In contrast to Plato, then, who thought about literature through the categories of knowledge and belief, Aristotle made it possible to think about believability and probable knowledge through the category of literature.

It's a premise of these lectures that this history of thinking about the relationship between poetic making and believing shaped subsequent literary history in the West and has had at least two consequences. First, literature in the Western tradition—which is to say the activity of poetic making or what Aristotle called poiesis—has almost always stood in a vexed relation to the question of belief. By belief, I mean in the first instance the philosophers' justified true belief, or religious belief in the transcendent God of the Hebrew Bible and the New Testament.[2] But I also mean probable knowledge in Aristotle's sense, and believability, in Cicero's sense of verisimilitude. To say that literature stands in a vexed relation to belief, then, means to conjure up the way philosophical or religious "true belief" may be qualified or subverted in literary texts by plots involving probable knowledge or rhetorical believability.[3] Second, in the Western tradition, any form of writing that rejects the authority of philosophy or theology for the autonomy of human making risks acquiring the attributes of literature or, in our modern parlance, literariness.[4] Literature in this sense questions the authority of philosophy or theology in the Western tradition. From the perspective of such culturally dominant discourses, then, literature is the name of a disturbance in the relationship of making and believing that is uniquely troubling. One of the effects of this disturbance is that belief itself comes to be seen as a made thing, a human artifact. Of no period was this truer than the English Renaissance, as I hope to have shown by the end of these lectures.

In this first lecture, I want to say more about the problem of literariness, understood as the essence of literature. I'll begin with the ways it has been defined in modern literary theory, and the problems I have with these definitions. I'll then turn to the very different Renaissance idea of literariness. In conclusion, I'll address the specific problem of literature during the English Reformation. The next three lectures proceed chronologically. In the second lecture, I will discuss a test case for the definition of literariness, Thomas Hobbes's *Leviathan*. In the third lecture, I focus on John Milton's late great poems, *Paradise Lost*, *Paradise Regain'd*, and *Samson Agonistes*, all towering examples of the problem of literature in relation to belief. And, for the last lecture, I will look at three figures who address the relationship of belief to aesthetic experience: Immanuel Kant, Søren Kierkegaard, and J. M. Coetzee in his intensely philosophical novel, *Elizabeth Costello*, which brings us right up to the present.

1. Modern Literariness

I think it's fair to say that the twentieth-century trouble with literature has taken two prominent forms: the first, a formalist account of the self-reflexivity of the literary text; the second, a critique of this notion of self-reflexivity, one that emphasizes instead the socio-political work of literature. If the first camp emphasizes literariness, the second tends to ignore it; but both sides are working with an entrenched, seemingly transhistorical dichotomy: the literary on one side, the socio-political on the other.

The first version of the twentieth-century trouble with literature is best articulated by the Russian formalist notion of literariness. In an important essay entitled "Linguistics and Poetics," the Russian linguist Roman Jakobson explained how for him the whole question of the literary began as a puzzle about the fact that the same devices that we find in poetry—alliteration, assonance, and other rhetorical effects— also appear in streetcar conversations, political sloganeering, and gossip. Jakobson argued that all these devices are instances of the poetic function, which he also called literariness or poeticity, and which he defined as a "focus on the message for its own sake." By message, Jakobson meant not thematic content but attention to the language of the text apart from its referential function. The poetic function, he wrote, promotes "the palpability of signs, [and] deepens the fundamental dichotomy of signs and objects." In poetry, the poetic function is the "dominant function"; in other genres and modes of writing, the poetic function can be found but always in a subordinate role.[5]

Equating poetry with the dominance of the poetic function might seem to suggest that poetry is a matter of the quantity of literariness, while equating the poetic function with the palpability of the sign might seem to suggest that literariness is simply a matter of figures of speech, such as assonance and alliteration. Jakobson tried to put these misunderstandings to rest. Literariness is, in his words, "not a supplementation of discourse with rhetorical adornment but a total reevaluation of discourse and of all of its components whatsoever." It is not a matter of tropes and figures, but a new mode of perception.[6] Jakobson added this illustrative—and, at first glance, offensive— anecdote:

> A missionary blamed his African flock for walking around with no clothes on. "And what about yourself?" they pointed to his visage, "are not you, too, somewhat naked?" "Well, but that is my face." "Yet in us," retorted the natives, "everywhere it is face."

Jakobson then drew the analogy to poetry: just as "everywhere it is face" for the natives, so in poetry "any verbal element is converted into a figure of poetic speech." Note that Jakobson uses the term "figure of speech" figuratively. He is referring not to technical figures of speech like assonance but to the self-referential dimension of poetry, the way poetic language is always commenting on itself, as the African does in responding to the missionary.[7] While the African's "my body is your face" is technically a metaphor, it is also a metalinguistic comment on how poetry works by calling attention to itself and so inviting us to see differently.[8] If, at first glance, the anecdote makes one uneasy, because it is playing on cultural stereotypes of the cultured white missionary versus the barbaric black African, the point is ultimately to illustrate the provincialism of the white man. What counts as a face, or the literary, it appears, depends on context, even one's cultural perspective.

Yet, even with this definition, the relationship between literature and literariness, poetry and poeticity, remains a source of trouble. Jakobson argued that "The content of the concept of *poetry* is unstable and temporally conditioned," by which he seemed to mean something like the fact that new genres arrive—or fall by the wayside—at particular historical moments (750). But the poetic function, poeticity or literariness, is transhistorical. It is also both more specific and more general: more specific because it is not subject to the law or concept of genre, more general because it is not limited to works of literature but a way of organizing our attention to language across periods, genres, and even disciplines.[9] Minimally, we can say that, for Jakobson, literariness is not reducible to isolable formal features of a text; it is not equivalent to the formal qualities or practices foregrounded by any particular literary regime, but always involves a kind of reflection on those features, a second-level reflection which may be dramatized by the author, or performed by the reader.[10] But what is already clear at this point is that the relation between literature and literariness is itself paradoxical and unsettling: the paradox is that the essence of literature is literariness, but literariness exceeds the category of literature. And this in turn implies that literature "itself" has no essence, no propriety, which is not the least of the troubling things about it.

I think Jakobson is right as far as he goes. But here and in the lectures that follow, I want to suggest that he doesn't go far enough. Following Jakobson, I will use literature in these lectures to name the institution of a specific kind of textual production, governed by a set of rules, which includes a set of recognizable genres (epic, lyric, tragedy, etc.) and a set of expectations about how these genres work. I will use literariness to refer to the literary quality of a text or a kind of literary reading that can be elicited by a text, whether or not that text fits under the rubric of literature. But I also want to quarrel with Jakobson and his followers. Jakobson invites us to attend to the shifting historical definitions of literature and their relation to literariness. But in Jakobson's own work and in the works of those he influenced, it seems fair to say that the historical dimension of this argument fell by the wayside. Jakobson's understanding of the poetic function remains primarily structuralist and formalist. He defines literariness in ahistorical terms as a focus on the palpability of the sign for its own sake, as though it could remain untouched by the shifting historical understanding of poetry.[11] At best, a focus on the palpability of the sign produces semantic ambiguity and heightened perception, but not deep historical or cultural knowledge.[12] I now want to suggest that the same is true of deconstruction, the dominant paradigm for thinking about literature in the 1970s and 1980s. Jakobson's definition of literariness as a quality of linguistic self-reflexivity, narrowly defined, reappears in deconstruction's concern with the self-referentiality of figurative language as the sign of the literary.

Deconstruction, in the American variant represented by Paul de Man, equated rhetoric with figurative language—that is, schemes and tropes. To perform a rhetorical analysis was to attend to the way figurative language complicated any effort to read language as denotative or referential. What Derrida called deconstruction was for de Man the interference between the rhetorical and grammatical levels of a text, or what he would later call with speech act theory the performative and constative dimensions. Texts were not imitations of the "real world," and reading could not be modeled on the perception of this world. Instead, literary texts performed the subversion of such naïve assumptions of referentiality. Collapsing the distinction between literature and literariness, de Man argued that literature simply named those texts that self-consciously (whatever that might mean) performed this subversion of reference.

In advancing this argument, de Man referred frequently to Romantic and modern poetry. But he was equally interested in texts that straddled the division between philosophy and literature, texts by writers such as Montaigne, Benjamin, Hegel, Kant, and Rousseau. Although de Man never put it this way, he seemed to think that a figure like Rousseau fit uneasily into the history of philosophy, even political philosophy, because his texts were so self-consciously literary.[13] It was as though Rousseau knew that philosophy was always already a form of literature. But literature, in this sense, was not a more convincing mode of philosophical argument; it was instead the allegory of the impossibility of such argument.

Because I was interested in this line of thought, I decided to do more reading in the history of rhetoric, and this reading ultimately helped propel my dissatisfaction with formalism and deconstruction, and their accounts of literariness. In the texts of Aristotle, Cicero, and Quintilian I discovered a whole new world of rhetoric, much larger than the world of schemes and tropes discussed by de Man—a world in which persuasion was a social and political activity, in which practical reason was front and center, and in which one could find a comprehensive technology of argument, including not only logos but ethos and pathos. This, as it turned out, was the sense of rhetoric that was important to my chosen field, the Renaissance, and above all to Renaissance literature. (It is arguably also the sense of rhetoric that was important to Rousseau.) Gradually, deconstruction and its definition of literariness began to seem arid and predictable. Rhetoric, as I now understood it, had a social, ethical, and political dimension; at least, it was available for social, ethical, and especially political uses.

This enlarged understanding of rhetoric was encouraged by habits of reading and paradigms of interpretation that were just beginning to surface in the United States in the 1970s, in what we called "theory." Initially an offshoot of structural linguistics and its application to literary texts, theory soon came to encompass a variety of approaches including Marxism, semiotics, and psychoanalysis.[14] Here, the second paradigm for thinking about literature finds its most powerful articulation. In contrast to the formalist notion of literariness, we now see an emphasis on the socio-political work of literary texts, which we might describe as their rhetorical and pragmatic dimensions. This emphasis was fostered by Michel Foucault's insistence on the inseparability of knowledge and power; by Jürgen Habermas' work on the public sphere and communicative reason; by Richard Rorty's pragmatism; and by a generation of feminist critics, including Sandra Gilbert, Eve

Sedgwick, Luce Irigaray, and others. In time, some of these influences were absorbed by New Historicism, and cultural materialism. Ironically, in time, they even affected deconstruction, which was reborn in a newly political form: deconstructing binary opposites was a useful strategy, it turned out, for dismantling political hierarchy and gender difference—at least in theory.

From one perspective, these developments aggrandized the role of literature, as when Richard Rorty argued that once the pretensions of philosophy are unmasked, one is left with literature; or when Stephen Greenblatt gave literature pride of place in the cultural poetics of New Historicism.[15] From another perspective, these developments diminished the distinctiveness of literature by making everything available to the kind of reading that used to apply to literature alone. (This was already the case, of course, with Derrida, who famously insisted that there is no "hors texte.") Thus, for example, Jean-François Lyotard argued that something like the discourse of the sublime informs not only avant-garde aesthetics but also the incommensurability of discourses in the field of politics. Art, for Lyotard, was not so much the object of analysis but a paradigm for thinking about larger political issues. The same can be said of Jacques Rancière, who has recently explored the relationship between politics and aesthetics in terms of the "distribution of the sensible." To be sure, Rancière has an argument about how the paradigm of poetics was replaced by that of aesthetics in the eighteenth century, but he seems chiefly interested in using the aesthetic as a model for thinking about class relations and political exclusions in modernity.[16] In this climate, literariness—which was so central to Russian formalism and deconstruction—is no longer of abiding interest.

I think it's fair to say that, in literary studies, at least in the Anglophone world, a reaction has now set in—which we could call a return to a more familiar notion of literature, and of literariness.[17] I'm thinking here of the influence of a figure like Derek Attridge, who has defended "the singularity of literature," and of Charles Altieri, who has defined the experience of literature in terms of a non-cognitive form of attention to the particular. Both draw on Kant's definition of aesthetic experience as the experience of a particular that cannot be subsumed under a general concept. For Attridge, literature is a singular "event," by which he means that it can't be located simply in a text but requires completion by the reader in the act of reading. But literature is also a particular kind of event, one that dramatizes the inventiveness of the author and produces inventiveness in the reader, not least of all through what Attridge calls the work's "invitation to alterity."[18]

Drawing on Wittgenstein as well as Kant, Altieri defines literature as a language game: individual works of literature are instances of that game, though—in Kantian fashion—they cannot be subordinated to a general concept of literature.[19] Instead, literature works by inviting us to attend to and appreciate the particulars, including sensory particulars, of the text at hand, to see them anew as significant but not as illustrations of a general principle. As formal accounts of literariness, the approaches of Attridge and Altieri have a lot to recommend them, but they also share many of the deficits of formalism and deconstruction. In particular, they assume the equation of the literary with a non-instrumental experience of the particular, to the exclusion of a wide range of cognitive or practical effects of literary experience. In this respect, they remain within the Kantian tradition of aesthetics.

I've rehearsed this history to illustrate what I meant when I said that the advanced graduate student who was troubled by Coleridge could be read as an allegory of our profession. Literature *is* troubling, not least of all in terms of how to define it, where to locate it, how to read it, and what to do with it. I've also rehearsed this history to show some of the limitations of the modern discussions of literariness and to argue for a longer view. On the one hand, Jakobson, de Man, Attridge, and Altieri all discuss literariness as though it were an ahistorical, formal property of literary texts, as though literariness were the same as self-reflexivity, narrowly construed. But if one equates literariness with self-reflexivity in this way—with, for example, a focus on language for its own sake, as Jakobson did—one has already, by definition, excluded earlier ways of understanding literature as a form of making that has the power to affect and transform cultural and political life. On the other hand, those critics who have expanded our understanding of theory to encompass such broad cultural relations of knowledge and power have very often left literariness by the wayside. In this divided landscape, we would do well to remember that literature has a history, specifically a history of relation to other disciplines. The trouble that literary critics and writers have with literature is inseparable from this tangled history of relation.

2. Poetics and Rhetoric

From my perspective as a Renaissance scholar, one of the striking things about most of the arguments I've canvassed is how little engaged they are with the dominant categories through which literature was conceptualized in the West before Kant. From this longer historical perspective, the specific twentieth-century trouble with literature is only possible as a result of forgetting its earlier conceptual location. I am thinking especially of poiesis and rhetoric, as well as the questions that come in their wake: questions about the relationship of literature to reality, about the human capacity to construct new artifacts, and about the conviction, persuasion, or belief that may inform or follow from engagement with a literary text.[20] To think historically about literature and literariness means taking up these concepts and attendant questions about the relationship between making and believing that, I have argued, are central to Western thinking about literature beginning with Plato and Aristotle. It means coming to understand that self-reflexivity and autonomy have different meanings in different periods. In the formalist or deconstructive understanding of the self-reflexivity and autonomy of literature, literature calls attention to its own linguistic makeup and its non-instrumentality; but self-reflexivity may also take the form of literature's reflecting on the authority of other belief-based discourses, just as it may take the form of calling attention, through its form, to our more general capacity to construct the world in which we live. This alternative, instrumental view of autonomy and self-reflexivity, I will suggest, is one powerful strain of thinking about literariness in the Renaissance.

In advancing this argument, I am building on a distinguished body of scholarship concerning the shared resources of literature and rhetoric, especially forensic rhetoric, from antiquity through the Renaissance.[21] Historically, both were concerned with the production of probable or convincing arguments, and both were concerned with persuasion. Whereas Plato criticized rhetoric for its appeal to the passions, which could only distort the auditor's judgment, Aristotle made engagement with the passions and their catharsis central to his account of poetry's positive effects.[22] And whereas Plato denigrated the lesser epistemological value of probable knowledge, relegating it to the status of opinion (*doxa*) or mere belief (*pistis*) in contrast to truth (*aletheia*), Aristotle granted literature the power to give us universal knowledge of what was likely to happen.[23] Probable knowledge was not mere belief in Plato's sense; instead it rose to the level of a philosophical universal, involving a logical judgment of likelihood, one that took into account a range of contingent circumstances, including the character and intention of the actor. In their attention to contingent or mitigating circumstances, such judgments were analogous to equitable judgments in a law court. In this way, Aristotle recast probable knowledge (*eikos*) as a positive effect of literature, as of rhetoric. The poet is not only a "maker of images" (1460b) but also a "maker of plots" (1451b)—that is, a structure of coherence that confers meaning on experience. Thus, when Aristotle describes tragedy as "the imitation of an action," we need to understand the productive or *poietic* dimension of such imitation.[24]

Here it's important to note that Aristotle distinguished poiesis or poetic making from labor on the one hand and action on the other. In contrast to the laborer, whose work was repetitive, ephemeral, and concerned with the realm of necessity or everyday needs, the poet was concerned to make an artifact capable of enduring in the world. In contrast to the man of action who was judged by the ethical quality of his acts, the poet was a craftsman and was judged by the excellence of the product he produced.[25] But poetry also shared something with the man of action insofar as it was thought by Aristotle to facilitate the equitable judgment of the audience. This emphasis on equitable judgment would be transmitted to the Renaissance through the Latin rhetorical tradition,[26] while the understanding of poiesis as making would be reinforced (as we'll see) by multiple currents of Renaissance thought.

Already in Aristotle, however, poetic making was a two-edged sword in relation to the question of belief. Aristotle's emphasis on formal coherence might seem to suggest (as Philip Sidney did centuries later) that, because the poem doesn't assert propositional truths as philosophy does, it cannot lie. And in some ways this is true. But precisely because Aristotle identified the response of the audience with a certain kind of logical inference, he was forced to admit the possibility of faulty reasoning and thus deception. More striking, Aristotle reported that Homer actually taught poets how to create such deceptions:

> It is Homer especially who has taught the other poets how to tell lies as they should be told. This is done by paralogism. That is, when the existence of one thing entails the existence of a second thing, or one occurrence entails a second occurrence, people assume that if this second thing exists, the antecedent also exists or occurs; but this is not so. If, then, the antecedent is a lie, but there is something else that would necessarily exist or happen if it were the truth, one should add this thing to the lie, for knowing this second thing to be true, our mind wrongly infers that the antecedent is true also. The Bath Scene [in the *Odyssey*] provides an example. (1460a)

Aristotle is referring to the moment when Odysseus finally returns to Ithaca disguised as a beggar. Modern readers of Erich Auerbach's *Mimesis* remember the bath scene as one of genuine discovery rather than deception: the nurse Eurycleia recognizes Odysseus by the hunting scar on his ankle. But, as James Hutton persuasively argues, the faulty reasoning that Aristotle describes here involves Penelope. The beggar claims to have met Odysseus many years ago in Crete. By way of proof, he tells Penelope what Odysseus was wearing, including a cloak of purple wool and a gold brooch. In Hutton's gloss, he "correctly describes Odysseus' dress and ornaments and his squire Eurybates. Penelope knows that the description is true and hence wrongly accepts as true the lie [that the beggar met Odysseus] to which it is 'added.'"[27] Paralogism or faulty reasoning creates the mere effect of truth and thus false recognition and unwarranted belief. Terence Cave has referred to paralogism as the scandal of literature: the fact that belief can be manufactured. And Christopher Prendergast has extended this analysis to society, arguing that our ideas of probability—which determine what we find believable in literature—may be a product of the coercions and deceptions of ideology.[28] Aristotle, however, doesn't simply condemn such deception and false belief as Plato did. Instead, he turns his attention to the way genre shapes our understanding of probability.[29] And he goes on to assert, "What is impossible yet probable should be preferred to that which is possible but incredible." Poetic believability may be influenced by society's idea of the probable but ultimately it is a consequence of poiesis, the art of making poetry or what we moderns would call literature.

It's here that we see the considerable overlap between Aristotle's *Poetics* and his *Rhetoric*. Both were arts of making and both were concerned with the production of belief. Just as Aristotle defended poetry as an art, so he defined rhetoric as the faculty or art of finding all available means of persuasion. "Persuasion," he asserted "is clearly a form of demonstration" (1.1). In so doing, he took issue with Plato's attack on rhetoric as mere sophistry. Instead, Aristotle argued, rhetoric taught forms of inference from shared opinion and produced conviction, though not logical certainty. In the *Rhetoric*, as in the *Poetics*, Aristotle also sanctioned the appeal to the passions. The orator must be able "to understand the emotions—that is, to name them and describe them, to know their causes and the way in which they are excited" (1.2). Style, including figures of speech, was only one part of rhetoric, and not the most important. Instead, the most important form of proof was the enthymeme or rhetorical syllogism:

> There are few facts of the "necessary" type that can form the basis of rhetorical syllogisms. Most of the things about which we make decisions, and into which therefore we inquire, present us with alternative possibilities. For it is about our actions that we deliberate and inquire, and all our actions have a contingent character; hardly any of them are determined by necessity.... Now the materials of enthymemes are Probabilities and Signs, which we can see must correspond respectively with the propositions that are generally and those that are necessarily true. A Probability is a thing that usually happens; not, however, as some definitions would suggest, anything whatever that usually happens, but only if it belongs to the class of the "contingent" or "variable." It bears the same relation to that in respect of which it is probable as the universal bears to the particular.[30]

Aristotle went on to divide proofs into artistic and inartistic: the former are intrinsic to the art of rhetoric and include all sorts of verbal argument (logos, ethos, and pathos). The latter are extrinsic to the matter of rhetoric, and include material signs such as contracts, witnesses, oaths, and other such material signs—such as scars (1.2.2–11, 1.2.14–18, 1.15, 1.33). As this discussion suggests, the proofs or forms of probable reasoning that Aristotle explored in the *Rhetoric* are precisely the ones at issue in the construction of a tragic plot in the *Poetics*.[31] The aim of such proofs (*pisteis*) was to produce belief (*pistis*) in the hearer (*Rhetoric*, 1356a19; 1367b30).[32] It was undoubtedly because of these shared forms of proof that for centuries the *Poetics* was read through Aristotle's *Rhetoric*, thereby assimilating his conception of poetry to the rhetorical art of persuasion.[33] At the same time, the long history of attacks on the rhetorical conception of poetry as misleading and seductive suggests that the threats of paralogism and of the manufacture of belief were always just below the surface.

For Cicero, too, rhetoric combined making and believing insofar as it was an art or *technē* designed to produce belief. Even as Cicero departed from Aristotle in emphasizing the civic and moral dimensions of rhetoric, he also drew on Aristotelian ideas of probability and persuasion.[34] In book 1 of *De inventione*, Cicero described the role of rhetoric in the founding of society:

> After cities had been established, how could it have been brought to pass that men should learn to keep faith [*fidem colere*] and observe justice and become accustomed to obey others voluntarily and believe that they must not only work for the common good and even sacrifice life itself, unless men had been able by eloquence to persuade [*eloquentia persuadere*] their fellows of the truth of what they had discovered by reason?[35]

Accordingly, the most important part of rhetoric was invention (*inventio*), the finding of "valid or seemingly valid arguments to render one's cause plausible" (*rerum verarum ac rerum similium quae causam probabilem reddant*; 1.7.9). Building on Aristotle's claim that rhetoric deals with matters that are contingent and disputable, Cicero explained that every dispute involves a question about facts, definitions, the nature of the act, or the legal process, and he proceeded to explore the techniques by which the orator can make his argument (1.8.10). Just as Aristotle emphasized the role of the enthymeme or rhetorical syllogism in producing proof or belief (*pistis*), so too Cicero stressed that the goal was to persuade the audience, to produce a state of conviction or belief (1.17.25: *fidem*) through the use of rhetorical proofs (1.37.67ff.; see *De oratore*, 2.27.116–17). As is already clear in Cicero, the protocols for constructing a rhetorical argument provided rules for interpreting written texts as well. In later centuries, these protocols would fuel the discipline of hermeneutics, including the interpretation of the Bible.[36]

For Cicero, too, the appeal to the passions was crucial to the art of persuasion. Like Aristotle's *Rhetoric*, Cicero's work would become a compendium of commonplaces about the passions which later writers would recycle and revise. But the techniques were formal as well: almost two millennia before eighteenth-century arguments about the use of the cool passion of economic interest to calm the violent passions of pride and ambition, the rhetorical tradition taught the use of one passion to counteract the harmful effects of another. Arguably, an even more powerful insight of this tradition was that the emotion of the speaker could be feigned and the emotions of the audience could be manufactured by rhetorical technique.[37] Such rhetorical techniques might, in the end, even persuade the orator who impersonated a speaker to be moved by his own passion. To make the point, Cicero drew an analogy to the theater: "What can be so unreal as poetry, the theater, or stage-plays? However, in that sort of thing, I myself have often been a spectator when the actor-man's eyes seem to me to be blazing behind his mask, as he spoke those solemn lines."[38] Manufacturing emotion was an essential part of manufacturing belief.

Quintilian took issue with the Aristotelian definition of rhetoric as the art of persuasion, since this neglected the requirement of moral virtue.[39] Rhetoric, in his definition, was the art of speaking well (*bene dicendi scientiam*; 2.15.34), where "well" describes both the skill of speaking and the virtue of the speaker, since no one can speak well who is not good (*bene dicere non possit nisi bonus*; 2.15.34). This means that the orator is a good man whether or not he persuades (2.15.4). Nevertheless, Quintilian devoted quite a lengthy discussion to the various forms of proof in book 5 of the *Institutio oratoria*, noting that "to all these forms of argument the Greeks give the name of πίστεις [*pisteis*] a term which, though the literal translation is *fides*, 'a warrant of credibility,' is best translated by *probatio*, 'proof'" (5.10.8). And he observed, with Aristotle, that "proof and credibility are not merely the result of logical processes, but may be equally secured by inartificial arguments," that is, arguments that do not derive from the art of rhetoric itself but are extrinsic to it, such as material signs of the sort Aristotle comments on in his discussion of paralogism.

Among the crucial supports of proof for Quintilian was "delivery" or rhetorical performance, aided by the passions: "All emotional appeals will inevitably fall flat, unless they are given the fire that voice, look, and the whole carriage of the body can give them.... A proof of this is given by actors in the theatre. For they add so much to the charm of even the greatest poets, that the verse moves us far more when heard than when read...."[40] Although Quintilian tried to hold the line by asserting that "appeals to emotion are necessary if there are no other means for securing the victory of truth, justice and the public interest" (6.1.8), shortly after this he allowed that such appeals were warranted in every part of rhetoric, insofar as they helped produce conviction or belief (6.2.1). The extreme case illustrates the rule:

> The peculiar task of the orator arises when the minds of the judges require force to move them, and their thoughts have actually to be led away from the contemplation of the truth. No instruction from the litigant can secure this, nor can such power be acquired merely by the study of a brief. Proofs, it is true, may induce the judges to regard our case as superior to that of our opponent, but the appeal to the emotions will do more, for it will make them wish our case to be the better. And what they wish, they will also believe (*quod volunt, credunt*). (6.2.5)

Here, too, the appeal to the passions helps produce belief, even a belief that may not be warranted.

In the centuries after Cicero and Quintilian, the rhetorical tradition lived on but Christianity repurposed the criterion of believability as a matter of religious faith. Specifically, the New Testament commentators self-consciously appropriated the classical and especially Hellenistic rhetorical concept of *pistis*, meaning persuasion or proof regarding disputed matters, to refer to the Christian's belief in and assent to the promise of salvation.[41] For some figures, this notion of persuasion paradoxically revived the Platonic critique of rhetoric and poetry as superfluous to true knowledge. In the words of George Kennedy, "Since Christian truth cannot be demonstrated by rational argument, conversion and persuasion result from the grace of God, which allows acceptance or rejection of the message, and not from anything the orator can do."[42] This was the case with Saint Augustine, who lamented his education in rhetoric and his love of Virgil, attributing his liberation from both to his reading of Plato and the New Testament. For others, including Augustine at a later point in his career, the Christian notion of faith as persuasion, along with the figure of Christ as the incarnate logos, could help to revalue the arts of language.[43]

Along with a revaluation of the arts of language went what we might call a revaluation of the passions.[44] While recommending the appeal to the passions in his rhetorical works, Cicero struck the pose of a Stoic sage in his works of moral philosophy. But Christ's exemplary suffering—his passion—gave new dignity to the human experience of the passions. In the later Middle Ages, the imitation of Christ involved imaginatively participating in his sorrows,[45] but already in the *Confessions* Augustine's struggle was not to extirpate the passions entirely, but to channel those passions into the love of God. Marjorie O'Rourke Boyle has argued that Augustine conceived of rhetoric at best as an illustration of a truth conceived on the model of dialectic or logic, and at worst as verbal "fornication," though she also sees in "Augustine's mature doctrine of the Holy Spirit as charity the premise for a rhetorical theology" which Augustine himself did not fully articulate. Although it's well beyond the scope of these lectures to amplify this point, this is a premise that would be developed by Augustine's rhetorically inclined Renaissance readers.[46]

Augustine's concessions to rhetoric can help us understand the Janus-faced nature of Christian faith, one side pointing toward doctrine, the other toward the believer. In *De Trinitate* Augustine distinguished between *fides quae creditur*, faith as belief in doctrine, and *fides qua creditur*, the faith by which the believer believes.[47] It was this second kind of faith that could be aided by the art of persuasion. As Kennedy notes, the fact that faith was a gift of God "might seem to render the Christian orator superfluous, and some Christians thought that attempts at artistic expression were idle ... but the Church always believed that the preaching of the gospel was necessary and came to understand it as part of the process by which God works among men."[48] After all, Christ and Paul were themselves exemplary preachers.[49] For Christians, accordingly, belief was not simply a lower form of philosophical knowledge, nor was it the same as rhetorical believability.[50] Instead, belief or faith referred to the divine gift of persuasion regarding Christian dogma. It was also a form of practical knowledge, and assent to knowledge: knowledge of the promise of salvation.[51] In the following pages, I will frequently use faith and belief interchangeably as my authors did, except when the text at hand clearly indicates otherwise. But I will also use belief or beliefs when doctrinal or epistemological content is at issue, and I will use faith (*fides*) when an author calls attention to the imbrication of religious credulity and rhetorical conviction.

3. Renaissance Literariness

While Renaissance authors inherited this rich history of thinking about persuasion from both classical and Christian texts, the chief influence on the Renaissance conception of literature was the recovery of the rhetorical works of Cicero and Quintilian.[52] Their influence on Renaissance conceptions of poetic making cannot be overestimated. In addition to the features outlined above and in contrast to medieval rhetoric, which was primarily an art of schemes and tropes, of letter-writing and preaching, classical rhetoric was designed to be used in the political forum, the law courts, and public celebrations. This new civic conception of rhetoric was enthroned at the center of the humanist curriculum, and poetry was itself defined as an art of imitation and persuasion that produced practical wisdom and moral effects. In line with the Latin rhetorical tradition, Renaissance humanism introduced a different conception of rhetoric from that of Socrates and a different conception of poetry from Aristotle's. Unlike Socrates, Renaissance humanists construed the art of rhetoric in positive terms; unlike Aristotle, they construed poetry in terms of its rhetorical power to persuade to action. Moreover, whereas Aristotle equated mimesis with the imitation of an action, Renaissance humanists were equally interested in the imitation of prior texts. In fact, one of the things that literariness means in this period is just this allusion to and revision of earlier works of literature and earlier genres.

Here it's important to note that Renaissance writers and readers had a more capacious understanding of literature than our modern notion of imaginative fiction.[53] What was called *bonae litterae* in Latin encompassed a wide range of genres, from moral philosophy to history to epic, from political pamphlets to collections of letters. Sometimes also called *litterae humaniores*, this conception of letters anticipated our modern notion of the humanities, and even perhaps some of the fields now included in the social sciences. There was, to be sure, also a narrower conception of literature and literary fame, as when Petrarch banked his reputation on his epic poem the *Africa*, and Machiavelli—thinking of his own plays—complained that Ariosto left him out of his list of great authors. In Renaissance England, this narrower conception of imaginative literature tended to be called "poetry" or "poesy." But "letters" broadly conceived referred to elite Latin and, later, vernacular culture that was not restricted to literature in our modern sense of the term. By this broader criterion, Thomas Hobbes could think of himself as a literary figure, as could Francis Bacon, John Selden, Anne Halkett, and Lucy Hutchinson. David Hume was still using literature in this sense when he wrote in his autobiography that "literature" was "the ruling passion" of his life, and then went on to equate literature with "the pursuits of philosophy and general learning."[54]

If this was the adult view of letters, what did the practice of literature look like to Renaissance schoolboys just beginning their formal education? With the exception of the Bible and manuals of Latin grammar, the curriculum consisted almost entirely of letters in the broad sense just described: Cicero, Quintilian, Virgil, Caesar, Cato, Pliny, and others. At an early age, roughly between seven and fourteen, schoolboys learned about literature by learning to imitate and thereby make literature. Such exercises took the form of composing speeches modeled on Cicero, translating verse to prose and vice versa, generating copious prose in the manner of Erasmus, or arguing pro and contra after Aphthonius. The student was also instructed to collect commonplaces—memorable images and turns of phrase—which in turn could be used as sources of invention. This pedagogy hasn't received a good press in recent decades—from the early work of Anthony Grafton and Lisa Jardine, who described it as deadly rote learning, to more recent Marxist or psychoanalytic approaches, which have condemned the Renaissance schoolroom as a site of Althusserian interpellation, or a scene of trauma and abuse.[55] But if this pedagogy was so deadly, how did it yield such brilliant results? Judging from the work of Shakespeare, Jonson, Milton, and their contemporaries, it seems far more likely that the message of the Renaissance schoolroom was that writing is generative and that the relationship to the past is best negotiated not by deference but by imitation, understood as appropriation and transformation.[56]

Against modern critics of humanist pedagogy, I want to suggest that the radical, constructive implications of the humanists' rhetorical conception of literature have still not been fully digested. It's generally accepted that Renaissance literature is rhetorical because it flaunts its own rhetorical inventiveness, ostentatiously calling attention to its linguistic *copia* and its manifest fictionality.[57] But Renaissance literature is also rhetorical insofar as it draws on forensic rhetoric to produce persuasive plots, verisimilar characters, and effects of interiority. In so doing, it necessarily raises the question of the relationship between poetic making and believing, as well as between making and believability. Years ago, Joel Altman argued that the forensic structure of argument on both sides of a question (*in utramque partem*) was essential to the structure of English Renaissance drama, which was aimed not so much at producing belief as at generating deliberation about controversial matters on the part of the audience. More recently, in work on Shakespeare's *Othello*, he has suggested that Renaissance writers were equally obsessed with, and anxious about, rhetoric's power to produce false conviction or *fides*, especially on the basis of inartificial proof, such as Desdemona's handkerchief. Kathy Eden has taught us how the forensic rhetorical techniques of Aristotle, Cicero, and Quintilian shaped Renaissance ideas of poetic fiction, including plots whose intended effect was to elicit equitable judgments on the part of the audience or reader. But she has also shown that the flipside of this tradition was the recognition that, as in the Player's speech in *Hamlet*, "an actor in a *mere fiction* [can] 'so force his soul to his own conceit' that he moves both himself and his audience to extremes of passion" that are simply artifacts of rhetorical persuasion.[58] As we've seen, this ability to manufacture passion is closely linked to the ability to manufacture belief, even as, on another level, it calls attention to the artfulness or work of the orator or poet.

Lorna Hutson has also emphasized how the forensic dimension of Renaissance drama enabled the production of character and, in the process, drew attention to the production of the work of art itself. In earlier work, Hutson showed how rhetorical persuasion or *fides* between men served to underwrite the traffic in women in Renaissance culture, as well as to stigmatize women as figures of rhetorical calculation or bad faith. Women, we could say, represented not just the possibility that faith was a construct or an artifact, but also the threat of paralogism, manipulation, or deception.[59] In her recent *The Invention of Suspicion*, Hutson demonstrates brilliantly how rhetorical techniques of *inventio*—in particular the orator's elaboration of the topical circumstances of who, what, when, where, and why—shaped Renaissance dramatic practice, with important implications for the audience's reception.[60] Specifically, for Hutson, the plays of Shakespeare and Ben Jonson do not so much persuade to moral virtue as invite the reader to collaborate in the *production* of verisimilitude—or believability—by engaging in a process of inferential reasoning about the characters' motives for action. Like Altman and Eden, Hutson argues that these forensic techniques of reasoning were drawn from the works of Cicero and Quintilian that were at the center of humanist pedagogy and repurposed for the composition of literary texts. In learning to reason inferentially about motives, the reader or viewer comes to appreciate the act of composition by which the text has been made. In Jonson's words, "posterity will remember the poet and dramatist ... [whom] they can commend" for his "manly" art of composition. As Hutson comments, for Jonson to call attention to his manly composition "is always for Jonson to show—to those manly enough to see—exactly how [the work] has been composed."[61] It is fitting, given this emphasis on the *work* of composition, that Jonson was the first English Renaissance poet to publish a folio edition of his own writing and call it "Workes," after the Latin *opera* (see Figure 1.1).

If the plays of Shakespeare and Jonson show how Renaissance literature was produced under the regime of rhetoric, the quotation from Jonson dramatizes a tension within rhetoric that then affects the way we understand the relationship between rhetoric and poetics. This is a tension between being persuaded to moral virtue and being persuaded to appreciate the poet as a maker, who draws on rhetorical techniques to shape his text. In the first case, rhetoric is a tool of a moral pedagogy that solicits our conviction or belief (*fides*); in the second case, rhetoric calls attention to the autonomous poetic artifact, the activity of poetic making (poiesis), and the production of believability, with only an indirect, if any, relationship to ethics. I use the term "autonomous" here to encompass several related ideas. The poet has his own field of expertise, as Aristotle claimed; he is

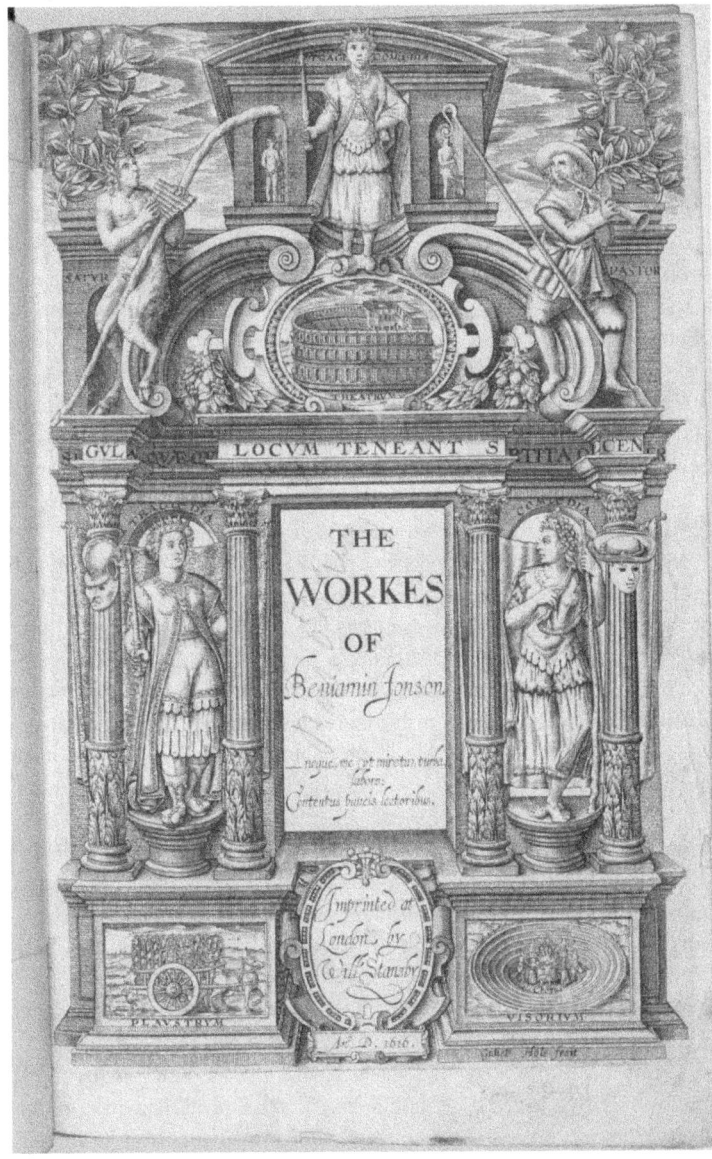

Figure 1.1 Title page of Ben Jonson's *Workes*. Royal Collection Trust. © Her Majesty Queen Elizabeth II 2018.

concerned with invention in the sense of making something new; and he is capable of creating an autonomous, imaginative world.[62] This view of the poet as autonomous maker coincided with Aristotle's view in the *Poetics*, a text that was lost to Western Europe during the Middle Ages (except in a Latin translation of a misleading Arabic paraphrase) but reintroduced in the late fifteenth century by Greek scholars fleeing the fall of Constantinople. Even as Aristotle was read through the Latin rhetorical tradition, he helped legitimize what was already a strong predisposition to describe poetry as a creative and productive activity.[63] In all these ways, the humanists' rhetorical conception of poetry amounted to a powerful rebuttal of Plato's philosophical disenfranchisement of art,[64] and a powerful redefinition of literature, as necessarily involving activities of rhetorical invention and persuasion on the part of the poet and cognition, judgment, and belief on the part of the audience or reader. Poetry, in this view, was not a lesser form of knowledge, but an exemplary one, because of both its capacity to invent and its power to persuade.

In the English Renaissance, the rhetorical and Aristotelian understanding of the poet as maker was intertwined with Neoplatonic ideas of the poet as a quasi-divine creator. There had been a long tradition among Church Fathers of describing God as an "artifex."[65] But it was not until the Quattrocento that humanists such as Marsilio Ficino and Cristoforo Landino drew on this idea to authorize the claim that the poet was himself like God by virtue of his creative powers.[66] Unlike their medieval predecessors, Quattrocento humanists emphasized the ambiguity of the Greek verb *poiein*, which could mean make or create, in order to stress the analogy between these two activities.[67] While this comparison was slow to take hold in the arts of painting, sculpture, and architecture, it was prominent in the literary arts.[68] Landino referred to the poet as a kind of divine maker.[69] Similar ideas can be found in Torquato Tasso, Julius Caesar Scaliger, and George Puttenham.[70] Philip Sidney famously compared "the highest point of man's wit with the efficacy of nature," and urged the reader to "give right honour to the heavenly Maker of that maker, who having made man to His own likeness, set him beyond and over all the works of that second nature: which in nothing he showeth so much as in poetry, when with the force of a divine breath he bringeth things forth surpassing her doings."[71]

This celebration of poetic invention occurred in the context of a general rehabilitation of all forms of making in this period. During the Renaissance, the humanists' understanding of poetry as a craft or art of construction was reinforced by the maker's knowledge tradition. This was the view that we can only know what we make ourselves, a view of knowledge usually associated with Bacon and Hobbes in England, and one that would have a powerful afterlife in the work of Vico and Herder.[72] There were glimmerings of this view in antiquity—Proclus, in his commentary on Euclid, argued that the geometer knows the truth about mathematics because he produces his mathematical constructs himself. The creator God of the Hebrew Bible and New Testament also provided a model of "the knower/ maker *par excellence*," and thus an analogy for the kind of knowledge the craftsman has of his work. But in antiquity, the prestige of contemplation was so high that maker's knowledge never came into its own. And in the Middle Ages the exclusive prestige of God as creator had a similar dampening effect.[73] As the intellectual historian Amos Funkenstein has argued, "the identity of truth with doing, or of knowledge with construction" was seen "in the Middle Ages, ... as the character of divine knowledge," but not of human craftsmanship.[74]

Things changed dramatically in the Italian Renaissance, with the new prestige of artisanal labor and the astonishing development in the arts. Craftspeople, Paolo Rossi argued long ago, "considered their operations to be 'a form of cognition.'"[75] Thus, Lorenzo Ghiberti, the goldsmith and sculptor who created the exquisite bronze relief doors of the Baptistry in Florence, thought of himself not as a mere craftsman but as "an imitator and knower of nature" (see Figure 1.2).[76] This preoccupation with artisanal maker's knowledge coincided with the humanists' interest in the art of rhetoric and its centrality to the reform of education.[77] The influence, that is, ran in both directions. The artisans drew on humanists to defend their newly elevated conception of craftsmanship, while some humanists described poetry itself as an organon of maker's knowledge. Sidney's *Defence of Poetry* is exemplary in this regard. The poet's achievement, he argues, is not only to make "a Cyrus," but to make many Cyruses if his reader will learn "why and how that poet made him"—that is, if the reader imitates the decisions and actions that went into the poet's production of the literary Cyrus.[78] Poetry is important for Renaissance writers not because it

Figure 1.2 Lorenzo Ghiberti, doors to the Baptistery of San Giovanni, Florence; image of Adam and Eve. © age fotostock.

produces in the spectator an aesthetic experience that models impartial contemplative judgment—as Kant would later argue—but because it is itself a form of productive action that is in turn imitated by the reader.[79] It's in this sense that poetry is a form of maker's knowledge.

By the seventeenth century, according to Funkenstein, maker's knowledge had become

> the mark of human knowledge, epitomized in the mathematical physics that showed not only how things are structured, but also how they are made. The identity of truth and fact was also claimed by a new brand of political [theorist] for whom the body politic seemed through and

through a man-made artifact: human society [was coming to be seen as] a spontaneous human construction. A new ideal of knowledge was born—the ideal of knowing by *doing*, or knowing by *construction*.[80]

Along with the rhetorical tradition, this ideal was to have profound implications for thinking about the constructive power of literary texts, not least of all their power to construct religious belief.

Let me try to clarify this last point. The historian of philosophy Jerome Schneewind has traced what he calls the invention of autonomy in the early modern period, the emergence of the idea of the morally autonomous, self-governing individual, whose faculties of judgment and reason can increasingly do without the active presence of God.[81] In the context of the literary tradition, we might characterize this development as one centered on the increasing autonomy of invention, understood as the human capacity for making artifacts, including artifacts of the human imagination. As we've seen, in the ancient rhetorical tradition that shaped so much of medieval and early modern poetics, invention referred to the finding of arguments in one's storehouse of commonplaces. Arguments so conceived were already existing bits of cultural wisdom that one could recombine in new ways, for one's own purposes.[82] The goal was to produce *fides*, conviction, or what the medievalist Mary Carruthers has described as "a confident consent to believe."[83] During the Renaissance, however, the increasing prominence of maker's knowledge gradually transformed invention into something new, something closer to our own modern sense of the term. Invention was less a matter of finding existing arguments and more a matter of making or creating them. Poetry was itself coming to have a new autonomy and new representativeness, precisely because maker's knowledge was no longer one form of knowledge among others (as it was for the medieval craftsman), but a new definition of human knowledge in general. For those who accepted this redefinition of knowledge as a form of making, the meaning of belief—at least, the kind of belief we direct toward texts—was itself transformed. And because the Bible was itself increasingly understood as a text composed by human writers, with a complicated history of redaction and transmission, religious belief also ran the risk of being thought of as a "made thing." This risk is central to the Reformation trouble with literature.[84]

4. Reformation Literariness

I now want to suggest that it was precisely the new centrality of rhetoric and maker's knowledge, and their influence on the contemporary understanding of poetry, that proved to be so explosive at the Reformation. As I mentioned at the outset of this lecture, the relationship between poetry and religious belief was newly vexed at the Reformation because belief itself was newly vexed. In the usual account of the period, belief was difficult because of the new emphasis on predestination, the uncertainty of grace, the conviction of sin, and the vitiation of human agency. The relationship between poetry and belief was also vexed because the dissenting religious movements that Luther hatched held conflicting views of the role of literature in the life of a Christian. For some, the Reformers' emphasis on a direct encounter with Scripture provoked new attention to the literary dimension of the Bible. And this in turn authorized and served as a model for secular poetry. For others, poetry was not only a distraction from religion; it might itself serve as evidence of the fall. In the late sixteenth century, Stephen Gosson, himself a playwright, notoriously referred to stage plays as a "school of abuse," and in the seventeenth century the Puritan lawyer, William Prynne, ranted against the licentiousness of the theater for more than 1,000 pages in his *Histriomastix*. All of this is familiar to students of the period.

My argument in these lectures is different. In my view, belief was difficult not simply because of the rigors of Reformation faith but also because of the challenge of poetic making. This is what I meant when I said at the beginning of this lecture that I am less interested in the effects of the Reformation on English literature than I am in the trouble posed by literature for the Reformation idea of faith.[85] For this reason, I am less concerned with figures like Gosson and Prynne than with a writer like Sidney who fully assimilated the new humanist vision of poetry. Even as Sidney allows for a poetry of divine praise, he insists that "right poetry," poetry correctly understood, involves a purely human art. If he also qualifies this heroic vision of art by insisting that the poet is a fallen creature, this proves to be a temporary concession. And when Sidney tells us that poetry has no rhetorical designs on the reader and does not solicit our belief, this too is double-edged. On the one hand, it amounts to a defensive maneuver against the critics of poetry, by insisting that poetry cannot seduce; on the other hand, the notion of right poetry implies the autonomy of secular poetic making and the sidelining of religious belief. Thus, in the witty peroration to the *Defence of Poetry*, Sidney flaunts the secular meaning of belief when he conjures his reader not only to believe "with Aristotle, that [the poets] were the ancient treasurers of the Grecians divinity" but also "to believe [the poets] themselves, when they tell you they will make you immortal by their verses."[86] Here Sidney ironizes the question of belief: he invites us not only to think of belief as a made thing, an artifact of rhetoric, but also to think of belief as the improbable effect of the poet's own self-aggrandizing claims for his poetic fictions. Through his hyperbolic rhetorical claims, Sidney encourages us to see that the act of reading poetry requires a skepticism about thematic claims—including the claim that poetry will make you immortal—that aligns the reader not with the believer but with the poet as maker. By this indirect route, Sidney intervenes in the heated Reformation discussion about the relationship between poetry and belief, and aligns himself with the recently recovered, chiefly Aristotelian view of the art of poetry.

Sidney is not the only English Renaissance poet who can be seen as resisting the Puritan censure of literature and, implicitly or explicitly, defending a purely human conception of making and invention. As I've already suggested, Shakespeare and Jonson also fit this bill, to cite only the most prominent writers between Sidney and Milton. Shakespeare is not immune to the Reformation, but his plays are more about belief than instances of it.[87] It's for this reason, I think, that Shakespeare has long been associated with what Keats called "negative capability." Despite the recent spate of studies that have attempted to revive a Christian Shakespeare who aims to "awake [our] faith," the faith that Shakespeare solicits is—as the statue in *The Winter's Tale* suggests—a faith in art. As for Jonson, it's hard to think of another English poet who cultivated more assiduously and with less religious angst the reputation of a learned maker, whose chief goal was to imitate and rival the works of the ancients. Not belief but judgment is at the heart of Jonson's credo. As he writes in *Discoveries*: "*Non nimium credendum antiquitati* [antiquity is not to be excessively believed]. I know nothing can conduce more to letters, than to examine the writings of the ancients and not to rest in their sole authority, or take all upon trust from them."[88] Jonson invites the same discriminating approach to—or, to use one of his favorite words, the same "understanding" of—his own works. Both Shakespeare and Jonson embrace a secular conception of literariness, just as they embrace belief as a matter of believability, in a way that throws into relief the struggle of their contemporaries.

While Sidney, Shakespeare, and Jonson represent the high point of secular literary culture in the English Renaissance, peacefully coexisting with religious belief, the same cannot be said of their most prominent successors. In the work of Hobbes and Milton, the humanist approach to poetic making becomes a sharply honed instrument for intervening in debates about religious belief. As we'll see in the next lecture, Hobbes drew on humanist rhetoric and maker's knowledge to argue for the invention of the commonwealth. But in a move that was far more challenging to his contemporaries, he also insisted that religious faith was an artifact of the sovereign's construction. Milton, too, I will argue in lecture 3, saw religious faith as a product of poetic invention. Although Milton's understanding of faith was very different from that of Hobbes, the results, from an orthodox Anglican perspective, were similarly mixed. Milton intended to work out his salvation in poetry but, as the reception of Milton has shown, many readers have felt that he instead substituted faith in poetry for faith in God. In both cases, religious belief was profoundly transformed—we might even say reinvented—by its encounter with poetic making.

Here, in conclusion, it may be helpful very briefly to compare my argument about the poetic reinvention of belief to that of the historian Ethan Shagan. In his recent book, *The Birth of Modern Belief*, Shagan argues that the meaning of belief underwent a transformation in the early modern period, partly in reaction to the rigors of the Reformation conception of faith. In the course of the late sixteenth and early seventeenth centuries in Europe, according to Shagan, belief morphed from purely religious belief to belief in the sense of opinion, based on reason, evidence, or experience. John Locke, for example, reduced belief to sovereign judgment, and argued that one believes in religion no differently from the way one believes any other truth claim. This evolution of the category of belief eventually made it possible for humans to believe in the products of their own imagination. Shagan cites as an example the Dutch emigré and political philosopher Bernard Mandeville, who considered much of religion to be a human invention. Nevertheless, Mandeville argued, we believe in religion because belief has social benefits.[89] This is a version of what I have called belief as a made thing. But Mandeville is an outlier for Shagan, who is far more interested in showing the breakdown of the categories of religious belief and opinion, belief and individual judgment, than in exploring arguments about the invention or purely human construction of religious belief.

In contrast to Shagan, my primary concern is not with the history of belief but with the history of literariness. I am less interested in religious practice and doctrinal disputes than in disputes about the nature and effects of literature. From this perspective, it is not possible to trace a simple shift from belief as religious faith to belief as opinion, since the latter conception was always already available within the rhetorical tradition. As I've explained, the Reformation heightened the tensions between making and believing that were constitutive of the idea of the literary from antiquity on. The trouble with literature in this period takes the specific form of a vexed relation between the new prestige of poetic creation and the new rigors of Reformation faith. For at least some of my writers, steeped in the humanist rhetorical tradition of poetics and maker's knowledge, faith itself becomes a human artifact, a product of poetic making. So while I am persuaded by Shagan's account of how it eventually became possible to believe in the products of one's own imagination, I argue that this transformation cannot be understood without attention to literary history, not least of all the history of the troubled relationship between poetic making and believing, rhetoric and faith, during the Reformation.

In the next three lectures, I will be exploring the specific form the trouble with literature took in the English Reformation and the centuries that followed. I take my point of departure from the humanist rhetorical notion of literature as an artifact that inevitably raises questions of persuasion and belief. I then trace the gradual emergence of the idea that religious belief is itself an artifact of human making. In the final lecture, I take up the eighteenth-century discourse of aesthetics, with its suspension of belief, and the emergence of the modern formalist notion of literariness which I canvassed at the beginning of this lecture. As we'll see, modern literariness has a history, one that is predicated on forgetting the more robust notion of the literary that reigned in earlier centuries. The large question I will be pursuing—and it is a genuine question—is whether there is a transhistorical notion of the literary in the Western tradition, understood as a tension between making and believing, that still allows us to respect differences between periods and authors. But, in keeping with my theme, I will also be exposing the many fault-lines in the troubled history of Western thinking about literature, beginning with Hobbes's *Leviathan*.

2
Hobbes and Maker's Knowledge

In the previous lecture I took us from ancient Greece, where Plato memorably articulated the trouble with literature, up to the European Reformation, where this trouble exploded anew, causing people to reconsider what literature could do, why one should read it, and what effects it might have. I would now like to turn to the mid-seventeenth century, when England was embroiled in civil war. In this time of heated political debate, we find an outpouring of pamphlets and newsbooks but very little poetry. In 1642, Parliament closed the theaters, explaining that the times were too serious for mere "stage-playes."[1] The sentiment was much the same during Cromwell's Protectorate. There were, of course, exceptions. One was Robert Herrick's *Hesperides* of 1648, a collection of short poems by a royalist who was sympathetic to some of Parliament's complaints. Another was Andrew Marvell's Horatian Ode on Cromwell (1650), which directly addressed the current political situation. In their different ways, both registered the ambivalence and uncertainty felt by many confronted by civil war and de facto political power. What could literature do but praise ambivalently or nostalgically celebrate a lost sense of community? In this literary wasteland, a relatively obscure figure named Thomas Hobbes burst on the scene with a new kind of writing, one that would decisively shape political conversation and literary activity in the later seventeenth century and beyond. In what amounted to a powerful anti-literary gesture, Hobbes declared his allegiance to Euclid and staked his claim to posterity on the invention of what was at the time an oxymoron: political science, a science of the contingent realm of politics.[2]

Hobbes, who was born in 1588, spent the first several decades of his adult life as a humanist secretary and tutor to members of the Cavendish family, strong supporters of Charles I. Sometime during this period, Hobbes read Euclid and credited this encounter with changing his sense of how to think about politics.[3] In 1640 he published *The Elements of Law* and in 1642 *De cive*, both of which offered early versions of his defense of absolutism. When the civil war broke out, Hobbes, fearing for his life, went into exile in France. In Paris, Hobbes found a group of royalist sympathizers and congenial interlocutors. It was there that he wrote *Leviathan*, which was published in 1651. Greatly expanding the analysis of political obligation that had appeared in his earlier work, Hobbes argued for absolute sovereignty based on the consent of the political subject to be represented or personated by the sovereign. The analysis was also far more polemical than his earlier work. In parts 1 and 2, in a shocking disavowal of his own humanist education, Hobbes blamed the entire civil war on the reading of Greek and Latin classics and proposed that logical reasoning alone could induce consent to political obligation. Then, in what appeared to be a 180-degree turn, in parts 3 and 4 Hobbes seemed to forget his rational, scientific analysis and become a Reformation theologian, taking on the Anglican Church and offering his own feisty interpretations of the biblical meaning of such vexed terms as "spirit," "angel," and "inspiration."[4] What do the two parts of *Leviathan* have to do with each other, and what do they tell us about Hobbes's antipathy to literature and his new mode of writing?

Literature for Hobbes was dangerous to the extent that it was informed by seditious beliefs and fostered them in its readers. Some of these beliefs were ancient and secular, such as the belief in a republican form of government that one could learn about from reading Aristotle and Cicero. Others were Christian and contemporary, such as the belief that God himself authorized political resistance and rebellion. Parts 1 and 2 of *Leviathan* deal with the first set of beliefs, parts 3 and 4 with the second set of beliefs. Or, as Hobbes described the topics of these chapters in the "Review and Conclusion" to *Leviathan*, the first two parts dealt with "the Venime of Heathen Politicians," while the last two addressed "the Incantation of Deceiving Spirits."[5] For Hobbes, then, literature and belief were deeply and dangerously intertwined. The solution to the political crisis was not literature, but political science.

Yet despite Hobbes's trouble with literature, *Leviathan* is one of the great literary works of seventeenth-century England, a work that deserves to be read and taught by literary scholars as much as by historians of political thought. *Leviathan* is not literary according to the twentieth-century definition of Roman Jakobson, for whom literariness involves a focus on poetic devices for their own sake. Nor is it literary because it brings to the fore the irreducible particularity or alterity of human experience, as Derek Attridge and Charles Altieri, among others, have argued in recent years. Rather, it is literary in early modern terms because rhetoric is at the heart of Hobbes's undertaking, both the attack on it and the repurposing of it to persuade the reader to a new view of political obligation and a new understanding of religious belief. It is literary as well because invention and fiction are central to its makeup. And it is literary in what I have suggested are trans-historical terms, because it takes up the question of the relation of poetic making to believing.

Hobbes himself says as much in the conclusion to *Leviathan*. There he ventriloquizes the view that "In all Deliberations, and in all Pleadings, the faculty of solid Reasoning is necessary: for without it, the Resolutions of men are rash, and their Sentences unjust: and yet if there be not powerfull Eloquence, which procureth attention and Consent, the effect of Reason will be little."[6] This sentence has often been taken to mean that, despite his antipathy to rhetoric, Hobbes finally conceded its pragmatic value, its usefulness in addressing one's audience.[7] In this view, rhetoric is an add-on, a mere adornment of the truth. This view fundamentally misconstrues Hobbes's argument in *Leviathan*, as well as his attitude toward rhetoric in his earlier works. When Hobbes declares a few lines later that "Reason, and Eloquence, (though not perhaps in the Naturall Sciences, yet in the Moral) may stand very well together," this is because it is the task of moral and political science to be persuasive. In the realm of politics, according to Hobbes, truth should be judged not by the philosophical criterion of logical consistency but by the rhetorical criterion of persuasiveness and the pragmatic criterion of social benefit.[8] Far from being a mere supplement to the truth, the literariness of *Leviathan*—in the Renaissance sense of its eloquence—is a key to its argument.[9] As we'll see, *Leviathan* is as much about the power of language, about the linguistic art of making or construction, as it is about politics. But this linguistic self-consciousness is always in the service of a practical goal. Specifically, Hobbes's verbal art is essential to constructing the commonwealth and disabling the competing authority of religious belief. For these and other reasons, we are justified in ascribing a quality of literariness to Hobbes's work, but one that in its embrace of the pragmatic dimension of rhetoric differs in important ways from modern conceptions of the literary.

In making this argument, I am intervening in the longstanding controversy about the relation between philosophy and rhetoric in Hobbes's work. The central problem of interpretation here is that Hobbes was critical of the seditious power of rhetoric, and explicitly declared that he had put the study of politics on a new scientific foundation. What then are we to make of the rhetorical brilliance of *Leviathan*?[10] I share the view of Timothy Raylor that Hobbes was from the beginning of his career skeptical of the civic humanist assumptions of Ciceronian rhetoric, according to which the ideal orator is a good man skilled in speaking. I agree that, for Hobbes, Aristotle's morally neutral conception of rhetoric as the technique of finding the best available means of persuasion was far more important. I take seriously Hobbes's claim that his goal was to put politics on a new scientific basis, by reasoning from agreed-upon definitions to certain conclusions. But I do not believe that Hobbes thought this dictated the exclusion of rhetoric. The question is, under what terms did he allow rhetoric a role in his argument?

Here I cannot agree with Raylor or, for that matter, Quentin Skinner, when they argue that, despite his allegiance to science, Hobbes in *Leviathan* nevertheless found a use for rhetoric understood as a means of dressing up philosophical truths or engaging in controversial argument. The conception of rhetoric as "dress" or "ornament"—as *elocutio* or style—doesn't do justice to Hobbes's practical conception of philosophy or to the centrality of rhetoric in the argument of *Leviathan*.[11] It doesn't do justice to the fact that for Hobbes, as Jeffrey Barnouw has argued, persuasion "wins belief by offering arguments that appeal to an audience on grounds less certain than logical demonstration, but are nonetheless seen as compatible and even continuous with demonstrative argumentation."[12] These "less certain" modes of argument include the crucial appeal to the passions, especially the passion of fear; the central role of legal and poetic fiction in *Leviathan*; and the analysis of political representation as fundamentally theatrical. For all of Hobbes's criticism of humanist rhetoric, he made skillful use of the techniques of rhetoric throughout *Leviathan* because he recognized that his science of politics had to grapple with the contingent realm of human action and the necessity of persuasion. As we'll see, rhetoric here is not simply a supplement to logical demonstration—that is, an illustration of truths that have already been proven—but an essential part of his argument. Ultimately, for Hobbes, political science as maker's knowledge is inseparable from the constructive power of language. Is this in contradiction with Hobbes's claim to have put politics on a new scientific foundation? Raylor refuses to consider how far Hobbes's philosophical practice in *Leviathan* is consistent with his scientific epistemology; he thereby suggests that *Leviathan* might not live up to Hobbes's stringent logical requirements. My argument is that Hobbes's conception of political science was more capacious than the strict definitions of Euclidean science; this for Hobbes was what it meant to adapt Euclidean science to the realm of politics.[13]

1. Hobbes on Literature, Rhetoric, and Maker's Knowledge

Let's begin with Hobbes's trouble with literature. As I've already suggested, Hobbes's complaints about literature were the complaints of a fellow traveler. In his early years as a secretary in the Cavendish household, Hobbes was engaged in humanist literary pursuits. It was at this time that he produced his translation of Thucydides, just the sort of writing a humanist secretary might undertake to advertise his rhetorical skills. As Hobbes was well aware, the humanist rhetorical regime of literature provided one version of practical knowledge—a view of how to make things with words—that was relevant to the sphere of politics. And yet, already in the Thucydides translation, we see Hobbes's ambition to reform humanist rhetoric from within. Like Hobbes, Thucydides viewed rhetoric as dangerous insofar as it fanned the flames of political dissent. What was required was a less heated, more reliable form of discourse, a dispassionate analysis of political events. Hobbes claimed to find this in what he called Thucydides' "contexture of narration"—that is, the way Thucydides insinuated his political views through his narrative account of historical events.[14] Hobbes's translation of Thucydides was a first attempt at this more reliable discourse about politics. But, in the account of his friend and biographer John Aubrey, Hobbes soon found an even more promising model for thinking about politics in the cool element of Euclidean geometry:

> He was 40 yeares old before he looked on Geometry; which happened accidentally. Being in a Gentleman's Library, Euclid's Elements lay open, and 'twas the 47th *El. libri*. I. He read the proposition. *By G—*, sayd he (he would now and then sweare an emphaticall Oath by way of emphasis) *this is impossible!* So he reads the Demonstration of it, which referred him back to such a Proposition; which Proposition he read. That referred him back to another, which he also read. *Et sic deinceps*, that at last he was demonstratively convinced of that trueth. This made him in love with Geometry.[15]

What impressed Hobbes about geometry was the fact that it offered certain knowledge because we construct the objects of investigation ourselves. Hobbes immediately saw the relevance of this kind of construction to politics: "Geometry, therefore, is demonstrable, for the lines and figures from which we reason, are drawn and described by ourselves; and civil philosophy is demonstrable because we make the commonwealth ourselves."[16] As we've seen, this conception of knowledge has come to be known in the secondary literature as "maker's knowledge." Maker's knowledge—as I argued in the first lecture—is not just one kind of knowledge among others; it is a new definition of knowledge, predicated on the claim that we can only truly know what we make ourselves.[17]

Knowledge here is a matter not simply of epistemological certainty but of power. Hobbes wanted to exert the same sort of power over his reader as Euclid had exerted over him, and he intended his political theory to have the force (though not the exact form) of Euclidean demonstration.[18] But he did not simply want to produce certain knowledge in the realm of politics of the sort Euclid had produced in geometry. He also wanted his political science to produce tangible benefits in the real world. As he wrote in *De Homine*, "the end of Knowledge is Power; and the use of theorems (which, among geometricians, serve for the finding out of properties) is for the construction of problems; and lastly, the scope of all action is the performing of some action, or thing to be done."[19] In short, it is precisely because the realm of politics is artificial or constructed, rather than natural, that it can be the object of science in Hobbes's sense. But the corollary is that political science is itself not just a matter of logical demonstration but also an art of making or construction, which is in turn a way of acting on the world.

Hobbes's conversion to Euclid might suggest that he subsequently abandoned his interest in rhetoric, but this is not the case. To the contrary, it's a striking feature of Hobbes's intellectual biography that he composed a "brief" or abstract of Aristotle's *Rhetoric* at the same time as he was developing his new political science. Hobbes's Latin digest of Aristotle's *Rhetoric* was composed sometime between 1631 and 1634, probably as an aid to tutoring the adolescent third earl of Devonshire, William Cavendish, and then published in revised form in English in 1637. As Timothy Raylor has shown, the Latin *Rhetoric* Hobbes was working with was the translation by Timothy Goulston of 1619, which placed particular emphasis on Aristotle's interest in "enthymematic belief"—that is, the production of persuasion by means of the rhetorical syllogism. Moreover, at the same time that Hobbes was teaching the young earl of Devonshire Aristotle's *Rhetoric*, he was also cross-referencing the discussion of metaphor in that text with the comparable discussion in Aristotle's *Poetics*. Hobbes's conversion to Euclid clearly did not preclude a continued interest in the uses of rhetoric.[20]

It's true that Hobbes himself frequently described his new scientific method as one of logic in contrast to rhetoric. The former, he argued, is concerned with reasoning from first principles or agreed-upon definitions to certain conclusions; the latter is concerned with persuasion, and draws on opinion, enthymemes, and appeals to the passions.[21] Yet Hobbes was also capable of allying his new science with eloquence, and absorbing the techniques of rhetoric into the discipline of logic. For example, in *De Cive*, Hobbes was more charitable toward rhetoric insofar as he distinguished between the right use and abuse of this skill:

> Now, *eloquence* is twofold. The one is an elegant, and cleare expression of the conceptions of the mind, and riseth partly from the contemplation of the things themselves, partly from an understanding of words taken in their own proper, and definite signification; the other is a commotion of the Passions of the minde (such as are *hope, fear, anger, pitty*) and derives

> from a metaphoricall use of words fitted to the Passions: That forms a speech from true Principles, this from opinions already received, what nature soever they are of. The art of that is Logick, of this Rhetorick; the end of that is truth, of this victory. Each hath its use, that in deliberations, this in exhortations; for that is never disjoyned from wisdome, but this almost ever.[22]

The eloquence that Hobbes praises is the eloquence that "explains things as they are," rather than one that appeals to the passions and prejudices of one's audience. Here and elsewhere, Hobbes tends to assimilate the right use of rhetoric to logic, thereby enlarging his conception of science to include a variety of modes of demonstration.[23] At the same time, as his equation of knowledge with power in *De Homine* and elsewhere suggests, Hobbes was also interested in appropriating for his new science the victory traditionally secured by rhetoric.

Here we begin to see that Hobbes's application of maker's knowledge to the realm of politics fundamentally changes both the scientific method and its object. This application in turn has implications for the art of rhetoric. As Hobbes was well aware, when Euclid's method was applied to the realm of politics, it had to engage with the matter of human nature. This included not only the passions and interests, but, above all, language. The new method had to avoid the abuse of language, while at the same time drawing on all the available means of persuasion to convince the reader of its conclusions. As in his earlier work, Hobbes approached the realm of rhetoric in *Leviathan* with the reforming zeal of a scientist. To apply maker's knowledge to politics was not simply to reason from established definitions to apodeictic conclusions; it also involved using the constructive power of Euclidean science as a model for the art of persuasion. Accordingly, in *Leviathan*, rhetoric is conceived of as a form of maker's knowledge, rather than as *elocutio* or illustration; instead, rhetoric involves modes of invention and demonstration that are crucial to the construction of the commonwealth. In his *Briefe* or précis of Aristotle's *Rhetoric*, Hobbes defined the art of rhetoric as the "Faculty, by which wee understand what will serve our turne, concerning any subject, to winne belief in the hearer";[24] and he went on to explain that "The beleefe, that proceedes from our invention, comes partly from the *behaviour* of the *speaker*; partly from the *passions* of the *hearer*; but especially from the *proofes* of what we alledge."[25] *Leviathan* is just such a proof designed to win belief in the hearer. And it does so, at least in part, by revising the tradition humanist notion of rhetorical invention, with implications for construction, fiction, and ultimately belief as well.

2. Hobbes on Invention, Construction, and Fiction

This revision of the traditional understanding of invention is explicit in chapter 3 of *Leviathan*, where Hobbes describes the essentially practical orientation of human thought. Hobbes calls this practical orientation "Invention, which the Latines call *Sagacitas*, and *Solertia*." In doing so, he departs from the humanist rhetorical definition of invention as the faculty of finding arguments from one's storehouse of commonplaces. Instead, invention comes to have the connotation of practical know-how, in particular the knowledge of how to produce the desired results. He then draws near to the modern sense of invention as creating something new when he asserts those faculties which "seem proper to man onely...proceed all from the invention of Words, and Speech. For besides Sense, and Thoughts, and the Trayne of thoughts, the mind of man has no other motion; though by the help of Speech and Method, the same Facultyes may be improved to such a height, as to distinguish men from all other living Creatures."[26] Language, which was first authored by God and then reinvented after the Tower of Babel, is the "the most noble and profitable invention of all other." Although we can abuse language by using misleading metaphors and senseless phrases, language is also the necessary condition of the development of our distinctively human faculties, including our rational capacity for logical deduction.[27] Finally, language is the precondition of those voluntary arrangements we know as the "Common-wealth," "Society," "Contract," and "Peace."[28]

Here we see that for Hobbes, language does not simply presuppose the will; it is also the occasion of the vast expansion of the will's powers insofar as it is the site at which new ideas can come into existence and be acted upon. Hobbes sees the development of reason and the will as dependent on language because it is language that allows us to conceive of general names and abstract concepts. These in turn allow us to transcend the limitations of sense. This transcendence may take the form of linguistic abuse, which Hobbes associates with rhetoric; but it may also produce the genuine knowledge that Hobbes associates with logic. As Hobbes writes in chapter 5 of *Leviathan*, "Reason is not as Sense, and Memory, borne with us; nor gotten by Experience onely, as Prudence is; but attained by Industry; first in apt imposing of Names; and secondly by getting a good and orderly Method in proceeding from the Elements which are Names, to Assertions made by Connexion of one of them to another" and so to science or "the knowledge of Consequences." It is important to see that this knowledge includes the knowledge of production: "For when we see how anything comes about, upon what causes and by what manner; when the like causes come into our power, we see how to produce the like effects."[29] The vehicle of both invention and deduction, language allows man to reason about the necessity of creating the commonwealth and then to bring that commonwealth into being. From this perspective, Hobbes gives us the single most powerful early modern example of what, in the first lecture, I called the autonomy of invention, that is, a newly powerful sense that invention is not tied to preexisting forms of argument, including political argument, but is capable of producing the commonwealth from new forms of argument and demonstration.[30]

Together, the frontispiece and the Introduction offer the most eloquent manifesto of the new maker's knowledge approach to politics and the new power of invention. In the frontispiece, the sovereign is literally made up of his subjects, thereby suggesting that the sovereign is constituted by the people. In the Introduction, Hobbes then dramatizes the linguistic dimension of maker's knowledge by comparing the creation of Leviathan to God's creative word: "the *Pacts* and *Covenants*, by which the parts of this Body Politique were at first made, set together, and united, resemble that *Fiat*, or *Let us make man*, pronounced by God in the creation." Invention here is a matter not of Euclidean demonstration but of the creative power of the word. Hobbes then tells us that he will analyze both "the *Matter*" of the commonwealth "and the *Artificer*, both [of] which is *Man*," and he will discuss "*How*; and by what *Covenants* [the commonwealth] is made." In this new science of politics, man is both matter and maker, and covenants are his art.[31]

Hobbes's celebration of the inventive power of language may seem at odds with his criticism of revolutionary rhetoric during the English civil war. But in a sense they are two sides of the same coin. Language is dangerous because it is powerful; that power must be harnessed to persuade to obedience rather than rebellion. While the Introduction celebrates the creative power of language, the frontispiece dramatizes Hobbes's ambition to counteract the revolutionary rhetoric of his contemporaries. He does so by borrowing the motto that is inscribed over the head of the sovereign from one of the culture's most compelling literary narratives, the biblical book of Job. God's powerful silencing of Job is Hobbes's model for his relation to the revolutionary reader, whose fiery ambitions he wants to quell. All of Hobbes's eloquence is designed toward this end. Once we are persuaded to reason about the abuses of speech and the other causes of civil war, we will accept the logical necessity of an absolute sovereign to put an end to the seditious use of rhetoric. Hobbes uses his "powerfull Eloquence" to convert the reader as political agent and orator into something like a passive aesthetic spectator, like one of the numerous spectators gazing up at the figure of the sovereign in the frontispiece to *Leviathan* (Figure 2.1).

Let me now turn to two examples of the role of rhetoric in part 1 of *Leviathan*. At the heart of Hobbes's argument for political obligation in part 1 is the narrative fiction of the state of nature, and the resulting political contract.[32] In rhetorical terms, Hobbes's story of the state of nature is a carefully wrought "argumentum," a "fictitious but plausible narrative" designed to persuade us to accept his argument.[33] As Hobbes would have been well aware, in the *Institutes*, Quintilian had discussed such narratives as instances of legal fictions, whose function was to elicit an equitable judgment on a case.[34] Quintilian was in turn drawing on Aristotle's discussion in the *Rhetoric* (1.13.17–19). As Kathy Eden has noted,

> the role of equity in Aristotle's legal and ethical theory not only includes the concept of legal fiction, but it also corresponds to the role of poetic fiction or *poiesis* in the literary arts. In the *Poetics*, poetry proves superior to history for the same reason that equity is superior to absolute justice. Whereas the historian treats only the particular instance ... —what Alcibiades did or suffered—the poet represents types of men engaged in the actions they are likely to perform.[35]

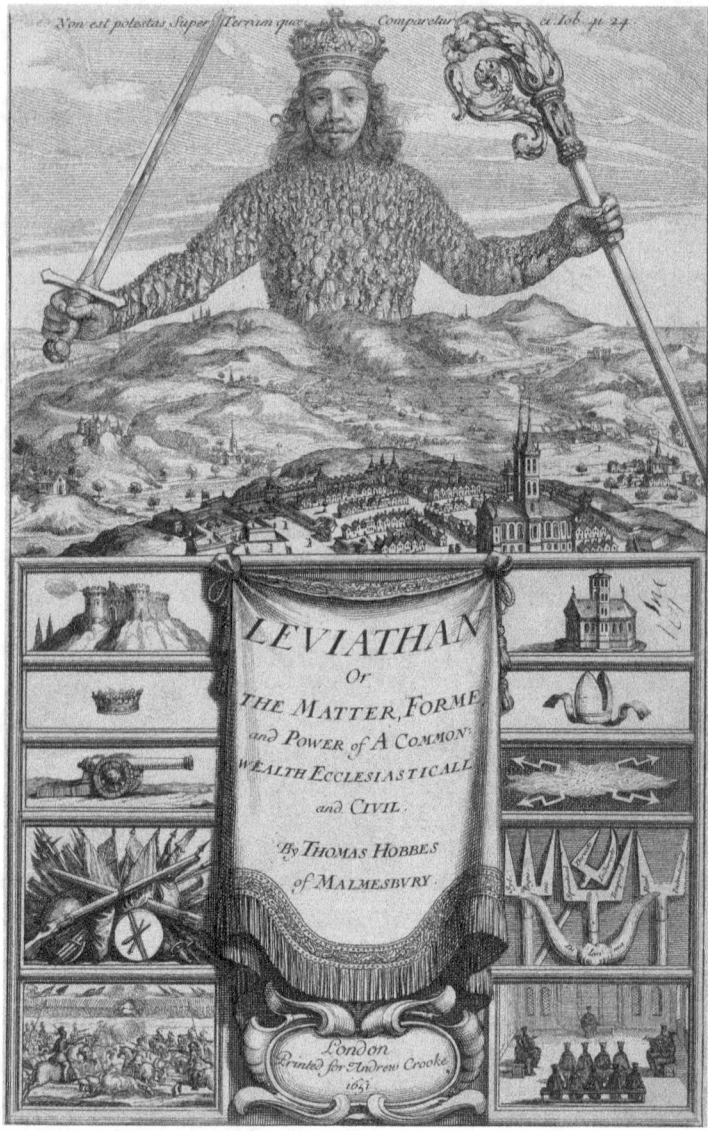

Figure 2.1 Frontispiece to Hobbes's *Leviathan*. © The Trustees of the British Museum. All rights reserved.

Hobbes's rhetorical and poetic fiction functions in a similar way insofar as it represents men in general engaged in the actions they are likely to perform under the extreme conditions of the state of nature. How does this argument work?

The first thing to notice about the description of the state of nature is that it is a synecdoche for the argument of *Leviathan* as a whole. The entire work is characterized by an avoidance of allusion, spareness of figuration, and fondness for understatement and irony, all of which serve to conjure up a world stripped of natural allegiance, historical precedents, and cosmic hierarchy. Hobbes's goal is to rid the reader of these moral and ethical commonplaces, these prejudices and misleading assumptions, in order to reestablish the state from the ground up. The best example of this is the paratactic description of life in the state of nature as "solitary, poore, nasty, brutish, and short," which gives us a vivid picture of our asocial condition, and a powerful impetus to construct a world of our own making. This rhetorical evocation of the desperate condition of individuals, fearful of their own violent death, is a crucial part of the argument that government and political obligation are necessary.[36] The appeal to the passions is thus not ancillary to Hobbes's argument but central to it, for as Hobbes tells us elsewhere, "the Passion to be reckoned upon, is Fear" (14.99). At the same time, it's important to see that this appeal is rhetorically designed to manufacture this passion in the reader, for if readers were already fearful of violent death, and thus already reluctant to engage in the civil war represented by the state of nature, there would be no need to write *Leviathan*.[37]

In short, the fiction of the state of nature is polemically designed to reject history in favor of the work of the imagination as more likely to produce the right judgment in the reader. Hobbes invites us to imagine ourselves in a state of nature—something not all that hard to do for those who had lived through the English civil war. Under these savage conditions, Hobbes asks, wouldn't we agree to delegate our power to an absolute sovereign rather than continue in that state? Wouldn't we want to become the aesthetic spectator, who has laid down his arms to gaze admiringly and fearfully at the sovereign in the frontispiece to *Leviathan*? As Hobbes's readers would have recognized, this fiction both alludes to and revises Cicero's own foundation myth of the origins of society in the eloquence of one powerful man. But instead of eloquence, Hobbes stresses the logical necessity of a contract; moreover, it is not society that is created by the contract but the sovereign.[38] If we are persuaded by this narrative, we then realize we have tacitly accepted the political contract of absolute sovereignty. As Hobbes writes,

> The only way to erect such a Common Power, as may be able to defend them from the invasion of Forraigners, and the injuries of one another, and thereby to secure them in such sort, as by their owne industrie, and by the fruites of the Earth, they may nourish themselves and live contentedly; is, to conferre all their power and strength upon one Man, or upon one Assembly of men, that may reduce all their Wills, by plurality of voices, unto one Will: which is as much to say, to appoint one Man, or Assembly of men, to beare their Person.... This is more than Consent, or Concord; it is a reall Unitie of them all, in one and the same Person, made by Covenant of every man with every man, in such manner, **as if** every man should say to every man, *I Authorise and give up my Right of Governing my selfe, to this Man, or to this Assembly of men, on this condition, that thou give up thy Right to him, and Authorise all his Actions in like manner*. This done, the Multitude, so united in one Person, is called a COMMON-WEALTH, in latine CIVITAS. This is the Generation of that great LEVIATHAN, or rather (to speake more reverently) of that *Mortall God*, to which wee owe under the *Immortal God*, our peace and defence. (17.120; my emphasis)

Hobbes's "as if" makes clear that the act of consent or authorization is itself a fiction, which is to say an imaginative act, which is implied by our obedience to the sovereign.[39] This crucial point was missed by one of Hobbes's most virulent critics, Robert Filmer, in his *Observations* on *Leviathan*. Filmer thought he was ridiculing Hobbes by pointing out the historical implausibility of his account of contracting, as though every citizen had to run up and down England contracting with every other. But Filmer's sarcasm revealed his own excessive literal-mindedness: the absurdity of his interpretation only served to make clear that Hobbes's narrative was a poetic and legal fiction designed to impress upon his readers the benefits of absolute rule. Here, as elsewhere, Hobbes's appeal to fiction is not at odds with his argument but an instrument of it, though with the added anti-rhetorical twist that we are invited to give up our own rights as agents and orators and accept the position of the aesthetic spectator. In his own way, Hobbes thus returns us to the etymology of theory as spectatorship, with the important difference that what we contemplate is not an a priori philosophical truth but rather an artifact of our own making.[40]

Chapter 16 of *Leviathan* also hinges on the notion of legal and poetic fiction, at the same time that it demonstrates and severely constrains what Hobbes means by political representation. As Richard Tuck has noted, the word "representation" does not appear in Hobbes's work before *Leviathan* (though Samuel Sorbière used it in his French translation of *De cive* with the approval of Hobbes), and he hypothesizes that this may be because the term conjured up parliamentary theories of the relationship between sovereign and subject that Hobbes wished to avoid.[41] But in *Leviathan* Hobbes famously devoted a whole chapter to this topic, and in doing so decisively claimed "representation" for his own absolutist political theory. He did so by showing that representation was—to return to Hobbes's own definition of civil philosophy as the knowledge of production—the means or "art" by which the commonwealth was itself produced: "A Multitude of men, are made *One* Person, when they are by one man, or one Person, Represented; so that it be done with the consent of every one of that Multitude in particular."[42]

Hobbes begins by defining a person as he "whose words or actions are considered, either as his own, or as representing the words or actions of an other man, or of any other thing to whom they are attributed, whether Truly or by Fiction."[43] He then tells us that the word person (*persona*) derived originally from the term for a theatrical mask and was then applied to tribunals and oratory, and he explicitly quotes Cicero describing how, as an orator, he speaks in the person or acts the role of the lawyer, his opponent, and the judge. This theatrical genealogy then allows Hobbes to distinguish between the author and the actor: the author is legally responsible for all actions he authorizes the actor to perform; the actor is neither responsible for the author's words, nor legally bound by the actions he performs in character.

The sovereign is created when individuals each authorize the same person or persons to represent or impersonate them, in the way that an actor impersonates a character. Hobbes calls this kind of person—a person who represents another—a feigned or artificial person. In so doing, he draws on the medieval law of corporations, which treated the corporation as a person, specifically a *persona ficta sive repraesentata*, governed by an *actor* or *rector*.[44] But the derivation of persona from the theatrical actor also revises the notion of the legal corporation. While preserving the crucial notion of acting on behalf of the represented, and thus allowing the sovereign's action to be taken as his subjects', the theatrical metaphor also guarantees the sovereign's independence.[45] Just as the actor is not legally bound by the character he represents, so the sovereign is not bound by his subjects. Once authorized, the sovereign is autonomous, literally a law unto himself.[46]

The sovereign as artificial person in turn subtends the powerful fiction that consenting individuals have been made into a unitary body politic: "A Multitude of men, are made *One* Person, when they are by one man, or one Person, Represented; so that it be done with the consent of every one of that Multitude in particular." In this way, Hobbes makes fiction central to his political theory: the commonwealth depends on the construction of the feigned or artificial person of the sovereign, who represents the multitude by "fiction." But fiction here is not equivalent to make-believe; instead, it involves an imaginative, linguistic, and in this case specifically political construction that has powerful effects in the real world. In short, the notion of the artificial person is not just a simile, and "as if" cannot be reduced to the "as" of comparison.[47] The artificial person is not a mere illustration of an argument that has already been made elsewhere. Instead, it is the essential vehicle by which the commonwealth is created. This is because representation is not a logical notion for Hobbes but a theatrical one, and its theatrical dimension is crucial to his argument. It is only after Hobbes has described both the state of nature and the nature of representation that he can proceed to the logical deduction of the laws of nature in part 2.

3. Hobbes on Private Belief and Public Faith

What is the relationship between the commonwealth as an artifact of our own making and the contemporary problem of belief? Hobbes's commonwealth is, in Philip Pettit's felicitous phrase, "made with words."[48] But if constructing the commonwealth had been Hobbes's sole concern, he could have stopped writing *Leviathan* at the end of part 2, which is pretty much where Pettit ends his otherwise compelling analysis.[49] In my view, and I think by the standards of Hobbes's own time, the commonwealth is not the most radical example of making in *Leviathan*. More shocking, I would argue, is Hobbes's application of maker's knowledge to the sphere of religious belief. As we've seen, Hobbes was horrified by the carnage wrought by competing beliefs in the English civil war. In parts 1 and 2 of *Leviathan*, he elaborated his own version of maker's knowledge to solve this problem. But in parts 3 and 4, Hobbes makes what appears to be an about-face and becomes a Reformation theologian.[50] This, I shall argue, is only apparently a rejection of the secular, rational analysis of the first half of *Leviathan*. For what has not been adequately recognized is that Hobbes's solution to civil war involved not only constructing the commonwealth from the ground up in parts 1 and 2 of *Leviathan*, but turning belief itself into a made thing in parts 3 and 4. In these chapters, Hobbes literalizes rhetoric's ability to "facere fidem" insofar as faith itself becomes a human artifact. At the same time, rhetorical persuasion is put in the service of suspending the power of religious rhetoric to incite politically incendiary passions and beliefs. In this respect, parts 3 and 4 are the corollary of the aesthetic spectator whom Hobbes fashions in the frontispiece of *Leviathan*. In these chapters, belief in the public sphere is framed as a matter of sovereign construction, which the reader is invited to contemplate and accept, but not actively contest. One of the more shocking implications of this argument is that God himself is, in the words of one scholar, "not a natural person. He exists only insofar as he is by fiction represented" by the sovereign.[51]

Hobbes's anxiety about seditious belief did not begin with *Leviathan*. In his early work, *The Elements of Law*, in a discussion of the ambiguity of language, Hobbes noted the equivocal meaning of the word "faith":

> [For example,] the word faith sometimes signifieth the same with belief; sometimes it signifieth particularly that belief which maketh a Christian; and sometimes it signifieth the keeping of a promise.[52]

The example is not innocent. Although in one sense the passage illustrates the general problem of the slipperiness of language, which then necessitates a sovereign interpreter to adjudicate the meaning of words, the particular example goes to the heart of Hobbes's project. As Hobbes notes, faith can simply mean belief in general. Sometimes it is equivalent to an individual's belief in Christianity, and sometimes it simply means keeping one's word. While the Christian meaning is dangerous, keeping one's word suggests a solution.[53] The goal of Hobbes's entire political theory, we could then say, is to strip the general term "faith" of its incendiary connotations of individual religious belief and make it instead unequivocally synonymous with the public "keeping of a promise," or contract.[54] From a subjective, potentially antinomian experience, faith must become a merely human artifact. This is the plot of parts 3 and 4 of *Leviathan*.

Hobbes begins the work of dismantling the power of private belief early on in *Leviathan*. In chapter 7, he argues that when we believe anything "not from the thing it selfe, or from the principles of naturall Reason" but from the authority of him who said it, then the real object of our belief is not so much the content of the discourse as the person who told us. This means that when we believe Scripture is the word of God, we do not so much believe in God as believe in the Church that taught us about Scripture. "And consequently, when wee Believe that the Scriptures are the word of God, having no immediate revelation from God himselfe, our Beleefe, Faith, and Trust is in the Church; whose word we take, and acquiesce therein." Hobbes then draws the subversive conclusion: "So that it is evident, that whatsoever we believe, upon no other reason, then what is drawn from authority of men onely, and their writings; whether they be sent from God or not, is Faith in men onely" (7.49). Hobbes thus takes a traditional Catholic argument about implicit faith—that when we believe the Church, we implicitly believe a number of doctrinal positions that are contained within that initial belief—and turns it on its head. Belief in the church is belief in men only.[55] This would seem to be a pretty devastating analysis of religious belief, and that is precisely the point. Hobbes demystifies religious belief as belief in men only in order to deprive it of its independent power, its claim to divine authority. But he also demystifies belief in order to prepare the ground for the argument that, in the public realm of the commonwealth, belief must itself be an object of construction, a made thing. This required a careful sifting of public faith from private belief, an artifact from a privately held conviction.

We see the explicit transition from the autonomy of belief to belief as a construction of the sovereign in Hobbes's discussion of Scripture in chapter 33:

> It is a question much disputed between the divers sects of Christian Religion, *From whence the Scriptures derive their Authority*; which question is also propounded sometimes in other terms, as, *How wee know them to be the Word of God*, or, *Why we beleeve them to be so*: And the difficulty of resolving it, ariseth chiefly from the impropernesse of the words wherein the question itself is couched. For it is believed on all hands, that the first and originall *Author* of them is God; and consequently the question disputed is not [one of authorship]... The question truly stated is, *By what Authority they* [Scriptures] *are made Law*. (33.267)

Here Hobbes tells us that the question of belief is a badly posed question, since everyone believes. Moreover, as Hobbes repeatedly says elsewhere, private belief or matters of conscience cannot be compelled. To the extent, then, that belief is merely private, it is irrelevant to the commonwealth. By contrast, belief in the public realm must instead be understood as something that is made or legislated by the sovereign.[56]

We see the same conversion of belief into a matter of sovereign construction or interpretation in the discussion of miracles in chapter 37. A miracle, Hobbes explains, is a supernatural event done for the purpose of procuring belief, specifically belief in the prophet who performed or predicted the miracle: "A MIRACLE, *is a work of God, (besides his operation by the way of Nature, ordained in the Creation,) done, for the making manifest to [God's] elect, the mission of an extraordinary Minister for their salvation*" (37.303). There is, thus, from the outset, the danger of imposture, given the great power that results from being considered a minister or lieutenant of God. Hobbes begins by analyzing miracles in terms of the criteria of likelihood, verisimilitude, or probability. Unusual events are often thought to be miracles, whereas usual events—even those for which we have no explanation—are taken to be consistent with natural law. "Therefore, if a Horse, or Cow should speak, it were a Miracle; because both the thing is strange, & the naturall cause difficult to imagin: So also were it, to see a strange deviation of nature, in the production of some new shape of a living creature. But when a man, or other Animal, engenders his like, though we know no more how this is done, than the other; yet because 'tis usuall, it is no Miracle" (37.300). Hobbes then turns to the ease with which men are deceived by impostors and fakes:

> A man that hath practiced to speak by drawing in of his breath, (which kind of men in antient time were called *Ventriloqui,*) and so make the weaknesse of his voice seem to proceed, not from the weak impulsion of the organs of Speech, but from distance of place, is able to make very many men beleeve it is a voice from Heaven, whatsoever he please to tell them. (37.304)

Because of "this aptitude of mankind, to give too hasty beleefe to pretended Miracles," Moses urged in Deuteronomy 13 and 18 "That wee take not any for Prophets, that teach any other Religion, then that which Gods Lieutenant, (which at that time was Moses,) hath established" (37.305). From this lesson in reading Scripture for what it has to tell us about false belief, Hobbes draws the conclusion that private belief in miracles must be judged by "the Head of the Church in all times," which in *Leviathan* means the sovereign. And then, just to make sure that we understand the absolute subordination of the Church to the State in such matters, Hobbes adduces as an example of a dubious miracle the Eucharist itself:

> For example; if a man pretend, that after certain words spoken over a peece of bread, that presently God hath made it not bread, but a God, or a man, or both, and neverthelesse it looketh still as like bread as ever it did; there is no reason for any man to think it really done; nor consequently to fear him, till he enquire of God, by his Vicar, or Lieutenant, whether it be done, or not.... A private man has alwaies the liberty, (because thought is free,) to beleeve, or not beleeve in his heart, those acts that have been given out for Miracles.... But when it comes to confession of that faith, the Private Reason must submit to the Publique, that is to say, to Gods Lieutenant. (37.305–6)[57]

In the case of the Eucharist, it is not private belief that confers the status of legitimate miracle but what we might call the "higher ventriloquism" of the sovereign, whom we have promised to obey. Hobbes thus marshals "the human capacity for art" against the artful craftiness of fake miracle-workers (37.304), thereby transforming private deception into a public benefit.[58]

As this critique of miracles shows, part of the way that Hobbes disables Scripture is by turning what he considers potentially seditious interpretation into "make-believe," a different construction of making from his own, one that is instead allied with a pejorative understanding of fiction. Here Hobbes inverts the usual arguments about poetic theology, according to which the first poets were theologians. Instead he implies that all theology is a kind of fiction. In chapter 12 he tells us that "the seed of *Religion* is... onely in Man" (12.75). On the surface, Hobbes is simply distinguishing here between man and other animals who have no sense of religion, but another equally possible construction is that religion is a purely human invention. This possibility shadows the rest of the chapter. Borrowing from Lucretius, he goes on to argue that curiosity about natural causes and fear of the natural world produced the first gods: "This perpetuall feare, alwayes accompanying mankind in the ignorance of causes, as it were in the Dark, must needs have for object something.... In which sense perhaps it was, that some of the old Poets said, that the Gods were at first created by humane Feare" (12.76). Although he distinguishes pagan gods created by fear from the one true God who excites only our curiosity (12.76–7), just as he distinguishes human invention from divine command (12.79), he also breaks down these distinctions by arguing that we can know nothing of God, so that any qualities we attribute to him—such as an incorporeal body—have no cognitive value but serve instead "*Piously*, to honour him with attributes, of significations, as remote as [possible] from the grossenesse of Bodies Visible" (12.77–8).[59] Despite their differences, then, both pagan religion and Christianity retail fictions in the realm of politics, where their shared aim is "to make those men that relyed on them, the more apt to Obedience, Lawes, Peace, Charity, and civill Society" (12.79). But fictions riddled with contradictions and absurdities, or manifestly self-interested fictions, will not do the trick. Hobbes attributes the dethroning of Catholicism in England not only to the corruption of ministers or the contradictions of scholastic theology, but also to the blatantly self-aggrandizing fiction "that a King hath not his Authority from Christ, unlesse a Bishop crown him." Finally, the Anglican Church is itself tarred with this brush: "So that I may attribute all the changes of Religion in the world, to one and the same cause; and that is, unpleasing Priests; and those not onely amongst Catholiques, but even in that Church that hath presumed most of Reformation" (12.85–6).

In part 3, Hobbes cleverly enlists Christ in support of his argument. In fact, it would not be going too far to say that Hobbes makes Christ a supporting character in the plot of *Leviathan*. As all readers of *Leviathan* know, a crucial part of the argument for absolute sovereignty is the disabling of competing claims to authority, above all the authority to interpret Scripture. This involves redefining the kingdom of God: instead of a kingdom coterminous with that of the earthly sovereign that might compete with it for allegiance, the kingdom of God refers to a literal kingdom on earth at the Second Coming. This means that Christ is no longer imagined as a present-day sovereign. His role is considerably more modest: "to proclaim the Kingdom of Christ, and to perswade men to submit themselves thereunto; and by precepts and good counsell, to teach them that have submitted what they are to do, that they may be received into the Kingdom of God *when it comes*" (42.341, my emphasis). A little further on, Hobbes emphasizes that Christ's task is one of persuading; his goal is "to make men Beleeve, and have Faith in Christ." Beneath Hobbes's definition of Christ's office, we cannot fail to hear the classical, secular description of the orator as one who produces faith in his hearers. As we've seen, the Latin phrase is "facere fidem," literally making faith, or making belief.[60] This rhetorical production of belief amounts to an evacuation of its potentially antinomian content: to have faith in Christ here means being persuaded by Christ of the sovereign's absolute authority.

Here we begin to see how Hobbes's rhetorical notion of Christ's office contributes to the making of the commonwealth. In *Leviathan* there is, crucially, a meta-dimension to Christ's rhetorical making. In his role as rhetorician, Christ doesn't simply persuade the individual to believe; he also persuades the believer that there is a separation between private belief and public action. He teaches that private belief—the realm of Protestant conscience—has no purchase on the political imagination of his hearers, and that the faith that counts in the public realm is the faith artificially constructed by the sovereign. In short, instead of acting like the incendiary parliamentary preachers, who used their sermons during the English civil war to stir up rebellion against Charles I, Christ as rhetorician counsels what we might called "the suspension of belief" and obedience to secular authority.[61] In this way, Hobbes uses Christ to construct his argument about private belief as politically disinterested and public faith as an artifact of the commonwealth.

In chapter 43, Hobbes then slyly attributes this construction to the reader. He adduces Christ to remind the reader that the sovereign's making and ultimately faith itself are contingent upon a human promise, specifically the human promise that set up the commonwealth. In the course of a few sentences, the meaning of faith is transformed from faith in Christ to keeping faith with or obeying the civil sovereign, and then to keeping the contract we have made with one another to set up the sovereign. Christ has not given us new Laws, Hobbes declares, but only "Counsell to observe those we are subject to; that is to say, the Laws of Nature, and the Laws of our severall Soveraigns" (404). He then clarifies that "The Laws of God are therefore none but the Laws of Nature, whereof the principall is, that we should not violate our Faith, that is, a commandement to obey our Civill Soveraigns, which wee constituted over us, by mutuall pact with one another" (404). This reduction of religious faith to keeping faith is in miniature the argument of the later chapters of *Leviathan*, according to which transcendental claims regarding the divine object of faith are replaced by the sociable institution of promising.

The conversion of belief into a made thing, and faith into a promise, is prosecuted at much greater length and with biting irony in part 4 of *Leviathan*, "Of the Kingdome of Darknesse." In Hobbes's vision, the world of politics is shot through with the imagination, which requires that we distinguish between good and bad images, enabling and deceptive fictions, appropriate representations and idolatrous ones. According to Hobbes, idols are made things that solicit false belief because unauthorized by the sovereign, whereas the fictions of absolute government are made things that we credit because we have promised to do so. Hobbes goes on to explain that there is "civil war in Christendom" because the enemy has introduced "the Daemonology of Heathen Poets, that is to say, their fabulous Doctrine concerning Daemons, which are but Idols, or Phantasms of the braine" (44.418). In keeping with this accusation, he describes Beelzebub as the "Prince of Phantasmes," and the Papacy as the "Kingdom of Faeries" (46.480). In case we missed the point, he adds

> that as the *Faeries* have no existence, but in the Fancies of ignorant people, rising from the Traditions of old Wives, or old Poets: so the Spiritual Power of the *Pope* (without the bounds of his own Civill Dominion) consisteth onely in the Fear that Seduced people stand in, of their Excommunication; upon hearing of false Miracles, false Traditions, and false Interpretations of Scripture. (47.482)

This critique is not limited to Catholicism, but applicable to the various Protestant factions in England, above all the Presbyterians who insisted on a degree of autonomy from the sovereign in religious matters and asserted their power by means of various politic fictions.[62] Chief among these is the "Doctrine, that the Kingdome of Christ is already come, and that it began at the Resurrection of our Saviour." "But," Hobbes immediately asks, "*cui bono?* What Profit did they expect from it? The same which the Popes expected: to have a Soveraign Power over the People.... The Authors therefore of this Darknesse in Religion, are the Romane, and the Presbyterian Clergy" (47.475–6).[63]

As in the earlier books, this analysis of conflicting interests and competing fictions motivates Hobbes's argument for an absolute sovereign. The sovereign alone must have the power to determine which products of the imagination should be allowed in the public realm (46.461). He is absolute, then, not only by virtue of his power to coerce, but also insofar as he controls the fictions promulgated in the commonwealth. In this way, the Hobbesian sovereign becomes a master of what later critics have called aesthetic ideology. Howard Caygill and Terry Eagleton have argued that aesthetics performed a policing function in the eighteenth century, one that supplemented the coercive force of the sovereign. Insofar as we construe aesthetics as a science of images and affects, one that suspends or hollows out the content of belief, and disables the seditious potential of rhetoric, this police-work is already evident in *Leviathan*.

How, then, can Hobbes pretend to rationally persuade his reader? Parts 3 and 4 of *Leviathan* offer a clue insofar as they implicitly take up the relation of public belief to the believability of a text, including not only Scripture but *Leviathan* itself. As we've seen, Hobbes goes out of his way to say repeatedly in these chapters that private belief cannot be coerced, even as he insists that, in the public realm, private belief must give way to public reason—that is, the sovereign's judgment. While this amounts to a radical constraint on the public confession of faith, it may also create space for Hobbes's own goal of educating his readers. As Jeffrey Barnouw has argued, there is a meta-dimension to Hobbes's argument in chapter 37, one that invites us to think about the relationship of these claims to the experience of reading *Leviathan*.

> To say that one can only be persuaded to belief means that the individual must reach his own judgment on the basis of arguments urged. The individual conscience which is secured by its privacy may seem to have lost its value for public religion. But it is an expression of a radical tendency in English Protestantism, as well as the opening of an inner space in which secular enlightenment can take root.[64]

The irony (which Barnouw doesn't note) is that the conclusion the enlightened reader is intended to draw concerns the necessity of an absolute sovereign. Earlier I discussed Hobbes's references to Deuteronomy 13 and 18, which warn against false prophets and insist on the necessity of believing only God or his lieutenant. In *Leviathan*, Hobbes interprets these biblical passages as subverting the authority of Scripture. That is, he uses Scripture to disable the notion that Scripture is self-evident and can be correctly understood by the individual reader. It is precisely because we disagree that we have consented to set up the sovereign to adjudicate our disputes, including our disputes about Scripture, and this means the sovereign has an exclusive right to interpret the biblical text publicly. In short, we have set up the sovereign precisely so that we can believe in him. What is true of the sovereign is even truer of the "fictitious person" of the commonwealth. To be rationally persuaded of the plausibility of Hobbes's argument is to come to understand Leviathan simultaneously as an artifact of the imagination and an object of our belief. Hobbes clearly hopes the same will prove true of *Leviathan* as well.

4. Aesthetics, Pragmatism, and Modernity

Let me now say a little bit more about the reception of Hobbes's work and its relation to later regimes of literariness, beginning with aesthetics. Hobbes's extraordinarily powerful doctrine produced many anxious responses in the decades that followed the publication of *Leviathan*. In the seventeenth century, the Cambridge Platonists Henry More, Ralph Cudworth, and Nathaniel Culverwell all sought to rebut Hobbes by emphasizing the divine order and rational harmony of the created universe. In the early eighteenth century, Anthony Ashley Cooper, the third Earl of Shaftesbury, went further and elaborated something like an aesthetic view of society in response to Hobbes's view of life in the state of nature as "solitary, poore, nasty, brutish and short."[65] Shaftesbury argued that humans were naturally governed not by fear or self-interest—as Hobbes had claimed—but by a disinterested love of beauty, which was both an aesthetic and ethical virtue. We experience disinterested pleasure when we perceive the beauty, order, harmony, and proportion of the universe—all attributes that point to the divine creator, who in turn underwrites the moral law.[66] Shaftesbury's account of disinterested pleasure was to have a great influence on subsequent descriptions of aesthetic experience by Addison, Hutcheson, Burke, and others. The emergent discourse of aesthetics, as a science and even ethics of beauty, appears here as a *reaction* to Hobbes's dystopian vision.

But there is another, contrary line of argument about Hobbes's relationship to the discipline of aesthetics. According to this view, there is an important *continuity* between Hobbes and the emergence of aesthetics. This is the argument of those twentieth-century critics who see in Hobbes's voluntarism, skepticism, and nominalism the beginnings of a crisis of rationalism. This crisis, it's argued, led to Kant's critical philosophy and the birth of modern aesthetics, both of which have in turn shaped our modern age.

The first thing to say is that there are both positive and negative versions of this argument for continuity between Hobbes and aesthetics. The negative argument is represented by Leo Strauss, for whom Hobbes's nominalism and voluntarism amounted to an attack on classical ideas of reason. For Strauss, Hobbes anticipates the subjectivism of modern philosophy so evident in the new discipline of aesthetics. A similar argument has been advanced by Howard Caygill, for whom Hobbes represents "the emergence of the problem of judgment in the early modern period and its violent resolution" by the sovereign.[67] If pre-modern philosophers believe in an objective order of the universe, modern philosophy—including that of Hobbes—rests on "the judgements of an autonomous subject," and truth is seen to be constituted by "the human intellect alone."[68] From here, according to Caygill, it is only a short step to the reflective judgment of Kantian aesthetics.

For both Strauss and Caygill, then, Hobbes anticipates aesthetics because he turns away from an objective order of knowledge to explore the ways in which the mind constitutes its own objects of knowledge. In this account, maker's knowledge lies between the objective order of pre-modern philosophy and the subjective orientation of modern philosophy. For Strauss, the result of maker's knowledge is relativism and historicism; for Caygill, the result is the loss of an objective standard of judgment.

But there is also a positive version of the role of aesthetics in the transition to modernity. Whereas for Strauss and Caygill, the aesthetic heralds the relativism and historicism of modern political theory, for Jürgen Habermas, the aesthetic is the realm in which we first encounter the modern philosophical project of rational self-legitimation, the project of constructing norms of judgment and interaction from within communicative rationality. In *The Philosophical Discourse of Modernity*, Habermas asserted that "Modernity can and will no longer borrow the criteria by which it takes its orientation from the models supplied by another epoch; *it has to create its normativity out of itself.*" He went on to argue that "The problem of grounding modernity out of itself first comes to consciousness in the realm of aesthetic criticism" in seventeenth-century Europe, when the "moderns" rejected the practice of imitating the ancients.[69]

As I've argued, for Hobbes the problem of grounding modernity out of itself first comes to consciousness in adapting the scientific method of geometry to political theory. At the same time, Hobbes's own equation of knowledge with making emphasizes the centrality of language to the new political science, which in turn anticipates the insights of aesthetics through its voluntarist emphasis on constructing the commonwealth. But in contrast to critics such as Strauss, for whom voluntarism is incompatible with a robust defense of values, Hobbes suggests that compelling values can only be constructed from agreed upon definitions. Values are not given to us a priori as the object of belief; they are instead invented or created, in the same way as we create new obligations by making promises. In this respect, Hobbes's work is perhaps less aptly described in terms of aesthetics than in terms of pragmatism.

Let me try to explain this last point by means of a few, concluding methodological reflections on the literariness of *Leviathan*. From one perspective, Hobbes's version of literariness could be described in terms of metalanguage, as I did in my earlier work. There I argued that *Leviathan* is metalinguistic, because it is about the ambiguity of language and the necessity of a sovereign to impose precise definitions of controversial terms, including "belief."[70] *Leviathan* doesn't simply analyze the role of language in the early modern crisis of judgment, but also calls attention to its own language in doing so. Seen through this lens, *Leviathan* has the quality of self-reflexivity that some twentieth-century critics see as the defining quality of literariness. But here's the problem with this way of thinking: wouldn't all self-reflexive texts then be literary according to this definition of literariness? And wouldn't this modern idea of literariness as self-reflexivity fail to capture Hobbes's ambition to construct a new commonwealth and persuade Englishmen and women to obey an absolute sovereign? The twentieth-century notion of self-reflexivity does scant justice to the creative dimension of Hobbes's conception of making and of autonomy. Above all, it cannot capture the rhetorical power of *Leviathan*, and Hobbes's determination to refashion his reader.

If we want a modern analogy, Hobbes's literariness is better described in terms of the philosophy of pragmatism. As Richard Rorty has written, the pragmatist refuses to accept the (loosely) Platonic distinction between appearance and reality, making and finding. He refuses to accept a representational theory of knowledge, where knowledge is a matter of correspondence to an objective state of affairs. The pragmatist doesn't simply appeal to existing beliefs but constructs them. He imagines not that science gives us access to what is "out there," but rather that it gives us the power to make nature responsive to our needs. Like the pragmatist, Hobbes too breaks down the distinction between making and finding. In this respect, as I've argued, he departs from the humanist rhetorical definition of invention as the faculty of finding arguments from an existing storehouse of commonplaces. Instead, invention comes to mean practical know-how, the knowledge of how to produce the desired results. Hobbes can then be seen as a pragmatist because, rather than treating language as a system of representation, he thinks of language as a tool to be used to solve certain problems and produce certain results.[71] In this context, belief is best thought of not as a matter of cognition but as what Charles Sanders Peirce called a "habit of action," and Hobbes's sovereign is a pragmatist because he wants to use his definition of belief to enforce the habit of obedience.[72]

What difference, ultimately, does pragmatism make to our thinking about literariness? It's arguable that once Hobbes pulls the rug out from beneath the traditional project of philosophy, we are left with a less grandiose, more conversational practice, which Rorty calls literature. This is a very different claim from the one that I advanced in my earlier work on Hobbes. There I argued that, by hiving off the humanist rhetorical conception of literature, Hobbes effectively aestheticized literature, in much the same way as he deprived rhetoric of its ongoing role in facilitating political deliberation. To aestheticize literature, in this earlier argument, was to defang it, to make it incapable of inciting disobedience and rebellion. A stronger argument, I now think, would be that Hobbes turned philosophy itself into literature—understood now as a distinctively Renaissance combination of humanist rhetoric and maker's knowledge. He did so by disabling philosophy's claims to metaphysical knowledge, indeed to any kind of knowledge that was not itself constructed.[73] Hobbes's work is not simply literary in the terms of the broad Renaissance definition of letters. It is literary in a more powerful way, insofar as he places making, rhetoric, and fiction at the heart of his new political science. In this roundabout way, even as he attacks literature, Hobbes recovers for his new political science something of the radically creative potential of literary invention.[74] Chief among those inventions is the argument that faith is a contract, a merely human promise. Hobbes thus implicitly poses the question of what it would mean to hold on to the power of literary invention while still preserving a devout commitment to religious faith. This is the question that obsessed John Milton and that I will take up in the next lecture on *Paradise Lost*, *Paradise Regain'd*, and *Samson Agonistes*.

3
Milton and the Problem of Belief

In the last lecture, we saw Thomas Hobbes stake a claim for a new mode of writing in the midst of the English civil war, a cool Euclidean rhetoric designed to quell the political and religious passions of his contemporaries. Hobbes, I argued, marshalled all the resources of literary invention, all available forms of "powerfull Eloquence," to make his case against the contemporary rhetoric of sedition. In this lecture, I take up the case of John Milton, Hobbes's younger contemporary and political antagonist. Like Hobbes, Milton was educated as a humanist. Unlike Hobbes, he repeatedly defended the humanist ideal of eloquence in his prose, as well as the humanist rhetorical and ethical vision of poetry.[1] And this was only the beginning of their differences. In his "Life of Milton," the seventeenth-century biographer John Aubrey wrote "[Milton's] widowe assures me that Mr. Hobbs was not one of his acquaintance, that her husband did not like him at all, but he would acknowledge him to be a man of great parts, and a learned man. Their interests and tenets did run counter to each other." This was an understatement. Hobbes supported the king in the civil war while Milton was on the side of parliament and defended the regicide in print. Hobbes was essentially a secular writer who argued that the sovereign alone has the power to interpret Scripture. Milton was by contrast a religious writer, who asserted the right of the individual to read and interpret the Bible for himself. Yet Milton's challenge to conventional religious, political, and literary authority was just as radical as Hobbes's.

Hobbes famously claimed that political science was "no older ... than my own book *De cive*"; Milton's claims for his own poetic achievement were even more outsized.[2] Who else would claim, as Milton did in the opening of *Paradise Lost*, to justify the ways of God to men? Who else would impersonate God speaking at such length and so unpleasantly in book 3 of the poem? But equally outsized was Milton's anxiety about the possible sinfulness of his ambition. One has only to think of the invocation to book 3, where the poet-narrator compares himself to Satan escaping the "*Stygian* Pool" and re-ascending to the light (*PL*, 3.14).[3] This anxiety was brilliantly captured by Andrew Marvell in his prefatory poem to *Paradise Lost*, where he describes his fear, upon first reading the poem, that Milton would "ruin the sacred truths to fable and old song." Milton, Marvell worried, ran the risk of reducing religion to fiction. In this worry, he was preceded by Milton himself, who (to cite just one example) compared Adam and Eve after the fall to "th' ancient Pair / In Fables old, less ancient yet then these / Deucalion and chaste Pyrrha" (*PL*, 11.10–12). If the only difference between the biblical story and the Ovidian myth of Deucalion and Pyrrha is that one fable is older than the other, the narrator prompts us to wonder, what does it mean to believe the story of the fall?[4] And what does it mean to believe in the Christian God? It's not surprising, given these questions, that Milton's own reputation as a poet has been shadowed by the question of his beliefs from the seventeenth century to the present. But what has not been sufficiently noted is that Milton's poetry does not simply articulate the problem of belief; it is also working out his own salvation.

As I noted in the first lecture, the question of belief has been entwined with the category of literature from Plato onward, even as the idea of belief undergoes significant revision in late antiquity and the Christian Middle Ages. Christianity appropriated the rhetorical vocabulary of persuasion to describe the conviction of religious faith. In the Renaissance, as we've seen, rhetoric was central to the humanist undertaking, which conceived of poetry itself as a vehicle of moral and, on occasion, religious persuasion. Milton intervenes decisively in this history not only by making poetry do the work of faith, but also by conceiving of faith on the analogy of poetry. In the process, rhetoric's preoccupation with persuasion or "making faith" (*facere fidem*) gives way to the poetic construction of Christian belief. This in turn will have radical and disturbing implications for how we think about belief.[5]

1. The Problem of Milton's Beliefs

Let me begin with a twenty-first-century example of the debate about Milton's beliefs. In the aftermath of the terrorist attacks on the World Trade Center and the Pentagon in the United States in 2001, John Carey cautioned us not to read Milton's late poem *Samson Agonistes* as a justification of revolutionary violence. In a scathing review of Stanley Fish's *How Milton Works*, Carey argued that Fish's positive interpretation of Milton's Samson was equivalent to a defense of terrorism. This amounted to putting Fish in the same camp as Osama bin Laden. Milton's Samson, in Carey's reading, is a figure of religious fanaticism, of belief ungrounded on any religious truth, a figure of Old Testament violence and revenge that Milton could not possibly have sanctioned. In Carey's words, "Milton's Samson cannot know whether his vengeance conforms to the divine purpose or not. But if he acts merely on the presumption that it does... then the lesson Milton's drama teaches is that if you suppose you have private access to God's mind, and act on the supposition, it can have hideous consequences."[6]

The Carey–Fish debate powerfully illustrates Milton's polarizing effect on his readers. In particular, it shows us that Milton's poetry demands that we take seriously the question of what to believe. But Milton went further than his critics insofar as he found *belief itself* a problem. We see this in Milton's treatise *On Christian Doctrine*, in which he defended a variety of heresies, ranging from mortalism to Arianism and subordinationism, the view that Christ was not coeval with God the father but created by him. These heresies clearly suggest that Milton was unhappy with mainstream Protestantism and struggling to make sense of Christian doctrine. But it is really in Milton's poetry that this struggle comes to the fore. In Raphael's speech about angelic digestion, Milton argues heretically for a continuity between matter and spirit. Adam and Christ both subscribe to mortalism, the view that the soul dies with the body (*PL*, 3.245–9; 10.789–92).[7] And, in his account of human history in book 12, Michael notoriously gives the crucifixion only half a line (12.413). Far more important than the crucifixion, Michael implies, is the conversation with Adam in books 11 and 12, which amounts to an extended lesson in scriptural interpretation. For Milton and Michael, faith is a matter of actively making sense of God's providence.

In his prose works, Milton drew a characteristically extreme conclusion from this active conception of faith. He declared that ostensibly correct beliefs, wrongly held, could themselves be a form of heresy. Thus, in a famous passage in *Areopagitica*, his defense of freedom of the press, Milton argued that what the Catholic Church called implicit faith, the simple acceptance of Church authority on matters of belief, was an abdication of the responsibility to interpret for oneself:

> A man may be a heretick in the truth; and if he beleeve things only because his pastor says so, or the Assembly so determins, without knowing other reason, though his belief be true, yet the very truth he holds becomes his heresie. There is not any burden that som would gladlier post off to another then the charge and care of their Religion. There be [many] ... Protestants and professors who live and dye in as arrant an implicit faith, as any lay papist of Loreto.[8]

For Milton, belief is not a matter of accepting Church authority. It is also not simply equivalent to justified belief in an objective state of affairs. It is above all a matter of subjective disposition and individual judgment. In *Areopagitica* as a whole, Milton tests this judgment by marshalling the same rhetorical figures to make contrary points. In doing so, he invites the reader actively to distinguish between them and to construct his belief by engaging with and rejecting the adversary's arguments.[9] But it is precisely this separation of belief from dogma or an externally imposed standard of truth, and the equation of belief with the activity of construction, that opens up the threat of heresy. It also opens the door to religious invention, or—to use a more general term—fiction.

The problems of implicit faith and fiction took on dramatic political relevance in 1649, when a text appeared, purporting to be written by King Charles I while he was imprisoned before his execution. In *Eikon Basilike*, or "The Image of the King," the figure of "Charles" lamented his treatment at the hands of the rebels, protested his faith, and recorded his prayers for divine assistance. He also drew an explicit comparison between himself and the suffering Christ, not least of all in the famous frontispiece which shows Charles holding a crown of thorns (see Figure 3.1).

In his response, the aptly titled *Eikonoklastes*, Milton impugned Charles' faith by noting that the king had cribbed his prayers from

Figure 3.1 Frontispiece to [King Charles I], *Eikon Basilike*. © The Trustees of the British Museum. All rights reserved.

the representation of pagan worship in Philip Sidney's popular prose romance, the *Arcadia*: "being at a loss himself what to pray in Captivity, [Charles] consulted neither with the Liturgie nor with the Directory [i.e., a pastoral handbook], but, neglecting the huge fardell of all thir honycomb devotions, went directly where he doubted not to find better praying to his mind with *Pammela* in [Sidney's] *Arcadia*."[10] From one perspective, there would be little difference between seeking one's prayers in an Anglican directory or the *Arcadia*. In either case, Charles would betray his inability to pray without an external prop, without, in fact, plagiarizing. But Milton seems particularly offended by the recourse to a text that involves pagan characters, suggesting that Charles can't tell the difference between true and false doctrine, Christianity and mere fiction. For Milton in 1650, Charles' religious hypocrisy was only one of the many reasons the idol of kingship needed to be destroyed and the English people needed to reassert their liberty. Right belief dictated political revolution.

Late in life, Milton was still articulating the grounds of this argument in his theological treatise, *On Christian Doctrine*. In book 1, chapter 2, "Of God," Milton equated faith with the knowledge of God, and belief with "assent to this truth" of "the doctrine of Christ." But he went on to explain, much as Hobbes did in *Leviathan*, that there can be no knowledge of God in the traditional sense of knowledge: "When we talk about knowing God, it must be understood in terms of man's limited powers of comprehension. God, as he really is, is far beyond man's imagination, let alone his understanding."[11] This means that

> It is safest for us to form an image of God in our minds which corresponds to his representation and description of himself in the sacred writings. Admittedly, God is always described or outlined not as he really is but in such a way as will make him conceivable to us. Nevertheless, we ought to form just such a mental image of him as he, in bringing himself within the limits of our understanding, wishes us to form. Indeed he has brought himself down to our level expressly to prevent our being carried beyond the reach of human comprehension, and outside the written authority of scripture, into vague subtleties of speculation. (133–4)

Here, knowing God means reading Scripture; such knowledge is metaphorical rather than literal, conditioned by God's accommodation of himself to human readers. The scope for individual interpretation—pejoratively described here as "vague subtleties"—would appear to be limited, by both the deficiencies of human understanding and the divine remedy. But, as we see in a later chapter, this is not the case.

In book 1, chapter 30, Milton makes Christ himself into an exemplary interpreter of the Hebrew Bible, with profound implications for the activity of reading. (Such, in fact, was already the case in *Paradise Regain'd*, as we'll see in section 3.) After arguing on the basis of scriptural evidence that reading the Bible is "prohibited to no one," Milton observes that "neither was Christ himself, whom we cannot suppose to have been considered as particularly learned in the law, forbidden to expound in the synagogue; much less, therefore, could it have been forbidden to read the Scriptures at home." A little later, he draws the conclusion: "whence it follows that the liberty of investigating Scripture thoroughly is granted to all." Milton insists that liberty is not license: while authorizing the individual interpretation of Scripture, he also scrupulously distinguishes between subjective interpretation and the object of faith—that is, the biblical text.[12] "It must always be asked how far the interpretation is in agreement with faith," by which he seems to mean the "analogy of faith," the notion that Scripture will interpret itself if the reader compares obscure passages with clear ones. And yet, in the very same chapter, Milton goes on to reject not only the authority of the Church in matters of interpretation, but even the authority of Scripture itself: "Nowadays," he writes, "the external authority for our faith, in other words, the Scriptures, is of very considerable importance and, generally speaking, it is the authority of which we first have experience. The preeminent and supreme authority, however, is the authority of the Spirit, which is internal, and the individual possession of each man" (1.30, 587).

From one perspective, Milton might seem here merely to be spouting commonplaces of the radical reformation about the anti-biblicist emphasis on the spirit, or the hidden text beneath the real text, ideas that were widespread among reformers in the sixteenth century and among sectarians of the 1640s and 1650s. But he goes further than these reformation commonplaces. Belief, for Milton, is not simply the result of trust in the Holy Spirit, or inspiration by the Holy Spirit. Instead, belief is something one does. Faith, he writes, is actually a form of work: "the gospel justifies through faith without the works of the law. So we, freed from the works of the law, follow not the letter but the spirit, not the works of the law but the works of faith."[13] In the phrase "works of faith" (*opera...fidei*), Milton deliberately and provocatively recalls the Catholic doctrine of works, good deeds that contribute to salvation, but in a way that challenges not only the Catholic conception of works but also the Protestant rejection of them. Works for Milton are not a matter of performing certain Catholic rituals, but neither are they inconsequential, as Protestants had argued. They are neither good nor bad in themselves: what matters is the spirit according to which they are done. Whereas the radical reformers acknowledged that there were such things as works of faith, good deeds that followed from the gift of grace, Milton turns this commonplace on its head. He suggests—no doubt scandalizing some of his readers—that faith itself entails work, specifically, the work of interpretation. We see this emphasis on the work of interpretation in an astonishing passage later in chapter 30 where Milton tells us that God deliberately made Scripture unreliable in order to provoke greater hermeneutical effort on the part of the faithful.[14] It's one thing to say, as Augustine did, that the obscurity of scriptural allegory is intended to engage the reader; it's quite another to say that God is responsible for both the poor state of Scripture, with its textual "corruption," and the "bad faith" of those entrusted with its transmission. Yet it's characteristic of Milton that he interprets God's mysterious ways as encouraging the reader to rely on the spirit rather than the letter.

We are now in a position to turn back to Milton's poetry, and specifically to *Paradise Lost*, where there is no better example of Milton's struggle to make sense of God's ways than the representation of God in book 3. Here, as Alexander Pope famously complained, God appears as an unpleasant "school divine," whom Christ must cajole into offering salvation to the fallen Adam and Eve. But this picture of God would not have surprised Milton's readers. Given his prelapsarian gift of free will, it's no wonder God angrily denounces fallen man: "ingrate, he had of mee / All he could have; I made him just and right, / Sufficient to have stood, though free to fall" (3.97–9). Instead, Milton's contemporary readers would have been shocked to find God defending his reasoning in a colloquy with the Son. Far from being the most repulsively orthodox part of the poem, as William Empson argued long ago, Milton here is at his most liberal and unorthodox.[15] God may look Calvinist insofar as he is a judge, but this God takes the time to justify his own decrees, including the decree that man "shall find grace" (3.131). Even more surprising, Milton presents God as open to persuasion regarding the precise meaning of such grace.

As I noted in the first lecture, arguments for equitable interpretation in the rhetorical works of Aristotle, Cicero, and Quintilian had been assimilated into the canons of biblical hermeneutics. In a Christian context, an equitable interpretation was a charitable one, an interpretation according to the spirit rather than the letter.[16] In book 3, Christ appears as an advocate and rhetorician, whose task is to persuade God that his decision to grant grace to Adam and Eve was correct. While tactfully insisting that God is the only judge, Christ also makes the case for equity:

> For should Man finally be lost, should Man
> Thy creature late so lov'd, thy youngest Son
> Fall circumvented thus by fraud, though join'd
> With his own folly? that be from thee far,
> That far be from thee, Father, who art Judge
> Of all things made, and judgest only right.
> Or shall the Adversary thus obtain
> His end, and frustrate thine, shall he fulfill
> His malice, and thy goodness bring to naught,
> Or proud return though to his heavier doom,
> Yet with revenge accomplish't and to Hell
> Draw after him the whole Race of mankind,
> By him corrupted? or wilt thou thyself
> Abolish thy Creation, and unmake,
> For him, what for thy glory thou hast made?
> So should thy goodness and thy greatness both
> Be question'd and blasphem'd without defense.
> (3.150–61)

Christ insists that God can't have intended the destruction of Adam and Eve; such a position would be morally indefensible. Instead, he argues that the correct judgment of the case would be a charitable one, and God agrees that this was his intention:

> All hast thou spok'n as my thoughts are, all
> As my Eternal purpose hath decreed:
> Man shall not quite be lost, but sav'd who will,
> Yet not of will in him, but grace in me
> Freely voutsaf't; once more I will renew
> His lapsed powers, though forfeit and enthrall'd
> By sin to foul exorbitant desires;
> Upheld by me, yet once more he shall stand
> On even ground against his mortal foe,
> By me upheld, that he may know how frail
> His fall'n condition is, and to me owe
> All his deliv'rance, and to none but me.
> Some I have chosen of peculiar grace
> Elect above the rest; so is my will:
> The rest shall hear me call, and oft be warn'd
> Thir sinful state, and to appease betimes
> Th' incensed Deity while offer'd grace
> Invites; for I will clear thir senses dark,
> What may suffice, and soft'n stony hearts
> To pray, repent, and bring obedience due.
> To Prayer, repentance, and obedience due,
> Though but endeavor'd with sincere intent,
> Mine ear shall not be slow, mine eye not shut.
> (3.171–93)

Even as God insists on his omnipotence, he also vows—against Augustine, Luther, Calvin, and others—to renew the free will of his fallen creatures. As a corollary, he declares that he is open to prayer, which he represents as an act of persuasion. Together, the renewed will and renewed possibility of persuasion constitute God's own equitable interpretation of his grace toward man. We see this activity of equitable interpretation dramatized in God's verbal repetitions: "sav'd who *will*, / Yet not of *will* in him, but grace in me; *Upheld* by me / By me *upheld*; Some I have chosen of peculiar grace / Elect above the *rest*; so is my will: / The *rest* shall hear me call; peculiar *grace* / offered *grace*; *To pray, repent, and bring obedience due* / *To Prayer, repentance, and obedience due*."[17] These lines distinguish between the rest who are saved and the rest who are damned; the grace that enables and the grace that is rejected. What finally makes the difference between superficially similar states is "sincere intent"; this is what triggers

God's equitable or charitable response to man, and enables the passage from the fallen will to the restored will.[18]

The colloquy in book 3 looks forward to books 11 and 12, which are essentially an extended lesson in rhetorical advocacy and equitable interpretation. As in book 3, Christ presents himself to God as the "advocate" of fallen Adam and Eve (11.33), and urges God to

> Accept me, and in mee from these receive
> The smell of peace toward Mankind, let him live
> Before thee reconcil'd, at least his days
> Number'd, though sad, till Death, his doom (which I
> To mitigate thus *plead*, not to reverse)
> To better life shall yield him, where with mee
> All my redeem'd may dwell in joy and bliss,
> Made one with me as I with thee am one.
> (11.37–44, my emphasis)

In reply, God grants Christ's plea and then again comments, with theological precision, "all thy request was my Decree" (11.47). Here, too, we see Milton working backward from divine omniscience and omnipotence to create a space of charitable or equitable interpretation. What does it mean to interpret the divine decree, and how can one make such interpretation compatible with equity? Even God seems preoccupied with this question when he explains why he could not allow Adam and Eve to remain in Eden:

> I at first with two fair gifts
> Created him endow'd, with Happiness
> And Immortality: that fondly lost,
> This other serv'd but to eternize woe;
> Till I provided Death; so Death becomes
> His final remedy, and after Life
> Tri'd in sharp tribulation, and refin'd
> By Faith and faithful works, to second Life,
> Wak't in the renovation of the just,
> Resigns him up with Heav'n and Earth renew'd.
> (11.57–66)

According to this reasoning, death might seem the worst of all punishments, but it is really a form of mercy, the theological and affective equivalent of equity. In the meantime, Adam and Eve are expected to have faith and perform "faithful works," a phrase that Michael echoes in book 12 in a passage I will turn to in a moment.

At the opening of book 11, Adam too emphasizes the problem of interpretation:

> *Eve*, easily may Faith admit, that all
> The good which we enjoy, from Heav'n descends;
> But that from us aught should ascend to Heav'n
> So prevalent as to concern the mind
> Of God high-blest, or to incline his will,
> Hard to belief may seem; yet this will Prayer,
> Or one short sigh of human breath, up-borne
> Ev'n to the Seat of God. For since I sought
> By Prayer th' offended Deity to appease,
> Kneel'd and before him humbl'd all my heart,
> Methought I saw him placable and mild,
> Bending his ear; persuasion in me grew
> That I was heard with favor; peace return'd
> Home to my Breast, and to my memory
> His promise, that thy Seed shall bruise our Foe;
> Which then not minded in dismay, yet now
> Assures me that the bitterness of death
> Is past, and we shall live. Whence Hail to thee,
> *Eve* rightly call'd, Mother of all Mankind,
> Mother of all things living, since by thee
> Man is to live, and all things live for Man.
> (11.146–61)

Here Adam almost seems to be ventriloquizing the Puritan reader, who is incredulous that God should care about "aught" of man that ascends to heaven. But, as Adam instructs the reader along with Eve, what is hard to believe is not impossible; it just involves work. As in book 3, prayer is then represented as a kind of rhetoric to which God bends his ear, and Adam's conviction—or faith—that God hears him with favor is itself described as "persuasion." This persuasion allows Adam to understand death in a new way, not as bitterness, but as the charitable promise of eternal life in the seed that "shall bruise our Foe"; that is, he comes to understand death in the way that God intends, not as a simple punishment but metaphorically, as the equitable resolution of a difficult case.

In book 12, Michael moves from showing Adam scenes of history to purely verbal instruction. These scenes do not illustrate dogma; rather, they are tests of Adam's hermeneutical skill. It is consistent with Michael's teaching that this is true even of Christ. In the course of their lesson, Michael tells Adam that knowledge of Christ is the "summe / of wisdom" which not even knowledge of the heavens or the secrets of nature could increase (12.575–6). But knowledge is not enough:

> only add
> Deeds to thy knowledge answerable, add Faith,
> Add Virtue, Patience, Temperance, add Love,
> By name to come call'd Charitie, the soul
> Of all the rest: then wilt thou not be loath
> To leave this Paradise, but shalt possess
> A Paradise within thee, happier far.
>
> (12.581–7)

Deeds here are explicitly contrasted to knowledge and placed in apposition to faith, virtue, patience, temperance, and love or charity. The syntax permits us to read the lines as suggesting that these theological virtues are either added to deeds or instances of them. Against the argument that deeds are contrasted to faith is the earlier line by Michael in which he speaks of "Faith not void of works" (12.427), as well as God's speech in book 3 about renewing Adam's lapsed powers. It is not enough to know about Christ; faith must take the form of action.

In a strange way, Milton's own poetic fascination with the work of belief in *Paradise Lost* has precipitated a kind of skepticism on the part of his readers. Because he stages his belief in poetry, Milton has been open to the accusation that the real object of his belief was poetry rather than God. William Blake famously claimed that "The reason Milton wrote in fetters when he wrote of Angels and God, and at liberty when of Devils and Hell, is because he was a true Poet and of the Devil's party without knowing it." Blake underestimated Milton, who was fully aware of the diabolic temptation of art and dramatized this awareness in many passages. Milton was also acutely aware of the temptation of revolutionary action, which is why he gave Satan, his most impressive poetic creation, the revolutionary rhetoric associated with the parliamentary cause. Moreover, it was precisely because he was aware of these temptations that he devoted so much time to clarifying, for himself, what it means to interpret Scripture and what role poetry has in the life of an educated believer. For these reasons, William Empson was wrong to think that Milton was reluctantly asserting the repulsive theology of orthodox Calvinism, just as Stanley Fish is wrong to think that Milton urges a pose of simple, even we might say Hobbesian, obedience to an authoritarian God. Neither could be further from the truth, further from Milton's emphasis on the work of interpretation that takes place in poetry.

2. Poetry and Belief at the Reformation

Let me now try to contextualize this argument with reference to the English Reformation. It's a striking feature of English literary history that the Reformation coincided with a remarkable flowering of English literature. But the relationship of this literature to belief has itself been the subject of considerable disagreement. In one take on the period, belief became newly problematic and so, as a result, did poetry. According to Malcolm Ross, this was caused by the internal transformation of Christian doctrine in the tumultuous years following Luther's break with the Catholic Church. In *Poetry and Dogma*, Ross claimed that seventeenth-century England witnessed the "dissociation between symbol and dogma."[19] Anglicans lost the Catholic sense of Christ's sacramental presence in history and, along with this, any sense of the sacramental power of language. Instead of modeling poetry on the Catholic idea of representation as real presence, Anglican poetry registered the "decline of the analogical symbol into simple metaphor."[20] The endpoint of this sad decline, according to Ross, was the work of John Milton: Milton, he wrote, "carries Christian poetry, and in particular the poetic uses of the Christian symbol, to a limit beyond which it cannot go and remain Christian."[21] While conceding that Milton's work is "distinctively Protestant," Ross claimed that it was just teetering on the brink of the "purely secular."[22] For example, he argued that Christ in Milton's poetry is no longer the perfect incarnation of Truth, Justice, and Order. Instead, Christ is one symbol among others, a symbol of an essentially secular, ethical truth. According to this argument, the Reformation did not simply pose a problem for Christian belief; it also resulted in the vitiation of literature.

Ross's view was challenged by the path-breaking work of Barbara Lewalski in the late 1970s. For Lewalski, belief was not so much a problem as a new source of literary energy. Specifically, Lewalski argued for a "Protestant poetics" in English Renaissance poetry that derived from the Protestant emphasis on the word of God and on the Bible as a compendium of literary genres and tropes. If the Bible was literature, it could then be seen to authorize secular literary activity. More recently, Brian Cummings has described how "the literary culture of the Reformation" emerged from a crisis in linguistic modes of interpretation and a revolution in theological vocabulary, both of which placed a new emphasis on the individual's encounter with and interpretation of the biblical text.[23] For both Lewalski and Cummings, the Reformation produced a new self-consciousness about figurative language and a new obligation for the reader to encounter that language directly, both of which contributed to the flourishing of English literature in the sixteenth and seventeenth centuries. In this way, religious belief fueled a new privileging of and attention to literature.

The most common approach to Protestant poetics, especially in the case of Milton, is to describe it as iconoclastic. According to this view, it is a satanic temptation to consider a work of art as an autonomous literary artifact. This was, after all, what pagan writers had done. The obligation of the Christian was by contrast to put art in the service of religion; the poet's paradoxical task was to make artifacts that deny their own workmanship precisely by foregrounding it—that is, by calling attention to poetry as an inadequate representation, something that needed to be moved beyond.[24] We can see this rhetorical strategy at work in *Paradise Lost* in those epic similes that stage and correct the reader's own misunderstanding—as when the narrator says after one particularly beautiful epic simile about the fall of Mulciber from heaven, "Thus they relate / Erring; for he with this rebellious rout / Fell long before" (*PL*, 1.738–48). It is a mistake, that is, to give any credence to classical myth, when the first instance of the fall was Satan's. Whatever kind of belief poetry elicits, it does so—according to this version of Protestant poetics—only to destroy the icon of art and point the reader (and artist) to True Religion.

I have a lot of sympathy with this position. I think it offers a compelling description of some of Milton's rhetorical strategies. Even more important, it gets Milton's ambitions right. As one critic has argued, all art worth its salt aspires to transcend the category of mere literature.[25] But I also think something more vexed and more interesting is going on in Milton's poetry. Milton's iconoclasm aims not so much at producing belief, or directing the reader to True Religion, as at reclaiming poetry as an act of invention and interpretation, not least of all because such invention is also consistent with his understanding of faith. From a Christian perspective, as we've seen, such invention amounts to a charitable or equitable interpretation. Such equitable interpretation is dramatized not only in the explicit verbal exchanges between God and Christ, Michael and Adam, and Adam and Eve that I explored earlier, but also in the very fabric of the poetic narrative, including the depicting of motive and passion that were essential to the construction of character.[26] As Regina Schwartz has argued with respect to *Paradise Lost*, "Painting descriptions, seeking causes, offering explanations, exploring motives, and delineating consequences to make a fairly unintelligible story intelligible: for Milton, these are the methods for interpreting according to the principle of charity." And yet, the more believable Milton made the story of the fall, the less it seemed to conform to orthodox Anglicanism and to the notion that true belief was a gift of God.[27] In this process, it's not so much that the religious culture of the Reformation helps to explain the creation of Milton's great poems, as that these poems threaten to undo the Reformation.

3. The Problem of Belief in *Samson Agonistes* and *Paradise Regain'd*

Earlier I discussed Milton's God and the representation of heretical doctrine in *Paradise Lost*. Let's grant that, in *Paradise Lost*, Milton created a great and partly heretical poem that directly challenged the nature of Protestant belief. I now want to argue that Milton's 1671 volume, entitled *Paradise Regain'd, to which is added Samson Agonistes*, is the poet's most powerful meditation on the dilemmas of faith. Together Milton's late poems address the problem that Marvell noted of ruining the sacred truths precisely because they privilege the activity of interpreting the biblical text over the text itself. In both cases, though in different ways, the poems are about the problem of interpretation, and its implications for belief.

For simplicity's sake, let me posit that there are three ways of reading the 1671 volume. First, there are those who read Samson as an exemplary hero. These readers sometimes argue that *Samson Agonistes* and *Paradise Regain'd* together present alternative, equally powerful responses to the Restoration of the Stuart monarchy: either iconoclastic violence or strategic withdrawal into the private realm.[28] Second, there are those who see the two poems as antithetical and who urge us to understand Samson as a failed exemplar of heroism, one that illustrates the inadequacy of the Old Testament ethic of revenge.[29] (This is the argument of John Carey whom I mentioned earlier, and who argues that Samson is simply a terrorist.) The inversion of typological order in the printing of the two texts—the fact that the Old Testament story comes after the New Testament one—could be adduced in support of this second argument: *Samson Agonistes* comes after *Paradise Regain'd* because Samson is antithetical to Jesus rather than foreshadowing him. But there is a third, biographical reading, which is that Milton places *Samson Agonistes* second because Samson's fate so closely resembles his own at the Restoration: both are blind, despairing, and surrounded by enemies. This is the argument I want to pursue here. In this reading, *Samson Agonistes* is added to *Paradise Regain'd* as an illustration of Milton's own fate, as an example of his own interpretation of Scripture, and as a test of the reader's judgment. According to this interpretation, *Samson Agonistes* shows us what Samson looks like from the Christian perspective of *Paradise Regain'd*—not a classical heroic figure but a Protestant hero of faith.[30] In this he is preceded by Milton's Jesus.

What does it mean to be a Protestant hero of faith and how would one show how faith works? In particular, how would one show this in poetry? Here we need to begin, as Milton's volume invites us to do, with the example of Jesus in *Paradise Regain'd*. Milton's Jesus is nothing if not an interpreter of the Hebrew Bible, who is literally working out his role as savior through his reading of Scripture. Hearing from his mother Mary that he is "no Son of mortal man," and that "Wise Men...from the East" have recognized him as the "King of *Israel*," Jesus says, "This having heard, straight I again revolv'd / The Law and Prophets, searching what was writ / Concerning the Messiah" (*PR*, 1.234, 250–4, 259–61). "Revolve" here means turning or unfurling the scroll of Scripture and diligently perusing it, as the Gospels will instruct later readers to "search" the Scriptures for the truth.[31] And this is what Jesus proceeds to do for the rest of the poem, pitting his own understanding of Scripture against Satan's literal-minded misunderstanding.[32]

In fact, it's a striking feature of the poem that the exchanges between Jesus and Satan often turn on whether to interpret the exact same biblical passage literally or figuratively. To cite just one example, the narrator of the poem tells us that when John the Baptist baptized Jesus, "Heaven open'd, and in likeness of a Dove / The Spirit descended, while the Father's voice / From Heav'n pronounc'd him his beloved Son" (1.30–2). In his meditation on his mission, Jesus also notes that "the Spirit descended on me like a Dove" (1.282). In contrast, Satan's own account of the same event is marked by a striking literary obtuseness: "I saw / The Prophet do him reverence; on him rising / Out of the water, Heav'n above the Clouds / Unfold her Crystal Doors, thence on his head / A perfect Dove descend, whate'er it meant" (1.79–83). Satan asserts that a dove literally descended, and in a casual aside confesses that he has no idea what this meant. If Jesus's doubt is an uncertainty about how to construe his mission and when to begin, Satan's doubt is an inability to believe that follows from an inability to understand poetic language. The narrator, by contrast, both asserts the poetic dimension of biblical language and offers an interpretation of its spiritual significance.[33] Once we see how the language of the Bible demands both belief and interpretation, or rather interpretation as the work of belief, we can also see how the Bible itself authorizes Milton's own poetic daring in *Paradise Regain'd*. Milton's *invention* of the dialogue between Satan and Jesus—a dialogue for which there is no biblical precedent and which the narrator describes as "unrecorded"—is itself both an act of belief and a powerful interpretation of the biblical text.

What kind of invention is this? It's well known that Milton drew on the biblical book of Job as a model for the structure of *Paradise Regain'd*.[34] Less well known is the fact that, in inventing or supplying the dialogue between Jesus and Satan, Milton drew on the exchange between Job and his comforters. In these exchanges, Job ironically reuses his comforters' own words to expose their superficiality. When Job's friends speak to him in the language of traditional Wisdom literature, Job parodies a line of Psalm 8, which reads, "What is man, that thou art mindful of him? And the son of man, that thou visitest him? For thou hast made him a little lower than the angels, and hast crowned him with glory and honour" (Ps 8:4–5). In Job's mouth, this marveling at God's elevation of man becomes an irritable wondering at God's excessive attention: "What is man, that thou shouldest magnify him? And that thou shouldest set thine heart upon him? And that thou shouldest visit him every morning, and try him every moment?" (Job 7:17–18). When Job's wife urges him to "curse God and die," Job responds ironically by playing on the fact that the Hebrew word for praise—*barek*—could also mean "curse." In a sharp rebuke to his wife's temptation to distrust, Job asserts that he will praise God, even though God has persecuted him (Job 2:9–10). Like Job's ironic treatment of his comforters, Jesus likes to echo Satan and, in the process, reveal the false assumptions underlying Satan's temptations:

> Said'st thou not that to all things I had right?
> And who withholds my pow'r that right to use?
> Shall I receive by gift what of my own,
> When and where likes me best, I can command?
> (2.379–82)

In this reply, Jesus characteristically and ironically turns Satan's language against him, by showing that Satan himself cannot give him what the tempter concedes he already has. Similarly, when Satan offers Jesus wealth to achieve his kingly mission on earth, the Son replies by playing on the meaning of kingly: "to guide nations in the way of truth / By saving doctrine ... / Is yet more kingly" than the political office offered by Satan (2.473–6).

Milton draws out the radical implication of the Son's replies in the conclusion of book 4. Here Satan's effort to understand in what sense Jesus might be a "son of God" (Job 1:6) produces a battle of scriptural quotations. When Satan urges "Cast thyself down; safely if Son of God; / For it is written, He will give command / Concerning thee to his angels," he alludes to Psalm 91:11–12, and proleptically to Luke

4:10–11, but the phrase "Son of God" also refers us back to Job 1:6. When Jesus replies, "Also it is written, / Tempt not the Lord thy God," he alludes to Deuteronomy 6:16 and proleptically to Luke 4:12, but he also refers us to the distinction between a son of God and the Lord in Job 1:6. Satan and Jesus, that is, read the same text and use the same phrases, as though to dramatize that the difference between these two "sons of God" cannot be established dogmatically—with reference to particular quotations, doctrines, or signs—but only indirectly, with reference to the reader's intention or spirit. In this sense, there is never a literal or direct correspondence between text and meaning, only an indirect or ironic one.[35]

There is yet more at stake in this battle of quotations. From one perspective, the Son could be said to be dramatizing the way canonical Christian Scripture is created out of a process of interpretation.[36] But in reading backwards from Luke to its pre-texts in Hebrew Scripture, Jesus could also be said to be dismantling Scripture for the purposes of its dramatic exposition in poetry, his own and by extension Milton's. As an exemplary reader of the Hebrew Bible, Jesus not only demonstrates that Scripture itself is a thing indifferent that can be put to better or worse uses (as Stanley Fish argued long ago); he also engages in an ironic practice of repetition and quotation, one that conspicuously does not decide the question at issue. This foregrounding of undecidability is consistent with Milton's view that God deliberately made Scripture unreliable to force Christian readers to assume responsibility for interpretation, a practice that Milton then imitates in *Paradise Regain'd*. In this context, Milton's representation of Jesus as defeating Satan through faith and verbal wit rather than through the crucifixion easily becomes a model for our own interpretive labor. Such a representation of the Son corresponds to what Harold Fisch has described as "Milton's desire to naturalize, or [even] ... 'demythologize' the gospel narrative."[37]

In the prologue to the poem, Milton went out of his way to call attention to the specifically literary dimension of his achievement. Strikingly, he did so with reference to classical rather than biblical texts. Here the poet describes his singing "Recover'd Paradise" in lines that allude to the opening of Renaissance editions of the *Aeneid*:

> I who erewhile the happy garden sung,
> By one man's disobedience, now sing
> Recovered Paradise to all mankind,
> By one man's firm obedience fully tried....
>
> (1.1–4)

Just as the Son will save mankind by passing the test of obedience that Adam failed, so Milton will save the epic by recasting the classical epic of empire as the epic of self-mastery. *Paradise Lost* now appears as mere pastoral ("the happy garden"), that is, as a mere prelude to the serious work of *Paradise Regain'd*. In this way, Milton activates the allusion to Virgil's *Georgics*, whose four-book structure informs Milton's own poem. As Anthony Low has noted, there are striking parallels between Milton's Jesus and Virgil's laborer, as well as between Virgil's reluctance to write epic before the time is ripe and the Son's own waiting for the right occasion to act.[38] The poet's argument that the end of the Golden Age was beneficial insofar as it prompted human beings to invent new arts, which famously ends with the maxim "labor omnia vincit / improbus" (1.145–6), also applies to the Son. These allusions to the *Georgics* are just one of the ways Milton invites us to see that the Son's Job-like patience also involves a kind of labor, specifically a labor of interpretation. For Milton, paradise regained is not the literal-minded paradise of the martyr, who imagines heavenly rewards in the afterlife. Nor is it the earthly paradise of the biblical Job who, at the end of his trials, receives such rewards in this life. Instead, paradise regained is a specifically ironic mode of understanding. The effect is not to disable the scriptural idea of the covenant, but rather to enable the secular version of it, one that can rival the greatest achievements of classical literature.

To understand this validation of Milton's own poetry in *Paradise Regain'd*, we need to turn to the temptation of wisdom, where Satan offers Jesus classical learning and eloquence, including the classical poetry that Milton loved and imitated, and Jesus appears to reject them. One standard response is to assert that, late in life, Milton came to believe in the incompatibility of humanist literature and faith, or the irrelevance of the former to the latter. Another—and in my view, more compelling—response is to argue that the Son didn't really reject all of classical learning, only some of it: when he condemns pagan literature, he explicitly makes an exception for literature in which "moral virtue is express'd / By light of Nature, not in all quite lost" (4.351–2). Just as some Christians saw Job as a pagan figure whose faith could serve as a supplement—however redundant—to Christian faith, so pagan literature is imagined as a supplement—however unnecessary—to Scripture. It is unnecessary not only for doctrinal but also for literary reasons, not only because the man of faith doesn't need to be instructed by pagan writers, but also because Scripture is already poetry:

> All our Law and Story strew'd
> With Hymns, our Psalms with artful terms inscrib'd
> Our Hebrew Songs and Harps in *Babylon*,
> That pleas'd so well our Victors' ear, declare
> That rather *Greece* from us these Arts deriv'd;
> Ill imitated....
>
> (4.334–9)

Jesus's claim here conforms to the patristic and Renaissance view that the Bible was a compendium of literary forms. As we've seen, the effect of such literary reading of the Bible was not simply to assert the superiority of Scripture to the classics, but also to authorize the writing of poetry. In the patristic tradition, Job was regularly singled out as one of the most poetic books of the Hebrew Bible.[39] Thus when Milton describes the book of Job as a brief epic in *The Reason of Church Government*, his point seems to be not just that Scripture uses tropes and figures, but that poets may use Scripture to authorize their own intervention in the specifically literary tradition inherited from the ancients. This is precisely what happens in *Paradise Regain'd*, where the Son articulates what Robert Alter has called "the double canonicity" of Hebrew Scripture, its literary as well as doctrinal exemplarity.[40] In arguing that Scripture alone is the repository of all the wisdom that is necessary for faith, Milton makes his own poetry not only redundant but also autonomous. If Scripture is self-sufficient and doesn't need Milton's poetry, it follows that the poet is not bound by what Scripture "records."

Ironically, what has been left "unrecorded" in the New Testament, judging from *Paradise Regain'd*, is the Son's own poetry. Poetry is what Milton adds to the biblical account of Jesus. In this way, Milton suggests that poetry is the rhetorical mode most appropriate to the

Son's ambiguous nature, most appropriate to his existence in the *saeculum*. At the same time, Milton makes it clear that poetry is also the proper mode for ordinary human beings to understand their own ambiguous location in secular life, including their relation to sacred texts. Poetry is privileged in this way because, for Milton, the secular realm is not defined by the absence of faith or religion (as it has often been in modern discussions) but rather by the absence of dogmatism, in the form of detachable pronouncements that bear only "a single sense." Milton's Jesus is thus a redeemer in more than one sense of the word (as is appropriate for a poem in which so much turns on double senses). He will ultimately redeem mankind, but in the meantime he redeems the independent activity of poetry, which we might think of as the counterplot to the authorized version of Scripture.

Turning from *Paradise Regain'd* to *Samson Agonistes*, it seems appropriate that this labor has to be performed all over again, both by Samson and by Milton. At the beginning of the poem, Samson is literally a laborer chained to a mill and, although at first this is a sign of his literal enslavement, very early in the poem it comes to signify his efforts to make sense of his dilemma.[41] On the day represented in the poem, the Philistines are celebrating their God "Dagon" and so have "forbid / Laborious works." Samson is thus at rest, but—he tells us—while he finds "ease to the body," he finds "none to the mind / From restless thoughts" and questions:

> Why was my breeding order'd and prescrib'd
> As of a person separate to God,
> Designed for great exploits; if I must die
> Betray'd, Captiv'd, and both my Eyes put out,
> Made of my Enemies the scorn and gaze;
> To grind in Brazen Fetters under task
> With this Heav'n gifted strength?   (30–6)

Samson can make no sense of his predicament: if there is truth to the prophecy of his great exploits, why is he suffering like Job? If he is responsible for his downfall, then is there no truth in prophecy?

Samson, in short, is a riddle, an occasion for debate, and ultimately a test of the reader's understanding. In the rest of the poem, Samson and his visitors try out various interpretations of his fate. Samson wonders "what if all foretold / Had been fulfill'd but through mine own default [?]" (44–5); the Chorus glibly proposes that "wisest Men / Have err'd, and by bad Women been deceived" (210–11); Samson's father Manoa laments his "ever failing trust / In mortal strength," and blames Samson, even while complaining about God's mixed signals: "For this did th'Angel twice descend?" (348–9; 361); Dalila pleads conjugal affection: "And what if Love, which thou interpret'st hate / ... / Caus'd what I did" (790–3). When Samson rebuffs her, she tries the argument from cultural relativism: "in my country ... I shall be nam'd among the famousest / Of women" (980–3). In short, just as Satan, in *Paradise Regain'd*, tempts Jesus to misread Scripture and to doubt his mission, so Samson's various visitors—his father, Dalila, the Chorus, and the Philistine Harapha—tempt him to despair about making sense of God's prophecy. In this dialectical colloquy, Samson learns to reject his own earlier incorrect interpretations by hearing them articulated by his false comforters, and gradually comes to see his own efforts to make sense of God's ways as the working out of his own salvation.[42] Samson, then, is not at rest on this day of rest but hard at work making sense of—or, to use the language of *Paradise Regain'd*, "revolving"—God's design.

Milton himself makes the connection to *Paradise Regain'd* when he describes Samson before he pulls down the temple "as one who prayed / Or some great matter in his mind revolved" (1637–8). But as the "as" suggests, Milton also aggravates the problem of interpretation in the conclusion of the poem. In the famous scene where Samson decides to go to the Philistine temple, it's hard to know whether the "rousing motions" he feels are divine inspiration or not (1382). And when Samson bows his head "as one who prayed / Or some great matter in his mind revolved," it's hard to know whether prayer is in apposition to the "revolving" of mental cogitation or in opposition to it. Milton's deliberate obfuscation of Samson's state of mind and his apparent nervousness about the subjective dimension of faith are in striking contrast to his confident assertion of the superiority of conscience to the text of Scripture in *Christian Doctrine*. They are also a far cry from the Son's insistence on the authority of the "spirit" (4.323). This is not, in my view, because Samson is a fallen Old Testament figure. Instead, it is because Samson is like us. In this respect, we could say Milton's Samson is the logical consequence of his demythologization of Jesus in *Paradise Regain'd*. Milton wants us to remember the messy imbrication of Samson's limbs with those of his enemies; he wants us to work to sort things out rather than be passive spectators at the flowery monument proposed by Manoa. He wants us to struggle to make sense of the final chorus, which pronounces that "all is best" (1745) and concludes:

> His servants he with new acquist
> Of true experience from this great event
> With peace and consolation hath dismist,
> And calm of mind, all passion spent.   (1755–8)

As readers, we must determine for ourselves our "acquist" of experience, as well as what course of action, if any, is dictated by "calm of mind." In this effort, we are not aided by the gesture toward Aristotelian catharsis in the last line of the poem: as Milton was well aware, the meaning of the catharsis clause was as much debated in the Renaissance as in our own time. Rather, the final line directs us back to the prefatory note to the poem, which stresses the labor of composition.

In his defense of tragedy in the prefatory note to *Samson Agonistes*, Milton writes, "Men in highest dignity have *labor'd* not a little to be thought able to compose a Tragedy" (my emphasis). While *labor* here might have a touch of irony insofar as it points to the many who have failed in this high undertaking, it also helps to highlight Milton's sense of the work of poetry. The Latin epigraph on the poem's title page gives Aristotle's definition of tragedy as the "imitation of an action that is serious, complete, and possessing magnitude" (1449b). In the prefatory note, Milton adds that such imitation of an action also includes the representation of "the passions," as he might well do for a poem in which despair, doubt, anger, and erotic ambivalence are so much on display, and in which much of the action consists of experiencing and then revisiting and channeling those passions to new ends.[43] As Milton would have known, a little later in the *Poetics*, Aristotle clarifies that "The imitation of the action is the Plot. By plot I here mean the combination of events" (1450a). Action then does not refer to a single action by a single individual, but rather a structure of coherence and significance imposed by the author. Aristotle even suggests that plot has a revelatory quality: "For tragedy," he writes "is not an imitation of men but of actions and of life. It is in action that happiness and unhappiness are found, and the end we aim at is a kind of activity, not a quality" (1450a). In juxtaposing the labor of composition with Aristotle's definition of tragedy, Milton implicitly equates labor with making a plot, which he defines as "nothing indeed but such economy [arrangement], or disposition of the fable as may stand best with verisimilitude and decorum."[44] The poet is a maker of plots, which is to say a producer of significant forms.[45] The same could be said of Milton's Samson.

In fact, we might say that what Milton—and Samson—achieve in *Samson Agonistes* is the transcendence of brute labor—grinding at the mill—by poiesis or poetic making. As many scholars have noted, poiesis for Aristotle sits between physical labor and action.[46] It is one of the productive arts, but it differs from the kind of labor that reproduces mere life. Moreover, it is notable that, as a productive art, it involves the imitation of action, which as we've seen may include the passions. In so doing, poiesis models action and ideally gives rise to it. Whereas Plato had made a distinction between the craftsman who is judged by the product of his labor and the ethical agent who is judged by the quality of his action, Aristotle—and even more, his Renaissance interpreters—imagined the poet as engaging in and fostering a kind of work that might also be conceived of as an ethical and intellectual activity. Milton went one step further and dramatized this work in the figure of Samson, who learns to reject his debilitating passions by seeing them represented by others, and for whom emotion eventually becomes a principle of action in the form of "rousing motions."[47]

In both of his late poems, then, Milton foregrounds the hermeneutic dimension of poetic making by constructing plots that are centrally *about* interpretation. In *Paradise Regain'd*, Jesus struggles to understand his prophesied role as messiah; in *Samson Agonistes*, Samson struggles to understand his current enslavement. As we've seen, Milton also foregrounds his own interpretive activity by narrating events in the Bible that strictly speaking did not occur. The dialogue between Satan and Jesus, and Samson's own despairing dialogue with the Chorus, Dalila, Manoa, and others are Milton's invention. The entire plot of *Samson Agonistes* occurs in the gap between verses 24 and 25 of the biblical book of Judges, between the capture of Samson and his arrival at the Philistine temple. The plot then is not mimetic, if by this we understand copying or mirroring; it is mimetic in Aristotle's or Philip Sidney's sense of making something new.[48] In this poetic expansion of the biblical text, Milton thematizes the link between equitable interpretation and the exploration of the character's motives. Just as all of the characters are trying to make sense of Samson's exceptional situation, so we are as well. Samuel Johnson once complained that the plot of *Samson Agonistes* has no middle. In response to Johnson, we could say that Milton foregrounds the reader's own contribution to the plot by making us determine the relationship of the "end" of the poem to what comes before—that is, the relationship of Samson's final decision to pull down the temple to his earlier exchanges with his visitors. In this respect, *Samson Agonistes* is one of those texts that force the reader to become a maker of plots, to impose significance on the order of events.[49] Milton's forcing the reader to become a maker is entirely consistent with his strenuous vision of interpretation. It is almost as though he were saying to the reader of *Samson Agonistes* what he writes of the reader of Scripture in *On Christian Doctrine*: no one can do this work for you, not even God.

What, then, is the difference between Scripture and literature, between a sacred text and a secular one? In the first instance, it may seem that Scripture is the inspired word of God and secular literary texts comment on or interpret Scripture, when they do not turn their attention elsewhere entirely. But, in another way, we could say that the implication of both *Samson Agonistes* and *Paradise Regain'd*, and perhaps of Milton's oeuvre as a whole, is that there are no privileged sacred texts. In appropriating the text of Scripture through the ongoing activity of interpretation, Milton also breaks down the distinction between Scripture and poetry. Like the angel Michael, who instructs Adam to attribute sanctity to no particular place (*PL*, 11.836-37), Milton does the same to the boundary between sacred and secular texts and in the process produces, though not for the first time, the secular activity of literature.

4. The Temptation of Fiction

The great emphasis Milton put on the activity of interpretation raises the question of the relationship between the act of interpreting and its object. In *On Christian Doctrine*, as we've seen, Milton scrupulously distinguishes between interpretation and the object of faith; at the same time, he asserts that the spirit must take precedence over the authority of Scripture. But, one might ask, if Scripture cedes its authority to the spirit—if Scripture must be supplemented by the activity of interpretation—doesn't this suggest that Scripture is incomplete? Doesn't it suggest a kind of Derridean logic whereby the Bible cannot then be the autonomous, self-sufficient word of God?[50] At times, Milton comes close to articulating something like this, as when he says that God made Scripture unreliable so as to prompt greater hermeneutical effort on the part of his creatures.[51] At other times, he seems acutely aware that poetic making (poiesis) taken to its logical conclusion might imply that God himself was a human invention—as Marvell feared in his poem on *Paradise Lost*, when he described Milton as "ruin[ing] the Sacred Truths to Fable and old Song."[52] If Milton were the American philosopher Richard Rorty, this reducing of sacred truths to fable would not be a problem: he would simply reject the notion that there was one fixed truth or divinely authored text, and embrace the ongoing conversation concerning the things we care about. Theology as talk about God would then be one discourse among many others, and God would be a metaphor not for the absolute but for the metaphysical ungroundedness of any of our intuitions, concepts or values. It may be that *Samson Agonistes* registers something like this intuition in the description of Samson's "rousing motions," the feelings that compel him to go to the Philistine temple, even though to do so is technically forbidden since it amounts to false worship. What some critics see as Milton's portrayal of the dangers of antinomianism may instead signal Milton's skepticism about his own rationalism.[53] In "A Note on Poetry and Belief," T. S. Eliot argued that doubt is part of any serious belief.[54] Milton's doubts seem to be directed at his own conviction that Scripture is entirely available to rational interpretation and that God's ways can in fact be justified. In either case, literature for Milton is the vehicle for inciting and registering the work of belief in interpreting sacred texts; at the same time, literature names a disturbance in the relationship between making and believing, as it has from recorded time.

Here we begin to get at the tragic dimension of *Samson Agonistes*. Many years ago, George Steiner argued that Christianity signaled the death of tragedy. This is because, according to Steiner, there is nothing tragic about the plot of divine redemption. Critics of *Samson Agonistes* have picked up on this line of argument, declaring that Samson is tragic precisely because he is not Christian. The logical endpoint of this argument is that Milton writes *Samson Agonistes* as a tragedy to show that tragedy is dépassé in the same way that classical epic is in *Paradise Lost*. To understand the world in tragic terms is, accordingly, a sign of misunderstanding, of reading that is guided by the Old Testament rather than the New.

In contrast to this reading, I believe that Milton in *Samson Agonistes* makes a powerful case for the intrinsic tie between tragedy and Christianity, beginning with the prefatory note to the poem in which he mentions the book of Revelation and Gregory Nazianzen's poem entitled *Christ Suffering* as exemplary tragedies. This intrinsic tie is not typological; Milton does not present Samson as a Christ figure whose passions and suffering prefigure the passion of Christ. Instead, he goes out of his way to present the story of Samson in terms that are faithful to the Hebrew Bible. The tie is rather analogical. In *Samson Agonistes*, Milton stages a drama of interpretation that every believer must enact for himself in his confrontation with Scripture. Tragic action is internalized in the activity of interpretation, which is inseparable for Milton from the work of faith.

We could then say that tragedy for Milton is the genre most appropriate to the dilemmas of believing.[55] In the first instance, we could see Samson's dilemma as that of all believers: the believer by definition believes in something external—God—which he doesn't produce and may not understand. This inscrutability itself gives rise to a tragic dilemma in which one is compelled to act with faith but without certain knowledge. But we could also say there is a metapoetic dimension to Milton's tragedy, which is premised on a greater skepticism about the reality of the object of one's faith. Here we could say *Samson Agonistes* enacts the conflict between poiesis—the act of making or conferring meaning—and the hermeneutical pathos of doing so, that is, the inability to ground that making on any metaphysical certainty.[56] I've argued that belief, for Milton, is inseparable from poetic making or invention. But the danger is that a "strong" poet—as Marvell described Milton—may also make-believe. It is not plot—and its elevation of human action—that is the temptation for Milton (as Stanley Fish argued long ago). Rather, the temptation is fiction. It is this temptation that Marvell referred to when he wrote of Milton ruining "The sacred Truths to Fable and old Song"; and it's this temptation that Milton referred to when he castigated Charles I for drawing his prayers from Sidney's prose romance. In his *Defence of Poetry*, Sidney defended "fiction" as "the imaginative ground-plot of a profitable invention."[57] But for Milton, this kind of invention stood in an uneasy relation to belief. This is because he did not aspire to write literature, if by this we understand mere fiction or imaginative artifacts that inhabit a realm of their own, unmoored from politics and religion. He aspired to write something more than literature, something that would engage without at the same time displacing, would interpret without at the same time replacing, the sacred Truths.

What does this mean for the "literariness" of Milton's 1671 volume? Critics have sometimes argued that Milton's ambition to produce more than literature resulted in something less. In his late poems, it's argued, Milton deliberately turned away from the conventionally literary to adopt a sparer style. This is particularly the case with *Paradise Regain'd*, in which Jesus rejects the temptation of pagan literature and Milton himself all but abandons the epic simile, the signature device of literary imitation and emulation in this genre. But there is a kind of painful spareness to *Samson Agonistes* as well. Lines such as "O dark, dark, dark, amid the blaze of noon / Irrecoverably dark, total eclipse / Without all hope of day!" (80–2) seem to declare not only the eclipse of Milton's own literary ambitions after the Restoration, but perhaps also the inadequacy of literary expression to Samson's crisis of faith. In both *Samson Agonistes* and *Paradise Regain'd*, it's argued, Milton's chastened style dramatizes the subordination of his literary ambition to his religious beliefs. And yet it's hard to reconcile this argument with the fact that both poems conclude with an explosion of epic simile. In *Paradise Regain'd* the final contest between Jesus and Satan is compared to Hercules fighting with Antaeus, and to Oedipus confronting the Sphinx, in an epic simile that unfurls for some twelve lines (563–75). Milton then outdoes this in *Samson Agonistes*, where Samson's "fiery virtue" (1690) is famously compared to an evening dragon, an eagle, and a phoenix over the course of seventeen lines (1690–1707). It's almost as though Milton were insisting on the poems' literariness, in anticipation of later critics' complaints. But what kind of literariness is this? And what do these questions of epic diction have to do with the more capacious sense of literariness I introduced in the first lecture?

Here it may be helpful to contrast two different ways of thinking about *Samson Agonistes* in relation to Hobbes's *Leviathan*. A modern, formalist reading that attended to diction, meter, genre, and other such features would, I think, stress the important differences between the two texts. To put it in the simplest terms, *Leviathan* is a prose treatise; *Samson Agonistes* is a poem: it has meter and line breaks. Similarly, Hobbes's argument is conventionally rhetorical: it is designed to persuade the reader to accept an argument about political obedience. In contrast, Milton's *Samson Agonistes* is not an explicit political argument, nor does it act like one. If Milton were alive today, this argument runs, he would not be unhappy to learn of the intense debate fostered by his poem, because the poem is *about* interpretation. That is, it is not simply an argument *for* Samson as exemplary hero; it is instead *about* Milton's and our activity of making sense of Samson, and Samson's activity of making sense of himself. In this first account of the literariness of *Samson Agonistes*, this quality of aboutness—that is, the rejection of explicit argument in favor of a self-reflexivity about the text's formal features and interpretive procedures—is what makes *Samson Agonistes* literary.[58]

But, if we think of literariness instead in the more capacious early modern sense of making that I introduced in the first lecture, then a self-reflexivity about poetic making is precisely what *Samson Agonistes* and *Leviathan* share, and this kind of self-reflexivity is not only compatible with, but contributes to making a rhetorically strong argument. Although one is a political treatise and the other a poem, one an argument for obedience, the other a dramatization of resistance, both enact in their attention to linguistic artifice (whether on the level of syntax or diction, irony or figuration, plot or fiction) the self-consciousness about making that they want to impart to the reader: in the case of Hobbes, this making is the construction of the commonwealth and of faith as a public promise, in the case of Milton, it is the working out of one's own salvation and turning faith into a matter of poetry. In both cases, the authors take up the question of the relationship between making and believing, though with very different results.

To say that *Samson Agonistes* is literary in this sense, then, is not the same thing as saying Milton's poem has no designs on the reader, or that it elicits a state of disinterested contemplation, as modern literariness is sometimes seen to do. Nor is it to say that Milton intended us to be unsure whether Samson was a hero, or to think he might have been intended as a negative example, as Carey and others have argued. To the contrary, it's saying that the poem both dramatizes Samson's exemplary heroic struggle to make sense of God's ways and is designed to provoke a similar activity on the part of the reader, which Milton equated with the work of faith. At the same time, the poem calls attention to the dangers inherent in its making or what we might call its artfulness. Because belief is for Milton inseparable from interpretation, it is also inseparable from art. But the interpretation of belief in art also runs the risk of ruining the sacred truths—that is, demystifying our engagement with the supernatural as a product of human artifice.

In conclusion, let me sum up some of the claims of this lecture. I've argued that Milton intervenes decisively in the Western tradition of thinking about poetry, by shifting the grounds of religious belief from authority to interpretation and then making his late poetry about this shift. Belief, for Milton, was not justified belief about a true state of affairs, nor was it equivalent to belief in doctrinal propositions. It was not comforting nor was it passive. It was not, that is, the kind of placid belief Samuel Johnson says we feel when confronted by "the good and evil of Eternity," which are beyond human comprehension, so that "the mind sinks under them in passive helplessness, content with calm belief and humble adoration."[59] Milton's belief was not like Johnson's because, for Milton, belief was not a position one held passively or helplessly. Instead, it was something one did—and ultimately, something one made. It's striking that Johnson himself recognized this about Milton. While Johnson thought that "unknown truths"—truths that escaped human comprehension—produced a passive state of humble adoration, even he was impressed with what Milton could make of "known truths." "Whoever considers the few radical positions which the Scriptures afforded [Milton]," Johnson wrote, "will wonder by what energetick operation he expanded them to such [an] extent, and ramified them to so much variety, restrained as he was by religious reverence from [the] licentiousness of fiction."[60] In equating belief with doing and making, specifically with the activity of interpretation and the writing of poetry, Milton pried belief loose from the authority of dogma even as he also struggled against the licentiousness of fiction. In this respect, Milton could be said to follow the lead of God's representation of himself in Scripture, which Milton tells us is not mimetic but an artifact of divine accommodation, of God's choice to represent or interpret himself in a way the human believer can understand. This had consequences for Milton's theology, which at its extreme runs the risk of suggesting that God is himself a fiction, that is, a creation of the human mind. Yet, while making may not always be so easy to distinguish from make-believe, it's clear that Milton's ambition cannot be described by this term. Not make-believe, but instead a dialectic between making and believing was Milton's goal. Whether Milton's poetry of belief is successful in balancing on this tightrope, or—to borrow an image from the last temptation of Jesus in *Paradise Regain'd*—on this pinnacle, only the reader can judge.

4
Modern Literariness
Kant, Kierkegaard, and Coetzee

In previous lectures, I've discussed the concept of literature in the early modern period. I focused in particular on the work of Hobbes and Milton, and their negotiations of the tension between poetic making and believing. For Hobbes, the goal of constructing Leviathan was to make belief itself a made thing, a matter of the sovereign's judgment. Milton, by contrast, wanted to hold onto the individual religious faith that Hobbes thought he was circumscribing. But for Milton, too, the goal was ultimately to turn belief into a made thing, an artifact of poetry. For both, then, literature did not simply raise the question of belief; it was itself a tool for thinking about and ultimately a vehicle for reconfiguring the very meaning of belief. At the end of the Hobbes lecture, I argued that Hobbes's suspension of belief looked forward to the emergence of the discipline of aesthetics and to the anti-foundationalism of some modern philosophy. Milton, too, has been seen as contributing to the emergence of the discipline of aesthetics, contrary to what he intended. In the decades following his death, readers who feared the radical implications of his work preferred instead to focus on his sublime style as though it were a merely literary or merely aesthetic achievement.[1]

I now want to pick up this argument about aesthetics and look at its implications for literariness in the eighteenth century and beyond. In particular, I want to wade into philosophy proper, and deal with two figures, Kant and Kierkegaard, who are crucial to the history of aesthetics. I'll argue that Kant's version of aesthetics empowers the constructive imagination in new ways and that Kierkegaard's critique of Kant involves a revision of the aesthetic, which gives us another way

The Trouble with Literature. Victoria Kahn, Oxford University Press (2020).
© Victoria Kahn.
DOI: 10.1093/oso/9780198808749.001.0001

of thinking about modern literariness. I'll conclude by revisiting the question of literariness in J. M. Coetzee's strange and wonderful novel, *Elizabeth Costello*. Originally delivered as a series of lectures by Coetzee, and still preserving traces of its origin in the "lessons" that structure the text, *Elizabeth Costello* raises in its very form the question of the difference between philosophy and literature. The novel also takes up one of the central themes of these lectures, the relationship between literature and belief. I will argue that, despite the strong formal differences between the texts of Kant, Kierkegaard, and Coetzee, all are engaged in a conversation about the kinds of belief we address to things that we make, and all three contribute to the construction of a specifically modern, formalist idea of literariness that, I have argued, has recently undergone a revival in the Anglo-American academy. This modern idea of literariness represents a decline from the heroic early modern version of Hobbes and Milton, in which making and construction are invested with all the power of Leviathan. Although it's beyond the scope of this lecture to make this case, this modern idea also arguably represents a decline from the concept of literariness we find in figures such as Brecht and Benjamin, Adorno and Marcuse, for whom the formal aspects of literature always have a political and even, in the case of Brecht, instrumental dimension. Making for the modern figures I discuss in this lecture is still important but (with the possible exception of Kant) religious belief is no longer an object of construction. Instead, by the time we arrive at Coetzee, religious belief has been replaced by the belief in literature or by what Elizabeth Costello calls the special fidelity of the writer.

Here it's useful to quote the philosopher Richard Rorty. He writes,

> The transition from a philosophical to a literary culture began shortly after Kant, about the time that Hegel warned us that philosophy paints in gray on gray only when a form of life has grown old. That remark helped the generation of Kierkegaard and Marx to realize that philosophy was never going to fill the redemptive role that Hegel had himself claimed for it.[2]

By literary culture, Rorty meant a culture that is no longer governed by the search for absolutes. It is a culture where members of society are content to engage in conversation about the things that matter to them, without imagining that these things could ever receive anything like a transcendental justification. A literary culture—at least in the modern West—is, for Rorty, anti-metaphysical and anti-foundationalist. In this chapter, I argue that this culture—and modern literariness—are a product of the history I am about to recount, in which aesthetics is first a matter of disinterested judgment, then a matter of the interesting, and finally involves a suspension of belief in favor of simply attending to the strangeness of human experience. Literature then becomes a way of making strange, as Jakobson and the Russian formalists argued at the beginning of the twentieth century. But this notion of estrangement itself involves an alienation from literature's earlier, more robust powers to construct new societies and new modes of belief.[3]

At the same time, these later figures invite us to ask whether the early modern notion of maker's knowledge is adequate to the modern idea of the literary or even to a transhistorical notion of the literary. Isn't it possible that literature or literariness, considered transhistorically, are categories that exceed maker's knowledge, that literature acts upon us in ways that are non-productive, if also not quite contemplative or disinterested in Kant's sense of the term? Isn't it possible, these later figures ask, that belief always stands in an orthogonal or even ironic relation to the literary? Isn't it possible, finally, that the kinds of belief literature engages are not least of all the kinds of beliefs we have about literature? These are some of the questions I'll be considering in this lecture.

1. Kant and Aesthetics

Let me begin with Kant, who is widely recognized as the most important philosopher for thinking about the emergence of the discipline of aesthetics. In the *Critique of Pure Reason*, Kant set out to determine the limits of reason. In so doing, he delegitimized the traditional metaphysical concerns of philosophy—knowledge of God, the soul, and the order of the cosmos—as beyond our powers of cognition. Instead, he made it clear that the world we experience is a world of our own making, one that we construct through a priori categories. While, from one perspective, Kant deprived philosophy of its redemptive role, from another he can be seen as the apogee of the maker's knowledge tradition: our constructed knowledge derives from the nature of the human mind as a self-legislating spontaneity. At the same time, Kant argued for what he called ideas of reason, regulative ideas of such things as divine providence and the afterlife, which he thought had a positive practical role to play in human life. For all these reasons, Kant has been seen as the "constructionist" par excellence, to use Ian Hacking's term.[4]

This emphasis on construction became even more important in the course of Kant's career as aesthetic judgment came to the fore. Kant turned to aesthetic judgment at the end of his life, when he realized he needed to explain the relationship between the *Critique of Pure Reason* and the *Critique of Practical Reason*, that is, between the natural world, governed by the laws of causality, and our moral assumptions of individual freedom and human agency.[5] Kant thought he found the evidence for the bridge between these two worlds in aesthetic judgment—a kind of judgment, he argued, that illustrates the harmonious relationship between the faculties of the understanding and the imagination.

Kant's account of aesthetic judgment was enormously influential in the decades that followed the publication of the third Critique. It impressed the generation of German Romantic writers who influenced Kierkegaard, and it remains influential in contemporary understandings of aesthetic experience and practical judgment. Let me focus briefly on three features of Kant's account of aesthetic judgment that were to be important to later accounts of aesthetic experience and that can serve to frame my discussion of Kierkegaard and Coetzee.

The first is Kant's description of aesthetic judgment or the judgment of taste as a peculiar kind of subjective judgment, one that is disinterested rather than interested. Aesthetic experience for Kant involves a pleasurable, subjective judgment of a particular object, one for which there is no general concept.[6] But aesthetic experience is also not merely subjective as sensory experiences of pleasure are. Let me give a simple example: "I like this tomato" is a merely subjective judgment, according to Kant, but "I like this painting" makes a different kind of claim on the listener. This is because, in making a subjective judgment of the painting, we also claim that everyone should agree with us.[7] Kant calls this kind of judgment, which is both subjective and universalizing, reflective judgment because it involves "a faculty for judging that in its reflection takes account (*a priori*) of everyone else's way of representing in thought, in order **as it were** to hold its judgment up to human reason as a whole."[8] In its distance from immediate practical concerns and its taking account of everyone else's judgment, such reflective judgment is disinterested.

The second important feature of Kant's account is that we are interested in having disinterested experiences because there is a link between aesthetic judgment and practical, ethical judgments.[9] As he famously declares in section 59 of the *Critique of Judgment*, this is because beauty is a symbol of morality. The disinterestedness we experience in aesthetic judgment serves as an analogy for the disinterestedness that is for Kant a condition of moral judgment.[10] This analogy will be particularly important for Kierkegaard.

The third feature of interest to us is that the *Critique of Judgment* can be read as dismantling the firm distinction between the realm of cognition and the realm of aesthetic judgment that Kant initially presupposes. Needless to say, I don't have space here to argue this point as it deserves. Let me simply call attention to a remarkable confession of failure in the *Critique of Judgment*. Kant confesses that we can only *hypothesize* the existence of an aesthetic bridge between the realms of freedom and causality. In section 22, he writes: "Whether... taste is an original and natural faculty, or *only the idea of one* that is yet to be acquired and is artificial... this we would not and cannot yet investigate here" (124, my emphasis). He drives the point home when he writes in section 59, "Taste *as it were* [*gleichsam*] makes possible the transition from sensible charm to...habitual moral interest...." In other words, Kant assumes what he set out to prove, and in doing so lodges an enabling fiction at the heart of his critical project.[11]

In the twentieth century, the Kantian notion of the aesthetic was appropriated by figures like Theodor Adorno and Herbert Marcuse as a vehicle of radical social critique. Precisely to the extent that aesthetic experience is distanced from everyday practical concerns, they argued, it allows us critical distance on the everyday operations of ideology.[12] Conversely, figures such as Paul de Man and Terry Eagleton have argued that the aesthetic is itself an instrument of ideology because the tensions and fissures of social relations are covered over by the veil of beauty or recast as the experience of the sublime.[13] For still others, what is most interesting about Kant is the centrality of aesthetic judgment to the entire critical project.[14] For these readers, Kant could be said to inaugurate the aesthetic as a way of seeing that would eventually be seen as giving priority to literariness over philosophy. Among early readers of Kant, Kierkegaard was one of the first to take this step.

2. Kierkegaard's Literariness

In his many comments on the aesthetic sphere of life, Kierkegaard is involved in an intense dialogue with Kant.[15] This dialogue is largely critical: whereas Kant stressed the disinterestedness of aesthetic pleasure, Kierkegaard repeatedly equates the aesthetic with the interesting. For example, an aesthete such as Don Juan is far from disinterested or dispassionate. Instead, he is a seducer who is obsessed with manipulating others, with self-interested pleasure and immediacy. By definition, he refuses the obligations of the ethical life. Or perhaps it would be more accurate to say that the aesthete views his ethical obligations from the distance of the Romantic ironist, and this in turn has the effect of vaporizing them under the pressure of his critical eye. The same is ultimately true of everyday experience as well. As Kierkegaard writes of the aesthete's characteristic attitude of Romantic irony, "all historical actuality [is] negated to make room for a self-created actuality."[16]

At the same time, the realm of aesthetics is not simply negative for Kierkegaard. In his refusal of universalizing ethical categories, the aesthete is in some ways analogous to the religious man or what Kierkegaard calls the knight of faith, who also refuses these ethical categories.[17] The aesthete and the knight of faith both conceive of themselves as—in Kant's terms—particulars for which there is no general concept; both claim to be "an exception" to philosophical and ethical universals.[18] Kierkegaard sometimes expresses this positive insight about the realm of the aesthetic in terms of the particularity of poetry, which allows us to transcend the Romantic irony of the seducer: "If we ask what poetry is, we may say in general that it is victory over the world; it is through a negation of the imperfect actuality that poetry opens up to a higher actuality, expands and transfigures the imperfect into the perfect, and thereby assuages the deep pain that wants to make everything dark."[19]

Here we begin to see why, for all his reputation as a theologian, Kierkegaard thought of himself primarily as an author, and a literary author at that. He once wrote of his own work, *Fear and Trembling*—accurately, as it turned out—"Once I am dead, *Fear and Trembling* alone will be enough for an imperishable name as an author. Then it will be read, [and] translated into foreign languages as well."[20] Against Hegel's grey on grey, and Kant's even greater obscurity, Kierkegaard's wit shines like a multi-faceted diamond. A lover of maxims, parables, fables, and epigrams, of Ovid and Lessing, Byron and Shakespeare, the author of numerous pseudonymous meditations, lyrical expostulations, and conjectural essays, Kierkegaard has just as much claim on literary history as on the history of theology. In Kierkegaard's own idiom, we could say that his writing hovers between these two categories of literature and theology, and that, if one looks closely, one can see the slight uncertainty or imbalance as he touches pen to paper.[21] More important, Kierkegaard was himself aware of this odd balancing act and made it the subject of his writing. With the exception of Nietzsche, it is hard to imagine a more important European writer for thinking about the relationship of philosophy and religion to literariness after Kant (see Figure 4.1).[22]

In order to understand Kierkegaard's attitude toward his literary work, we need first to understand his antagonistic relationship to philosophy. Philosophy, for Kierkegaard, meant thinking in universals. The universal mediates our understanding of particulars and thereby makes conceptual knowledge possible. The preeminent contemporary example of philosophical knowledge was the work of Hegel, whom Kierkegaard condemned for his "incessant chatter about the universal."[23] But Kierkegaard was also resistant to Kant's account of the universal in the ethical realm, that is, the categorical imperative.[24] In either case, such abstract philosophical knowledge was, for Kierkegaard, antithetical to the intensely personal, individual experience of faith.

If philosophy is the wrong approach, then one needs to find a different way of writing about religious experience, one that resists the universalizing work of the concept. Here, Kierkegaard adapts Kant's argument about aesthetics for his own purposes. In the *Critique of Judgment*, as we've seen, the particular aesthetic object is that for which no general rule or concept can be given. Kierkegaard understood that this aspect of aesthetic experience has something in common with the religious. Both emphasize the particularity of experience; both

Figure 4.1 Image of Kierkegaard, courtesy of the Danish Museum. The Museum of National History, Frederiksborg Castle. Photo: The Museum of National History.

inhabit a realm resistant to philosophical logic; and both can be characterized paradoxically as "singular universal[s]."

This is why Kierkegaard turns away from philosophy to literary forms of writing: the "Dialectical Lyric" of *Fear and Trembling*; the "Venture in Experimenting Psychology" of *Repetition*; the diary, maxims, and dialogues of *Either/Or*; and the *Concluding Unscientific Postscript*—which announces its resistance to Hegelian system-building in all three words of its title. These works resist the notion that the truth can be simply, conceptually appropriated. They also resist the notion that truth can be authoritatively imposed by the author, as though from on high. Instead, truth—especially religious truth—is something that needs to be poetically—that is, figuratively or indirectly—conveyed and apprehended. It's this indirection for which Kierkegaard praised Socrates in *The Concept of Irony*, noting that by these lights Plato had something of a "poetic disposition."[25] In his *Journals*, Kierkegaard went further and described God himself as "like a poet."[26]

In pursuit of literary indirection, Kierkegaard adopts a variety of pseudonyms, such as Johannes de Silentio, Constantin Constantius, and Johannes Climacus. These are all Latin names suggesting the monastic life: Johannes of Silence, Constantin who is more constant, Johannes who climbs (this last name is taken from a seventh-century Greek monk who wrote a treatise called "The Ladder of Paradise"). There are also pseudonyms within pseudonyms, as when Hilarius Bookbinder copies the manuscripts "by sundry persons" left in his bookshop in *Stages on Life's Way* or Victor Eremita—aka Victor the hermit—edits the work of the aesthete and the judge in *Either/Or*.

What is striking about all of these characters is that, despite their wit and volubility, they are oddly hollow. It is as though Kierkegaard wanted to emphasize the externality of these figures, their lack of subjectivity, their purely verbal existence. At the same time, this hollowness coexists with tremendous particularity and psychological acumen, as when the aesthete in *Either/Or*, a Don Juan figure, writes a hundred pages of extraordinarily detailed analysis of the erotically charged musical structure of Mozart's *Don Giovanni*, or when the figure of Johannes in the *Diary of a Seducer* paints such a vivid picture of the object of his attentions, the sixteen-year-old Cordelia, or when "Anti-Climacus" depicts the intensity of existential despair in *The Sickness unto Death*.

As Kierkegaard suggests in his later *Point of View for my Work as an Author*, this combination of hollowness and particularity is precisely the point of these pseudonymous characters. There he writes that the goal of his "whole activity as an author" is "*Without authority* to **call attention** to religion, to Christianity."[27] In contrast to the magisterial mode of philosophy, then, Kierkegaard's thin literary figures are all designed to call attention to their lack of authority and indirectly to provoke the reader's own subjective experience. In his *Concluding Unscientific Postscript*, Johannes explains in a neat dialectical maxim why indirection is the proper mode of communication about subjective matters: "Inwardness cannot be directly communicated, for its direct expression is precisely externality." Instead, inwardness can only be evoked in the external form of poetry ironically or indirectly. In adopting an indirect method of communication, Kierkegaard puts literariness in the service of religion. But his goal is not to present authoritative religious doctrine. Rather, his aim is, through literary irony and indirection, to precipitate a decision in favor of the inwardness of faith. In this respect, Kierkegaard and his various pseudonyms respect the freedom of the reader, just as God does. Or as Johannes Climacus observes:

> To communicate in this [indirect] manner constitutes the most beautiful triumph of resigned inwardness. And therefore no one is so resigned as God; for He communicates in creating, so as by creating to *give* independence over against Himself. The highest degree of resignation that a human being can reach is to acknowledge the given independence in every man, and after the measure of his ability to do all that can in truth be done to help someone preserve it.[28]

Here, as Kierkegaard tells us in his *Journals*, he was influenced by Aristotle's *Poetics* where poetry has to do with the realm of the possible rather than the actual, and by Lessing's conception of poetry as a temporal art dealing with the transitory and contingent.[29] In its indirection, imaginative particularity, and concern with contingency, literature rather than philosophy is the right vehicle of religious address, the right way to address the possibility of the intensely subjective and contingent experience of faith, which cannot be directly represented. In an odd way, this means that literature, for Kierkegaard, succeeds by failing. Like the Kantian experience of the

Modern Literariness: Kant, Kierkegaard, and Coetzee

sublime, in which the failure of the imagination to encompass the grandeur or power of nature allows us to see that there is something in us that can recognize and thus transcend this failure, the trouble with literature points beyond itself to the sphere of faith. In this way, the failure of literature is also, for Kierkegaard, its peculiar advantage over philosophy.

3. Reading *Fear and Trembling*

We see this double movement of success and failure in *Fear and Trembling*, the work on which Kierkegaard staked his reputation. In this text, the pseudonymous author, Johannes de Silentio, struggles to make sense of Abraham's binding of Isaac on Mount Moriah, in Genesis 22 (see Figure 4.2). Precisely because he wants to understand Abraham and the meaning of this story for the life of faith, Johannes reads with acute attention to its details. In keeping open the question of the meaning of Abraham's story, he also signals his departure from the philosophical condemnation of Abraham by Kant and Hegel, both of whom refused to understand Abraham as an exception to the moral law, instead judging him to be guilty of murder.[30]

Johannes tries to make sense of the biblical story through various retellings, in which he imagines Abraham's thoughts and emotions, and Isaac's response. In the first version, Abraham fears that Isaac will lose faith when he understands he is about to be sacrificed, so he deliberately pretends to be acting of his own accord rather than in obedience to God. In the next version, Abraham sacrifices the ram but cannot recover his faith: "he could not forget that God had ordered him to do this. Isaac flourished as before, but Abraham's eyes were darkened and he saw joy no more." In the third version, Abraham himself cannot make sense of his willingness to sacrifice Isaac or God's willingness to forgive him; and in the final version, Isaac sees Abraham's face distorted in despair on Mount Moriah and Isaac himself loses faith.[31] In none of these four psychologically probing versions can faith and psychology happily coexist. In three of the four versions, either Abraham or Isaac loses faith; in the remaining version, Isaac can only retain his faith if Abraham pretends to be acting of his own accord. Ultimately, the extraordinary vividness of these short, spare narratives only serves to dramatize Johannes's failure to make human

Figure 4.2 Rembrandt van Rijn, *Sacrifice of Isaac*. The State Hermitage Museum, St. Petersburg. © The State Hermitage Museum. Photo: Vladimir Terebenin.

sense of Abraham's obedience to God. These retellings are all in a way literary imitations or interpretations of the Bible, but they are also about the inadequacy of such readings. Each of the retellings imposes a psychologically plausible account on the biblical story, but in the end each only serves to illustrate the incommensurability of such literary verisimilitude and the experience of faith. Abraham's faith will not yield up its secrets to Johannes's narratives.

This failure helps to explain why Kierkegaard characterizes *Fear and Trembling* as an aesthetic work in his late account of his writings, *The Point of View for My Work as An Author*. For Kierkegaard, Johannes's powerful vignettes are a merely literary achievement. He is able to appreciate the sublime incomprehensibility of Abraham's willingness to sacrifice Isaac, but he is not able to live this paradox as a believer. In this respect, he is still an aesthete. The aesthete experiences the incommensurability of everyday life and the life of faith, or of the particular exception and the universal, as a kind of irony, but he remains stuck there. He does not enact the existential commitment that true faith requires. While Johannes's retellings of the Abraham story reveal its intense literariness and narrative power, he does not escape the realm of the aesthetic. This, we could say, is Kierkegaard's initial trouble with literature.

And yet, on another level, this trouble catapults us beyond literariness. This is because the failure of Johannes's retelling points indirectly to what it cannot capture: the sublime exceptionality of Abraham. Whereas a man of lesser faith might perhaps have done as God commanded with stoical "resignation," Abraham had faith that God would not ultimately demand this sacrifice, even as he also prepared to obey. This double movement of faith—resigning Isaac but believing he would not be asked to do so—is not comprehensible from the position of ordinary ethics, according to which such a sacrifice would simply be murder.[32] This is to say it is not comprehensible from the position of reason, ordinary human psychology, or the narrative techniques adopted by Johannes. Instead, Abraham believed "by virtue of the absurd." And by virtue of the absurd, everything he was willing to sacrifice was given back to him. Kierkegaard calls this double movement of faith "repetition."

Repetition means that, strangely, ironically, Abraham returns from Mount Moriah to the sphere of ordinary existence. He returns to our world and mingles with us. How then does one identify a knight of faith, such as Abraham? Johannes tells us that, in this world, the knight of faith may in fact look like the most bourgeois of creatures, for example, a tax collector or a postman.[33] As he observes, with a hint of disappointment,

> [the knight of faith] is not a poet, and I have tried in vain to lure the poetic incommensurability out of him. Towards evening, he goes home, and his gait is steady as a postman's. On the way, he thinks that his wife will have a special hot meal for him when he comes home—for example, roast lamb's head with vegetables.[34]

Here we see that, in contrast to the life of the aesthete, the religious life involves a kind of irony to the second degree. Like the aesthete, the believer is aware of the difference between the particular and the general, between the exceptional life of faith and the universal sphere of ethics, but awareness of this irony paradoxically returns the believer to full immersion in the things of this world. He sacrifices aesthetic immediacy, we might say, but gets it back in full, insofar as the aesthetic involves the experience of the particular without the mediation of the philosophical universal or the concept. Ironically, in the passage just quoted, aesthetic immediacy is represented in the "petit fait vrai" of the realistic novel, the gratuitous detail of roast lamb's head with vegetables, that makes us believe in the fictional world of the narrative—or would, if *Fear and Trembling* were a novel. The repetition of faith, for Kierkegaard, is literariness in a higher key. Kierkegaard sacrifices literature on the altar of religion since the aesthetic dimension of literature is inadequate to the religious life; but he also gets it back, insofar as its irony and indirection allow him to communicate about the existential demands of faith. This is all very well for Kierkegaard. But here we need to pause and ask: what about for the modern, twenty-first-century reader? What about for us?

4. Faith versus Literariness

Kierkegaard's work gives us a powerful example of the way the aesthetic in the Western tradition has been defined over against philosophy, and a powerful illustration of how the aesthetic stands in an ironic relation to the religious life: the aesthetic is at once similar to the religious life in its emphasis on particularity and different insofar as it is a pale shadow of religious commitment. For Kierkegaard, as we've seen, the *difference* between the aesthete and the man of faith lies in the latter's capacity for repetition in a religious sense, which I've called a higher literariness or a higher irony.[35]

But what if there were a further irony, historically speaking, that Kierkegaard did not anticipate? What if there were less of a distinction between the life of an aesthete and that of a religious man than Kierkegaard thought? The philosopher Stanley Cavell has argued that both our concept of the aesthetic and Kierkegaard's are historically determined and that our modern concept of the artist is more like Kierkegaard's idea of the religious man than Kierkegaard could ever have conceived.[36] I think there's something here worth exploring. Following Cavell's lead, couldn't we think of the self-reflexivity and indirectness of modern art as inviting an ironic self-consciousness that enriches the world of everyday experience in the way Kierkegaard claims faith does? This is not to say that our modern experience of art is religious. Instead, it's to suggest that Kierkegaard's account of the irony of religious experience provides a structural analogue to our experience of art. The difference, of course, is that religious experience is predicated *on* belief, whereas works of art in Kierkegaard's sense can only be *about* belief. They do not so much mimetically reflect belief as reflect on it.

The understanding of literature as involving this kind of self-reflexivity is widespread in twentieth-century theory. We saw one rather limited version of this self-reflexivity in the first lecture, in the work of Roman Jakobson, who defined literariness as a focus on the message or the palpability of the sign, for its own sake. But, in other work, Jakobson, like his contemporary Victor Shklovsky, gave more attention to the semantic implications of literariness—the way literature's alienation from ordinary forms of communication enlivens our experience of the everyday world. The twentieth-century art historian Arthur Danto captured this semantic dimension of self-reflexivity when he wrote that works of art are "about" what they represent. By this, Danto meant that works of art, including literary works, are not simply representations that mirror the world; instead they are interpretations.[37] The philosopher Paul Ricoeur argued in a similar vein that literary representation must be understood as suspending traditional understandings of reference. Instead, he urged, "We must dare to form the paradoxical idea of a productive form of reference. The advantage of this paradox...is that it allows us...to affirm as vehemently as possible that...all discourse is about...[what it represents]."[38] Elsewhere, Ricoeur explicitly tied this notion of aboutness to the realm of fiction and the idea of literariness: "Word artisans... do not produce things but just quasi-things. They invent the 'as if.' In this median sense, the term *mimesis* is the emblem of that split...that opens up the world of fiction, or, to use a current vocabulary, that institutes the literariness of the literary work."[39]

Cavell, Danto, and Ricoeur could be said to describe the way that most of us, I think, now read Kierkegaard. Kierkegaard's brilliant imitations of various speakers are quasi-things that open up the world of fiction and invite us to think about the possibilities they represent. This is why Kierkegaard's pseudonymous works are such a terrific example of modern literariness. As he himself recognized, these works might precipitate a decision for faith—but they also might not. What they *do* tell us is that, once the pretensions of philosophy have been unmasked, we have to accept that any representation this side of revelation is literary.[40] This is the insight behind Kierkegaard's statement in *The Point of View for My Work as an Author* that "In all eternity, it is impossible for me to compel a person to accept an opinion, a conviction, a belief. But one thing I can do: I can compel him to take notice."[41]

5. Coetzee: About Belief

I want to end by exploring the relevance of this modern idea of literariness and self-reflexivity to a contemporary work of literature, J. M. Coetzee's *Elizabeth Costello*. I have chosen Coetzee for his formidable reputation as a modern writer who challenges the distinction between literature and philosophy, and who takes on the weightiest of philosophical issues: the nature of consciousness, embodiment, and desire; the meaning of artistic imitation; the relationship between literature and belief. I've chosen him as well because Coetzee's own sense of himself as a writer is explicitly indebted to Kierkegaard, whose maxim, "Learn to speak without authority" is quoted by one of his narrators.[42] Finally, I've chosen *Elizabeth Costello* in particular because it offers a meditation on the art of writing as a kind of making that is both indebted to the early modern idea of maker's knowledge, and different from it insofar as it infuses making with a new sense of irony, contingency, and risk. In the process, belief too undergoes a transformation. In all these ways, Coetzee helps us see how far we've come from the heroic making of Hobbes and Milton.

Literary historians of the novel have argued that the concept of fiction undergoes a sea change with the emergence of the novel. Lennard Davis has claimed that the novel does not owe its origins to the ostentatiously improbable adventures of prose romance. Instead, the novel explicitly distinguishes itself from romance by insisting on the putatively factual nature of its recorded events.[43] More recently, Catherine Gallagher has asserted that the Renaissance category of fiction was essentially equivalent to the marvelous or fantasy. Even a figure like Philip Sidney, who famously quipped that the poet never lies because he never asserts, still, according to Gallagher, distinguished the golden world of poesy from the brazen one of everyday reality. In the Renaissance, she argues, "fiction" meant "that which is fashioned or framed... whether for the purposes of deception or otherwise"; or "something that is imaginatively invented." It was only in the eighteenth century, Gallagher writes, that one begins to find "stories that were both plausible and received as narratives about purely imaginary individuals." At one and the same time, we see the emergence of "a *conceptual category* of fiction, and [of] believable stories that did not solicit belief."[44]

Gallagher is certainly right that the early modern period was happy to flaunt the made-ness of its fictions, although it is not the case that "poesy" in the Renaissance was always equated with fantasy.[45] Moreover, as I've argued, Renaissance writers were certainly capable of creating "believable stories that did not solicit belief," where belief is understood to mean crediting the story's representation of real historical events. One has only to think of the plays of Shakespeare and Jonson. Something certainly changes with the novel, but it is not the invention of the category of fictionality. If we follow the implications of my argument, a better candidate might be the different relationship between making and believing. As we'll see, at least one character in *Elizabeth Costello* attributes the modern reader's lack of religious belief to the early modern transformation of belief charted in the previous chapters, even as the novel also subjects the heroic idea of making to heightened scrutiny and irony.

Two chapters are particularly relevant to our exploration of the relationship of making and believing in the novel. In the first, "The Humanities in Africa," the main character—an Australian novelist named Elizabeth Costello—visits her sister Blanche, a nun working at a hospital in rural Zululand. The occasion is Blanche's receiving an honorary degree—a doctorate in humane letters—for her work on behalf of the poor. Much of Coetzee's novel takes the form of lectures that Elizabeth gives here and there as a distinguished writer and humanist—lectures in which she regularly, if unwittingly, offends her audience. In this chapter, instead, it's the nun Blanche who deliberately offends her audience of humanists by giving a lecture on the failure of the humanities.

Blanche begins by reminding her audience that the humanities or *studia humanitatis* had their origin in fifteenth-century century textual scholarship in Europe. According to Blanche,

> The text for the sake of which textual scholarship was invented was the Bible. Textual scholars saw themselves as servants in the recovery of the true message of the Bible.... The figure they employed to describe their work was the figure of rebirth or resurrection. The reader of the New Testament was to encounter face to face for the first time the risen, reborn Christ, *Christus renascens*, obscured no longer by a veil of scholastic gloss and commentary. It was with this goal in mind that scholars taught themselves first Greek, then Hebrew, then (later) other languages of the Near East. Textual scholarship meant, first, the recovery of the true text, then the true translation of that text: and true translation turned out to be inseparable from true understanding of the cultural and historical matrix from which the text had emerged. That is how linguistic studies, literary studies (as studies in interpretation), cultural studies and historical studies—the studies that form the core of the so-called humanities—came to be bound together.[46]

The problem with this philological study of ancient languages, according to Blanche, is that it proved ultimately to be a distraction. In the process of studying Greek in order to read the New Testament, Renaissance scholars necessarily came into contact with the classical texts of Greek antiquity. These texts exerted a powerful draw of their own and, in time, the humanists began studying these texts as ends in themselves. "Thus... did it come about," Blanche says with obvious distaste, "that biblical scholarship and studies in Greek and Roman antiquity came to be coupled in a relationship never without antagonism, and thus did it come about that textual scholarship and its attendant disciplines came to fall under the rubric 'the humanities.'"[47]

Here's where Blanche delivers her bombshell to the humanists in her audience, a message Blanche is also directing to us, as readers of Coetzee's novel:

> "The message I bring is that you lost your way long ago, perhaps as long as five centuries ago. The handful of men among whom the movement originated of which you represent, I fear, the sad tail—those men were animated, at least at first, by the purpose of finding the True Word, by which they understood then, and I understand now, the redemptive word.
>
> That word cannot be found in the classics, whether you understand the classics to mean Homer and Sophocles or whether you understand them to mean Homer and Shakespeare and Dostoevsky.... The *studia humanitatis* have taken a long time to die, but now, at the end of the second millennium of our era, they are truly on their deathbed."[48]

In this lecture, Blanche offers about as harsh an indictment of the humanities as one can imagine. For her, the humanities, or what she might have called secular literature, are themselves a fallen enterprise, in the sense that they portray human life in an unredeemed state. The trouble with literature is finally that it is a poor substitute for the word of God.

Ironically, Blanche's sister, the novelist Elizabeth, seems to agree, for her own defense of literature makes no normative claims. We see this particularly in the conclusion to the book, a Kafkaesque parable in which the novelist Elizabeth is asked to defend her writing. Kafka, it's well known, identified personally with Kierkegaard, with whom he shared a broken engagement and a tyrannical father. More to the point, he recognized a kindred spirit in Kierkegaard's work, writing in a letter:

> [Kierkegaard's books] are not straightforward, and even if he later developed towards a kind of straightforwardness [*Eindeutigkeit*], this too is simply part of his chaos of spirit, mourning and belief. His contemporaries may well have sensed that more clearly than we do. Moreover,

> his compromising books are pseudonymous and that almost to their very core; despite the amount which they explicitly admit, they can, in their totality, be very properly regarded as letters by the seducer, written behind clouds.[49]

The same, of course, could be said of Kafka himself—but with an important difference. This is because Kafka adapted Kierkegaard's account of the life of faith to the life of the artist.[50] In stories such as "The Hunger Artist" and "Josephine the Singer," Kafka replaced the decision for faith with a decision for literature.[51] In this respect, Kafka is an important precursor for Coetzee. Coetzee's character Elizabeth Costello, however, is quite dismayed when she finds herself in a world particularly reminiscent of Kafka's parable "Before the Law." She tells us explicitly that she has never liked Kafka's work. Judging from what transpires in the penultimate chapter, I think it's a safe bet she wouldn't like Kierkegaard either. How, then, can Kierkegaard help us understand Coetzee?

Here's a summary of the penultimate chapter which, like the rest of the book, is narrated by a not quite omniscient third-person narrator. Elizabeth Costello arrives at a gate with her suitcase.[52] She is told that, before she can pass through, she must make a statement of what she believes. "Belief," she replies, "Is that all? Not a statement of faith? What if I do not believe?" The guard replies, "We all believe. We are not cattle. For each of us there is something we believe." But Elizabeth demurs. "It is not my profession to believe, just to write. Not my business. I do imitations, as Aristotle would have said." She pauses, and then adds hopefully, "I can do an imitation of belief, if you like. Will that be enough for your purposes?" Later, when she is being interrogated by a panel of judges, she confesses that she has beliefs in the sense of ordinary opinions and prejudices, but she comments, with a kind of theological precision, "I do not believe in them. They are not important enough to believe in." Still later, reflecting on the demand that she state what she believes, she muses that she does not even believe in art. "If, in the end, she believes in her books more than she believes in that person (Elizabeth Costello), it is belief only in the sense that a carpenter believes in a sturdy table or a cooper in a stout barrel. Her books are, she believes, better put together than she is."[53] If this is not quite Samuel Johnson kicking a stone as proof of the empirical world, it is an appeal to poetics as a technē or art that, like other arts, produces well-made artifacts.

A little further on, Elizabeth thinks about a passage in the *Odyssey* that has always moved her. In her account, Odysseus is in the underworld and cuts the throat of his favorite ram and lets its blood flow in order to summon the spirits of the dead. "The pallid dead crowd around, slavering for a taste, until to hold them off Odysseus has to draw his sword."[54] Reflecting on why the scene haunts her, she comes to the conclusion that "she believes, most unquestionably, in the ram":

> The ram is not just an idea, the ram is alive though right now it is dying. If she believes in the ram, then does she believe in its blood too, its sacred liquid, sticky, dark, almost black, pumped out in gouts on to soil where nothing will grow? The favourite ram of the king of Ithaca, so runs the story, yet treated in the end as a mere bag of blood, to be cut open and poured from. She could do the same, here and now: turn herself into a bag, cut her veins and let herself pour on to the pavement, into the gutter. For that, finally, is all it means to be alive: to be able to die. Is this vision the sum of her faith: the vision of the ram and what happens to the ram? Will it be a good enough story for them, her hungry judges?[55]

The *Odyssey* says nothing about a "favorite ram" being sacrificed in the underworld. Odysseus sacrifices a herd of sheep and adds that he will sacrifice the best heifer he has when he returns home to Ithaca.[56] By adding "favorite" to her account of the ram sacrificed in the underworld, Elizabeth almost seems to conjure up the biblical ram that substituted for Abraham's sacrifice of Isaac. The Bible of course says nothing about the ram's "sticky" blood and neither does Kierkegaard, whose account Coetzee surely knows. "Sticky blood" may instead be an allusion to Dostoevsky, one of Coetzee's favorite writers. In *Crime and Punishment*, Raskolnikov imagines killing the old pawnbroker and feeling her "sticky warm blood"; "sticky" may also recall Ivan Karamazov, when he tells Alyosha about his love for "the sticky little leaves as they open in the spring."[57] For now, we can say that Elizabeth's focus on the ram's sticky blood is a moment of interspecies sympathy, and a desublimation of faith into an intense experience of earthly particularity, including the irreducible materiality of her own frail body.[58] The equivalent of this is not the Rembrandt painting of the sacrifice of Isaac, but Caravaggio's 1603 painting of the sacrifice, in which the focus is on Isaac's pain and horror at his imminent death (see Figure 4.3).[59]

Here we need to stay with Elizabeth and the ram a little longer. In the *Odyssey*, Odysseus performs a sacrifice in order to summon the hosts of the dead and hear their stories. This famous scene of conjuring is also about the power of literature to summon up the voices of the past. In contrast to Odysseus, Elizabeth imagines herself as both the sacrificial victim and the object of the hungry judges' demand for a story, which she resists, even as she also tries to respond. What then does it mean to believe in the ram? We should first note that Elizabeth characterizes her belief hypothetically and fictionally. "*If she believes* in the ram, then does she believe in its blood too?" "She *could do the same*, here and now." These hypotheses are linked to the activity of fiction-making: "The favorite ram of the king of Ithaca, *so runs the story*"; "Is this vision the sum of her faith...? *Will it be a good*

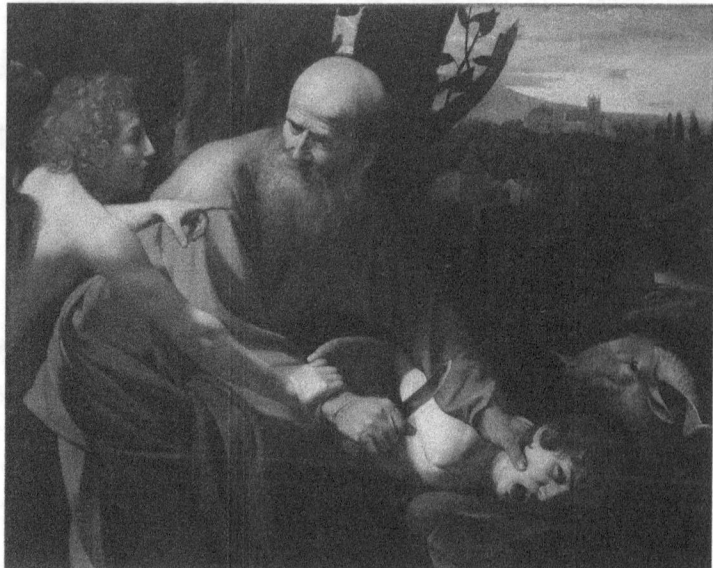

Figure 4.3 Caravaggio, *Sacrifice of Isaac*. Galleria delle Statue e delle Pitture degli Uffizi, Inv. 1890 n. 4659.

enough story for them . . . ?" Belief is ironized as a working hypothesis, a stage-prop of poetic making, almost as though Elizabeth were trying on a new identity as a believer, just as Kierkegaard explores identities through his pseudonymous creations. The modern literariness of the passage is, then, marked in multiple ways: it is not an instance of belief; it is *about* belief, and Elizabeth is self-consciously and thematically calling attention to this aboutness, just as her intertextual allusions make the point that the passage is also "about literature." On another level, Coetzee is himself signaling a specific version of aboutness, the link between hypothesis and fiction-making, in his use of free indirect discourse—the signature rhetorical device of the modern novel which one scholar has identified with the activity of hypothesizing.[60]

Elizabeth, then, believes in the ram if we put belief in scare quotes. Not surprisingly, then, she can't quite get herself to believe in the afterworld she seems to be in and the trial she seems to be undergoing, not least of all because the whole chapter is, to use Elizabeth's words, "a purgatory of clichés," "an elaborate set of dovetailing commonplaces," a parody of Kafka, and altogether too "literary." I refer to the chapter—rather than to Elizabeth's experience—as a purgatory of clichés, because it is one of the effects of this narration to get us to think about—because Elizabeth herself is thinking about—her own experience and her belief as literary constructs. Still later in her musings about belief, she says, "I cannot afford to believe.... In my line of work, one has to suspend belief." Finally, she says what we already knew from the passage on the ram: she believes in what is indifferent to her belief, life itself. But, in the end, none of these versions of belief does the trick; none allows her to pass through the gate. I think this must be because there is no heaven for someone of Elizabeth's beliefs or non-beliefs; as Kafka said in one of his aphorisms, "There is a goal but no way." Or, as Elizabeth herself says, anticipating another encounter with the judges, "What chance do I stand as a writer, with the special problems of a writer, the special fidelities."[61] Instead of propelling us into heaven, Elizabeth's ironic manner of belief, her artistic fidelity, returns us to this world, as well as to the literary world we can only know because we have made it ourselves. But in doing so in the mode of conjecture, Elizabeth's ironic manner amounts to what Kierkegaard called "speaking without authority." In this way, her fidelity amounts to a repetition of and ironic commentary on Kierkegaard's knight of faith, who also returns to this world.

This brings us to the ethical dimension of *Elizabeth Costello*. Like all of Coetzee's novels, this one raises profound questions about such ethical issues as animal rights, as well as attitudes toward the old, and toward death and dying. In her "confession," Elizabeth also asks us to think about the nature of this quasi-religious act in a secular context. But it is also part of the ethical work of the novel—if this generic term is still accurate—to move us beyond the question of what is represented to how: to raise questions about the nature of fiction and representation, and the ethical work the suspension of belief may produce. This is what I meant earlier in this lecture when I wrote that the kinds of belief that literature engages are not least of all the kinds of belief we have about literature. Coetzee seems to have some ethical concerns about what the novel has become. Perhaps he is tired of the self-reflexivity of the postmodern novel for its own sake, even though he has himself written a postmodern novel.[62] Perhaps, like Kierkegaard or for that matter Beckett, another favorite of Coetzee, he wants to call attention to his own lack of authority. As Gabriel Josipovici has written of this Kierkegaardian writing "without authority," "The only way for some semblance of truth and clarity to emerge is for the author to recognize that the conclusion, that which would finally give authority to the book, is lacking, to feel this quite vividly and make us feel it as well."[63]

The scene in the afterlife, if that is what it is, ends there. But the book *Elizabeth Costello* ends with a letter from Elizabeth, Lady Chandos, to the seventeenth-century humanist, lawyer, and statesman, Francis Bacon. I think it's worth devoting some attention to this afterword by way of conclusion, since it places so much emphasis on poetic making as a kind of knowing. Coetzee is playing here with Hugo von Hofmannsthal's "Letter of Lord Chandos to Lord Bacon" (1902). Hofmannsthal Lord Chandos describes a spiritual crisis in which he loses confidence in the ability of language to convey our deepest experiences. I say spiritual, even though Chandos tells Bacon he doesn't believe in God, because there is a quasi-mystical dimension to Chandos's experience. He tells us how alienation from language and common-sense understanding proves to be a threshold to an entirely new kind of perception:

> A watering can, a harrow left in the field, a dog in the sun, a shabby churchyard, a cripple, a small farmhouse—any of these can become the vessel of my revelation. Any of these things and the thousand similar ones past which the eye ordinarily glides with natural indifference can at any moment—which I am completely unable to elicit—suddenly take on for me a sublime and moving aura which words seem too weak to describe.

And later he observes, "At those moments an insignificant creature, a dog, a rat, a beetle, a stunted apple tree, a cart path winding over the hill, a moss-covered stone mean more to me than the most beautiful, most abandoned lover ever did on the happiest night."[64] While rejecting language, Lord Chandos's letter restores to language the literary power of making strange, making us see the world anew. And yet, even as he records his experiences, he tells Bacon, he cannot commit this vision to words because "the language in which I might have been granted the opportunity not only to write but also to think is not Latin or English, or Italian, or Spanish, but a language of which I know not one word, a language in which mute things speak to me and in which I will perhaps have something to say for myself someday when I am dead and standing in front of an unknown judge"—just as Elizabeth Costello had to justify herself before the bench of judges in the afterlife.[65]

Coetzee gives us a very different picture. Elizabeth Chandos's letter is an appeal to Lord Bacon for help with her distracted husband. It describes her husband's experiences of intense rapture and revelation, along with the trials of other "extreme souls." Echoing Hofmannsthal, she writes that a rat, a beetle, a mangy dog might be the vessel of such revelation, but for herself she asks "how... can I live with rats and dogs and beetles crawling through me day and night... tugging at me, urging me deeper and deeper into revelation—how? *We are not made for revelation.*" Then she pleads with Bacon: "Save me, dear Sir, save my husband! Write! Tell him the time is not yet come, the time of the giants, the time of the angels," adding "Yet he writes to you, as I write to you, who are known above all men to select your words and set them in place and build your judgements as a mason builds a wall with bricks. Drowning, we write out of our separate fates. Save us." The letter ends there.

It would take considerably more time than I have even to begin to unpack this stirring meditation on writing and the writer's life. But at the very least we can say that, like the scene in the afterlife, Elizabeth Chandos's letter is about the relationship of poetic making to belief. Elizabeth appeals to Bacon, the patron saint of scientific maker's knowledge, to save her from revelation. Whereas, in Hofmannsthal letter, Chandos tells us there is no human language adequate to the simplest revelation offered by the world, in Elizabeth's letter, language is a sturdy wall between us and the pulsating universe. The same is true for Elizabeth Costello, who believes in her books as she believes in a sturdy, well-made table. For this reason, Elizabeth can offer a defense of literature as mimesis, as when she says of her confusing experience in the afterlife: "How beautiful it is, this world, even if it is only a simulacrum!" And for this reason she can believe "unquestionably" in the ram in the *Odyssey*. Writing for Elizabeth, and also, it seems, for Coetzee, does not involve religious belief or even belief in the sense of opinion; instead, it involves a kind of attending to the strangeness of the world. With Kierkegaard, Coetzee seems to be saying, "In all eternity, it is impossible for me to compel a person to accept an opinion, a conviction, a belief. But one thing I can do: I can compel him to take notice." In this way, Coetzee seems to reduce making to making-strange, but not without some sense of pathos, infused with a recognition of the creative possibilities that have been lost.

In my first lecture, I recounted an anecdote from my time as a first-year graduate student. I was struck then by the affectation of advanced students who regularly declared they were troubled by some aspect of a literary text. "What really troubles me," one student said, "is Coleridge's use of the figure of the albatross." Coleridge is usually remembered for recommending to the reader the suspension of disbelief when she encounters literally incredible characters or events—such as supernatural creatures or the killing of an albatross that stops the sea breeze from blowing.[66] Elizabeth Costello riffs on Coleridge's phrase when she speaks of her suspension of belief. In either case, we have a very different notion of literariness—and of the dialectic between making and believing—from the robust sense of construction that we encountered in early modern texts. As I hope I have now convinced you, this modern notion of literariness has a history, one that is unimaginable without the literary transformation of belief in the early modern period. Against this backdrop, Elizabeth Costello helps us to see that the modern suspension of belief amounts to a different kind of belief, which she calls the writer's fidelity. This is why Elizabeth Costello can say that, even though there is nothing she believes in, she believes unquestionably in Homer's ram.

Notes

Lecture 1

1. Derek Attridge, *The Singularity of Literature* (New York: Routledge, 2004), 4. See also W. H. Auden, "In Memory of W. B. Yeats": "Poetry makes nothing happen."
2. In *The Body in Pain: The Making and Unmaking of the World* (New York: Oxford University Press, 1985), Elaine Scarry argued for a different kind of vexed relation between making and believing in the Hebrew Bible, insofar as "the Scriptures can be understood as narratives about created objects that enable the major created object, namely God, to describe the interior structure of all making" (181). To put this another way, belief is itself a product of making (see 190).
3. On the various meanings of verisimilitude, especially in the Renaissance, see Baxter Hathaway, *Marvels and Commonplaces: Renaissance Literary Criticism* (New York: Random House, 1968), 54–87; and Bernard Weinberg, *History of Literary Criticism in the Italian Renaissance*, Index: s.v. "Verisimilitude."
4. On the relationship between poetry and belief in the Western tradition, see M. H. Abrams' wonderful essay, "Belief and the Suspension of Disbelief," in *Doing Things with Texts*, ed. Michael Fischer (New York: Norton, 1989), 88–110. To the opposition of poetry to philosophy and theology, Abrams adds science in the early modern period and later.
5. Roman Jakobson, "Linguistics and Poetics," in *Selected Writings*, vol. 3: *Poetry of Grammar and Grammar of Poetry*, ed. Stephen Rudy (The Hague: Mouton Publishers, 1981), 25.
6. Ibid., 50. See also Yury Tynyanov, "The Literary Fact," in *Modern Genre Theory*, ed. David Duff (London: Longman, 2000), 29–49; and Victor Shklovsky's comment on defamiliarization in art: "its purpose is not to make us perceive meaning, but to create a special perception of the object— *it creates a 'vision' of the object instead of serving as a means for knowing it.*" See "Art as Technique," in *Russian Formalist Criticism: Four Essays*, ed. Lee T. Lemon and Marion J. Reis (Lincoln: University of Nebraska Press, 1965), 18.
7. In this way, the anecdote seems to respond to those passages in the *Critique of Judgment* in which Kant exempts "[Maori] New Zealanders . . . with their

tattooing" from judgments of beauty. Kant, that is, is the missionary and the New Zealanders are like the African flock in posing problems for his Eurocentric aesthetic judgment. See the *Critique of Judgment*, trans. Paul Guyer and Eric Matthews (Cambridge: Cambridge University Press, 2001), §16, 115. Alex Walton has reminded me that Jakobson's anecdote resembles one in Michel de Montaigne's essay, "De l'usage de se vestir" (book 1, chap. 35): "Je ne sçay qui demandoit à un de nos gueux, qu'il voyoit en chemise en plein hyver, aussi scarbillat que tel qui se tient ammitonné dans les martes jusques aux oreilles, comme il pouvoit avoir patience: Et vous monsieur, respondit-il, vous avez bien la face descouverte: or moy je suis tout face." John Florio translates this as: "A certaine man demanded of one of our loytring rogues whom in the deep of frosty Winter he saw wandering up and downe with nothing but his shirt about him, and yet as blithe and lusty as another that keepes himselfe muffled and wrapt in wanne furres up to the eares; how he could have patience to go so. '*And have not you, good Sir*' (answered he) '*your face all bare? Imagine I am all face.*'"

8. In another essay entitled "What is Poetry?," Jakobson takes another stab at defining literariness. He now compares poeticity to a way of tasting. The poetic function is like the effect of olive oil on a dish: "oil is neither a complete dish in and of itself nor a chance addition to the meal, a mechanical component; it changes the taste of food and can sometimes be so penetrating that a fish packed in oil has begun to lose...its original genetic name [e.g., sardine] and is baptized anew as [olive fish]." "But how" he goes on to ask, "does poeticity manifest itself? Poeticity is present when the word is felt as a word and not a mere representation of the object being named or an outburst of emotion, when words and their composition, their meaning, their external and inner form acquire a weight and value of their own instead of referring indifferently to reality." Jakobson goes on to ask, "Why is all this necessary? Why is it necessary to make a special point of the fact that the sign [is not identical with its] object?" And he answers, with a bracing humanism, "Because besides the direct awareness of the identity between sign and object..., there is a necessity for the direct awareness of the inadequacy of that identity.... The reason this antinomy is essential is that without contradiction there is no mobility of concepts, no mobility of signs, and the relationship between concept and sign becomes automatized. Activity comes to a halt, and the awareness of reality dies out" (750). Jakobson is clearly gesturing here to what the

formalists called the alienation effect of poetry, the way poetry makes us see the world anew. In this indirect way, Jakobson may unwittingly suggest that literariness is a function of the institution of literature. On this point, see Jonathan Culler, *Structuralist Poetics* (Ithaca: Cornell University Press, 1975): "If one uses linguistics as a critical tool . . . , how does that affect the definition of the poetic function? No longer the key to a method of analysis, it becomes a hypothesis about the conventions of poetry as an institution and in particular about the kind of attention to language which poets and readers are allowed to assume" (69, see also 74).

9. See Jakobson, "Linguistics and Poetics," on the difference between poetry and the poetic function: "Any attempt to reduce the sphere of the poetic function to poetry or to confine poetry to the poetic function would be a delusive oversimplification" (25); see also 28: verse exceeds the limits of poetry but verse always implies the poetic function. In "The Crisis of Comparative Literature," in *Concepts of Criticism* (New Haven: Yale University Press, 1963), René Wellek describes "the problem of 'literariness'" as "the central issue of aesthetics," but equates it with literature rather than seeing it as applying to non-literary texts (293). In "Exquisite Cadavers Stitched from Fresh Nightmares: Of Memes, Hives, and Selfish Genes," in *Comparative Literature in an Age of Globalization* (Baltimore: Johns Hopkins University Press, 1995), Haun Saussy argues for a more compendious notion of literariness as "a differential concept correlated with [i.e., defined by its departure from] ordinary language" (17). For Saussy, literariness emerges from methods of reading rather than being an inherent property of texts. Later he defines Comparative Literature not as the reading of literature, but as "reading literarily" (23). For a compatible discussion of literariness as a way of reading, see Jonathan Culler, *Structuralist Poetics*, chap. 6.

10. So far, this definition of literariness is both tautological and equivocal, begging the question of whether literariness is something in a text or something we confer upon it. Here I think it's helpful to keep in mind the argument of René Wellek and Austin Warren, for whom the work of art "is a system of norms of ideal concepts which are intersubjective," so that the question of what's in the text and what is imposed on it can't be so easily separated: both are functions of what they call a "collective ideology," a shared set of assumptions. See Wellek and Warren, *Theory of Literature* (New York: Harcourt, Brace, and Company, 1942), 141.

11. Other early twentieth-century theorists who are associated with the notion of defamiliarization don't necessarily fit into the formalist camp. This is the case, for example, with the early work of Victor Shklovsky, whose concept of estrangement was intended to capture the social function of art, its ability to rehabilitate our perception of lasting truths; and, in a different way, Bertolt Brecht, who clearly saw defamiliarization as part of a revolutionary historical project. See Galin Tihanov, "The Politics of Estrangement: The Case of the Early Shklovsky," *Poetics Today* 26 (2005): 665–96.

12. Consistent with this approach, Jakobson implicitly accepts the philosophical critique of literature when he writes that "truth values" are "extra-linguistic entities" that exceed the bounds of poetics ("Linguistics and Poetics," 19). Finally, because his understanding of the self-referentiality of the message in the poetic function has no cognitive content, he explicitly distinguishes the poetic function from metalanguage (27).

13. See Paul de Man, *Allegories of Reading* (New Haven: Yale University Press, 1979), 113. But, for a contrary argument, see de Man, "Kant and Schiller," in *Aesthetic Ideology* (Minneapolis: University of Minnesota Press, 1996), where de Man chastises Schiller for aestheticizing philosophy, for not being philosophical enough (144–5).

14. Jonathan Culler, *The Literary in Theory* (Stanford: Stanford University Press, 2006), 23.

15. See Richard Rorty, "Philosophy as a Transitional Genre," in *Philosophy as Cultural Politics*, vol. 4 of *Philosophical Papers* (Cambridge: Cambridge University Press, 2007), 91–5.

16. See Jacques Rancière, *The Politics of Aesthetics*, trans. Gabriel Rockhill (New York: Continuum, 2004),13. See also Rancière, *Disagreement*, trans. Julie Rose (Minneapolis: University of Minnesota Press, 1999).

17. I'm not thinking here of what in an American context is called the New Formalism—so-called in reaction to New Historicism—since I think New Historicism was always interested in formal analysis.

18. Attridge, *The Singularity of Literature*, 59. See also Charles Altieri, *Reckoning with the Imagination: Wittgenstein and the Aesthetics of Literary Experience* (Ithaca: Cornell University Press, 2015); and, for a representative collection of articles, see *The New Aestheticism*, ed. John J. Joughin and Simon Malpas (Manchester: Manchester University Press, 2003).

19. For Altieri, what is important about aesthetic experience is that it invites us to attend to the particular without subsuming it under a universal

concept. Accordingly, aesthetic experience cannot be judged by the usual standards of propositional truth. And, if we approach literature expecting ethical truths, we are guilty of mistaking what Kant called reflective judgments for determinate judgments.

20. It might seem that mimesis should also be part of this neglected vocabulary, but I think it's fair to argue that deconstruction amounted to an extended meditation on the classical problem of mimesis, beginning with Derrida's *Marges de la Philosophie* (Paris: Editions Minuit, 1972), and his *Dissémination* (Paris: Seuil, 1972).

21. See, among others, Wesley Trimpi, *Muses of One Mind: The Literary Analysis of Experience and its Continuity* (Princeton: Princeton University Press, 1983); Kathy Eden, *Poetic and Legal Fiction in the Aristotelian Tradition* (Princeton: Princeton University Press, 1986); Lorna Hutson, *The Invention of Suspicion: Law and Mimesis in Shakespeare and Renaissance Drama in the Aristotelian Tradition* (Oxford: Oxford University Press, 2007). Eden focuses on the Aristotelian tradition which sees poetry and forensic rhetoric as making use of the same techniques of reasoning and promoting the same kind of equitable judgments. Hutson shows how the techniques of forensic rhetoric, in particular, hypothesizing about an agent's intention, produced the characterological effect of interiority and subjectivity, and thus the illusion of verisimilitude, in Renaissance drama. For older but still influential treatments, see Owen Barfield, "Poetic Diction and Legal Fiction," *Essays Presented to Charles Williams*, ed. C. S. Lewis (Oxford: Oxford University Press, 1947), 106–27; and R. S. Schoeck, "Rhetoric and Law in Sixteenth-Century England," *Studies in Philology* 50 (1953): 110–27.

22. See Eden, *Poetic and Legal Fiction*, 61: "In an effort to answer Plato's objections to *mimesis*, and, in particular, its appeal to the irrational side of human nature, Aristotle aligns the undeniable emotional impact of tragedy with the participation of the emotions in legal and ethical judgment. In both settings—the theater and the law court—the proper operation of fear and pity contributes to the judging process. More precisely the transformation of fear into pity, when the act has been fully qualified, characterizes the psychological aims of both tragic fiction and equity."

23. See Rudoph Bultmann's article on "*Pisteuo*, etc." in *Theological Dictionary of the New Testament*, ed. Gerhard Kittel, trans. and ed. Geoffrey W. Bromily (Grand Rapids, Michigan: Eerdmans, 1964–76), 6:174–82, 197–228, here 176 n19: "Cf. esp. Resp. [*Republic*] VI, 511d-e, where *noesis* ('insight'),

dianoia ('understanding'), *pistis* ('belief') and *eikasia* ('probability') are listed in their graded relation to *aletheia* ('truth'). In Resp., VII, 533e–534a, the sequence is *episteme, dianoia, pistis, eikasia*, and the last two are summed up as *doxa* ('opinion'), the first two as *noesis*; the relation of *noesis* to *doxa* is that of *episteme* to *pistis*." See also Plato, *Timaeus* 29c–d: "for as Being is to Becoming, so is Truth [ἀλήθεια] to Belief [πίστιν]" (Loeb edition, 52–3).

24. A fuller discussion of what Aristotle means by poiesis would need to address Aristotle's discussion of mimesis in his *Physics*. Aristotle first says that art imitates nature (194a), and then that art completes nature (199a), thereby suggesting that mimesis is not simply a matter of imitation but also has a productive dimension. In the gloss of Philippe Lacoue-Labarthe, art "is the imitation of *phusis* as a productive force, or as *poiesis*." See Lacoue-Labarthe, "Diderot: Paradox and Mimesis," in his *Typographies: Mimesis, Philosophy, and Politics*, ed. Christopher Fynsk (Cambridge: Harvard University Press, 1989), 256. Paul Ricoeur also emphasizes the productive dimension of mimesis in Aristotle's *Poetics* and discusses plot as the conferring of meaning in "Mimesis and Representation," *Annals of Scholarship* 2 (1981): 15–32.

25. See Aristotle, *Politics*, 1278a2–12; 1280b32–4; 1328b32–45 on the difference between labor and action; *Poetics*, 1460b on the different standards of correctness in poetry and politics; and *Nicomachean Ethics*, 6.4 on the difference between making and acting. The literature on the Aristotelian distinction between labor, work, and action, and between poiesis and praxis, is vast, and complicated by the fact that poiesis included both poetry and artisanal labor. See, among others, Hannah Arendt, *The Human Condition* (Chicago: University of Chicago Press, 1958); Eden, *Poetic and Legal Fiction*, 30–6, 61; Richard Halpern, *Eclipse of Action: Tragedy and Political Economy* (Chicago: University of Chicago Press, 2017); Patchen Markell, "Arendt's Work: On the Architecture of *The Human Condition*." *College Literature* 38 (2011): 15–44. Cary J. Nederman argues that there is "a conceptual struggle in Aristotle's own thought" on the relationship of labor to productive activity and to action. See his "Men at Work: *Poiesis*, Politics, and Labor in Aristotle and Some Aristotelians," *Analyse & Kritik* 30 (2008):17–31, here 19. See also Hans Robert Jauss, "Poiesis," *Critical Inquiry* 8 (1982): 591–608; Kelvin Knight, *Aristotelian Philosophy: Ethics and Politics from Aristotle to MacIntyre* (Cambridge: Cambridge University Press, 2007), 4–40; and Tom Angier, "Aristotle on Work," *Revue internationale de philosophie* 4 (2016): 435–49. Some of the most interesting work on

Aristotle's distinction between poiesis and praxis, making and acting, is found in the secondary literature on Heidegger. See, for example, Jacques Taminiaux, "Poiesis and Praxis in Fundamental Ontology," *Research in Phenomenology* 17 (1987): 137–69.

26. On equity, see Eden, *Poetic and Legal Fiction*.
27. James Hutton, ed. and trans., *Aristotle's "Poetics"* (New York: W. W. Norton, 1982), 109, n113, commenting on *Odyssey* 19.165–260.
28. See Terence Cave, *Recognitions* (Oxford: Oxford University Press, 1988), 46; Christopher Prendergast, *The Order of Mimesis* (Cambridge: Cambridge University Press, 1986). Cave discusses the Renaissance reception of Aristotle's notions of mimesis and paralogism on pp. 55–83. It's notable that, for Cave, this scandal has an affective dimension: it is "sexually disquieting," insofar as it implies the possibility of sexual deception and infidelity.
29. Aristotle takes account of the way genre shapes ideas of probability at 1460a when he writes "The marvelous is an element that should of course be embodied in tragedies, but that which is a prime source of the marvelous—namely, the irrational—can be more freely introduced in epic poetry."
30. Aristotle, *Rhetoric*, W. Rhys Roberts trans., in *The Works of Aristotle*, ed. W. D. Ross, vol. 11. (Oxford: Clarendon Press, 1924), 1.2 (1357a).
31. This is one of Eden's arguments in *Poetic and Legal Fiction*.
32. On Aristotle's use of *pistis* to mean both proof and the listener's belief, see Joseph T. Lienhard, "A Note on the Meaning of Pistis in Aristotle's *Rhetoric*," *American Journal of Philology* 87 (1966): 446–54.
33. Eden, *Poetic and Legal Fiction*, 8–9. According to Eden, this reception of the *Poetics* through the *Rhetoric* minimized for centuries the influence of Aristotle's distinctive concept of fiction.
34. Eden argues that Cicero turned Aristotle's logical notion of probability into a psychological notion of verisimilitude. See Eden, *Poetic and Legal Fiction*, 15–16, and Cicero, *De inventione*, 1.21.29.
35. All references are to *De inventione*, trans. H. M. Hubbell, Loeb Classical Library, (Cambridge: Harvard University Press, 1949), here 1.2.3. On *fides*, see also Cicero, *Partitiones oratoriae*. 9.31; *Brutus*, 50.187; *De officiis*, 2.9.33; Quintilian, *Institutio oratoria*, 5.8.1.
36. See Kathy Eden, *Hermeneutics and the Rhetorical Tradition: Chapters in the Ancient Legacy and its Humanist Reception* (New Haven: Yale University Press, 1997). Also relevant is George Kennedy, *Classical Rhetoric and its*

Christian and Secular Traditions from Ancient to Modern Times (Durham: University of North Carolina Press, 1980).

37. See, for example, Cicero, *De oratore*, trans. E. W. Sutton and H. Rackham, Loeb Classical Library (Cambridge: Harvard University Press, 1948), 1.51.219–1.54.33, 2.16.68, and especially 2.42.182–2.53.216. The argument about exciting contrary emotions appears at 2.53.216. On eighteenth-century arguments about countervailing passions, see Albert O. Hirschman, *The Passions and the Interests: Political Arguments for Capitalism before its Triumph* (Princeton: Princeton University Press, 1997). I explore the classical rhetorical origins of this argument in "The Passions and the Interests in Early Modern Europe: The Case of *Il Pastor fido*," in *Reading the Early Modern Passions*, ed. Gail Kern Paster, Katherine Rowe, and Mary Floyd-Wilson (Philadelphia: University of Pennsylvania Press, 2004), 217–39.
38. Ibid., 2.46.193.
39. I quote from Quintilian, *Institutio oratoria*, trans. H. E. Butler, Loeb Classical Library, 4 vols. (Cambridge: Harvard University Press, 1979–86).
40. Ibid., 11.3.2–11.3.6; see also book 6, Preface, and 6.1.1–6.2.34.
41. See Eduard Fraenkel, "Zur Geschichte des Wortes *fides*," *Rheinisches Museum* 71 (1916): 187–99; Gérard Freyburger, *Fides: étude sémantique et religieuse depuis les origines jusqu'à l'époque Augustéenne*, 2nd ed. (Paris: Société d'Édition Les Belles Lettres, 2009); James L. Kinneavy, *Greek Rhetorical Origins of Christian Faith* (New York: Oxford University Press, 1987); and Teresa Morgan, *Roman Faith and Christian Faith: "Pistis" and "Fides" in the Early Roman Empire and Early Churches* (Oxford: Oxford University Press, 2015). Morgan argues there is no reason to believe that New Testament authors had the kind of specialized knowledge of Greek rhetoric that would suggest their concept of faith was informed by the rhetorical tradition or legal tradition (8). In contrast, Kinneavy argues that New Testament authors developed a new concept of faith (*pistis*) by combining the Hebrew Bible's notion of faith as trust with the Greek rhetorical notion of persuasion (*pistis*). In addition to the Hebrew idea of trust, the Christian idea of faith came to involve "the notion of faith as honorific..., the notion of an intellectual assent, and the notion of some corollary doctrine." Faith also included "the subsidiary concepts of faith as a gift, of faith as being a free assent, and of only a limited measure of certainty in faith" (92). Kinneavy also describes the difference between the Hebrew Bible's notion of faith and that of the New Testament as a

difference between "faith that" and "faith in." See 26–55, 100. Martin Buber made a similar point in *Two Types of Faith* (London: Routledge, 1951), when he argued that the Hebrew Bible's conception of faithfulness stresses "fidelity to the law," whereas the New Testament equates faith with belief in propositional truth (see Morgan, 9). Kenneth Burke discusses the use of the rhetorical term *pistis* to mean Christian faith in *A Rhetoric of Motives* (Berkeley and Los Angeles; University of California Press, 1969), 51–2.

42. George A. Kennedy, *Greek Rhetoric under Christians Emperors* (Princeton: Princeton University Press, 1983), 181.

43. The secondary literature on Augustine's rhetoric and his indebtedness to Cicero is vast. See, among others, C. S. Baldwin, "St. Augustine and the Rhetoric of Cicero," *Proceedings of the Classical Association* 22 (1925): 22–46; Maurice Tétard, *Augustin et Cicéron*, 2 vols. (Paris: Etudes Augustiniennes, 1958); Henri-Irénée Marrou, *Saint Augustin et la fin de la culture antique*, 4th ed. (Paris: Brocard, 1958); Harald Hagendahl, *Augustine and the Latin Classics*, 2 vols. (Göteborg: Göteborg University Press, 1967), 2: 479–588; W. R. Johnson, "Isocrates Flowering: The Rhetoric of Augustine," *Philosophy and Rhetoric* 9 (1976): 217–31. As Johnson points out, the fact that Augustine began his manual of Christian rhetoric, *On Christian Doctrine*, after his consecration in 395 and only finished it shortly before his death in 430 testifies to his enduring interest in rhetoric (219).

44. This is in part the argument of Erich Auerbach's *Mimesis: The Representation of Reality in Western Literature*, trans. Willard Trask (Princeton: Princeton University Press, 1953). See also Auerbach, "*Passio* as passion," in Auerbach, *Time, History, and Literature*, ed. James I. Porter, trans. Jane O. Newman (Princeton: Princeton University Press, 2014), 165–87; and Auerbach, "Camilla and the Rebirth of the Sublime," in *Literary Language and its Public*, trans. Ralph Mannheim (New York: Pantheon, 1965), 183–234.

45. For examples from the twelfth century onward, see Auerbach, "*Passio* as Passion."

46. See Marjorie O'Rourke Boyle, "Augustine in the Garden of Zeus: Love, Lust, and Language," *The Harvard Theological Review* 83 (1990): 117–39, esp. 139 n132. This notion of rhetorical theology would be taken up by many of Augustine's Renaissance readers. See n52 below.

47. Augustine, *On the Trinity*, trans. Stephen McKenna (Washington, D.C.: Catholic University of America Press, 1962), 375 (book 13, chap. 2, para. 5).

48. Kennedy, *Greek Rhetoric*, 181. Not only Augustine but also Gregory of Nazianzus, Basil, and many of the Latin fathers were trained in classical rhetoric and taught rhetoric before becoming Christians. On Gregory and Basil, see Kennedy, *Greek Rhetoric*, especially 215–39 on Gregory's use of technical rhetoric vocabulary to describe the role of the priest and preacher. Augustine addresses the objection that rhetoric might not be necessary and makes the case that it is in his *On Christian Doctrine*, 4.16.

49. On Jesus and Paul as preachers, and on the intersection of Christianity and classical rhetoric, see George A. Kennedy, *A New History of Classical Rhetoric* (Princeton: Princeton University Press, 1994), 257–70.

50. In *Greek Rhetorical Origins*, Kinneavy argues that both Augustine and Aquinas "placed the level of certainty of faith below that of science. Aquinas placed it between knowledge (*scientia*) and opinion [*Summa Theologica*, II-II, Q.4, Art. 8], and Augustine says that it only has a plausibility because it is based on authority." But in a footnote, Kinneavy adds that for Aquinas "the inferiority of faith to science and understanding and wisdom is, however, only true relatively, that is, in regard to human beings" (156 n43).

51. See Kinneavy, *Greek Rhetorical Origins*, 26–33, and 92. For a compelling recent treatment of the various meanings of faith in the Middle Ages, see Ian Forrest, *Trustworthy Men: How Inequality and Faith Made the Medieval Church* (Princeton: Princeton University Press, 2018).

52. Although a full history of the intersection of religious faith and rhetorical persuasion is well beyond the scope of these lectures, it's worth noting that Quattrocento Italian humanists and Northern humanists were also acutely aware of the imbrication of these two concepts and practices. For the former, see especially the work of Lorenzo Valla, and the scholarship of Salvatore Camporeale: *Lorenzo Valla: umanesimo e teologia* (Florence: Nella sede dell'instituto, 1972); "Umanesimo e teologia tra '400 e '500," in *Problemi di storia della chiesa nei secoli XV–XVII* (Naples: Edizioni Dehoniane, 1979), 137–64; "Renaissance Humanism and the Origins of Humanist Theology," in *Humanity and Divinity in Renaissance and Reformation: Essays in honor of Charles Trinkaus* (Leiden: Brill, 1993), 101–24; "*Institutio oratoria*, lib. I, cap. 6.3 e le variazioni su tema di Lorenzo Valla: *sermo e interpretatio*," in *Rhetorica: A Journal of the History of Rhetoric* 13 (1995): 285–300; *Lorenzo Valla: Umanesimo, riforma e controriforma: studi e testi* (Rome: Storia e letteratura, 2002); *Christianity, Latinity, and Culture: Two Studies on Lorenzo Valla*, ed. Patrick Baker and Christopher S. Celenza (Leiden: Brill,

2013); for the latter, see Erasmus, and Camporeale, "Umanesimo e teologia tra '400 e '500"; Marjorie O'Rourke Boyle, *Rhetoric and Reform: Erasmus' Civil Dispute with Luther* (Cambridge: Harvard University Press, 1983); Kathy Eden, *Friends Hold All Things in Common: Tradition, Intellectual Property, and the Adages of Erasmus* (New Haven: Yale University Press, 2001). I discuss the rhetorical dimension of Valla's and Erasmus's conceptions of faith in *Rhetoric, Prudence, and Skepticism in the Renaissance* (Ithaca: Cornell University Press, 1985).

53. See Raymond Williams, "Literature" in *Keywords* (Oxford: Oxford University Press, 1985), 185: literature appears in the fourteenth century to mean general learning; not until the eighteenth century did literature mean "the practice and profession of writing." On the history of the term literature, see also René Wellek, "Name and Nature of Comparative Literature," *Discriminations* (New Haven: Yale University Press, 1970); Wellek and Warren, *Theory of Literature*, chap. 1; Warren Boutcher, "Literature," in *Palgrave Advances in Renaissance Historiography* (Houndsmills, England: Palgrave Macmillan, 2005), 210–40; Walter Cohen, *A History of European Literature* (Oxford: Oxford University Press, 2017), 11–13. On the meaning of literature in the Renaissance, see Adrian Marino, *The Biography of 'The Idea of Literature' from Antiquity to the Baroque*, trans. Virgil Stanciu and Charles M. Carlton (Albany: State University of New York Press, 1996).

54. David Hume, *Principal Writings on Religion*, ed. J. G. A. Gaskin (Oxford: Oxford University Press, 2008), 3.

55. See Anthony Grafton and Lisa Jardine, *From Humanism to the Humanities* (Cambridge: Harvard University Press, 1986); Richard Halpern, *The Poetics of Primitive Accumulation: English Renaissance Culture and the Genealogy of Capital* (Ithaca: Cornell University Press, 1991); Lynn Enterline, *Shakespeare's Schoolroom: Rhetoric, Discipline, Emotion* (Philadelphia: University of Pennsylvania Press, 2011). The forerunner of the trauma theory of humanist pedagogy is Walter J. Ong, "Latin Language Study as a Renaissance Puberty Rite," *Studies in Philology* 56 (1959): 103–24.

56. For the Renaissance understanding of imitation, see especially Thomas M. Greene, *The Light in Troy: Imitation and Discovery in Renaissance Poetry* (New Haven: Yale University Press, 1982), and George Pigman III, "Versions of Imitation in the Renaissance," *Renaissance Quarterly* 33 (1980): 1–32.

57. See William Nelson, *Fact or Fiction: The Dilemma of the Renaissance Storyteller* (Cambridge: Harvard University Press, 1973), chaps. 3 and 4; and, on *copia*, Terence Cave, *The Cornucopian Text: Problems of Writing in the French Renaissance* (Oxford: Oxford University Press, 1979).

58. See Eden, *Poetic and Legal Fiction*, 180; and Lorna Hutson, *The Invention of Suspicion*, on the rhetorical production of effects of interiority. See also Joel B. Altman, *The Tudor Play of Mind: Rhetorical Inquiry and the Development of Elizabethan Drama* (Berkeley, Los Angeles, London: University of California Press, 1978), for a magisterial earlier work on the importance of rhetoric for the "controversial cast" of Renaissance literature, including the complex development of character. On persuasion by inartificial proof and anxiety about the power of rhetoric, see Altman, *The Improbability of Othello: Rhetorical Anthropology and Shakespearean Selfhood* (Chicago: University of Chicago Press, 2010). On the various meanings of verisimilitude, especially in the Renaissance, see n3 above.

59. Lorna Hutson, *The Usurer's Daughter: Male Friendship and Fictions of Women in Sixteenth-Century England* (London and New York: Routledge, 1994). Hutson argues that men displaced their anxieties about new socio-economic relations onto women, and linked the dangers of rhetorical persuasion to the imagined threat of female sexual promiscuity. On paralogism as figuring the threat of sexual promiscuity, see Cave, *Recognitions*, 13–15.

60. See also Lorna Hutson, *Circumstantial Shakespeare* (Oxford: Oxford University Press, 2015).

61. Ben Jonson, *Discoveries*, cited by Lorna Hutson, *The Invention of Suspicion*, 345, 346. Elsewhere, Hutson has explored the gender implications of Jonson's notion of manliness. See Hutson, "*Civility* and *Virility* in Ben Jonson," *Representations* 78 (2002): 1–27.

62. On the idea of the heterocosm, see Harry Berger, *Second World and Green World: Studies in Renaissance Fiction-Making*, ed. John Patrick Lynch (Berkeley and Los Angeles: University of California Press, 1990), chap. 1. In *The Mirror and the Lamp* (Oxford: Oxford University Press, 1971), M. H. Abrams locates the heyday of this idea of the poem as heterocosm in the eighteenth century (see 272–85).

63. See Marino, *The Biography of 'The Idea of Literature,'* 122–3 on the Renaissance conception of poetry as a productive activity. M. H. Abrams discusses the construction model of art in the Renaissance, in "Art-as-Such: The Sociology of Modern Aesthetics," in *Doing Things with Texts* (New York: Norton, 1989), 134–58. In *Poetic and Legal Fiction*, Kathy

Eden argues that, although the *Poetics* was relatively unknown in the Middle Ages, the Aristotelian tradition, with its emphasis on the similarities between poetic and legal fiction, was preserved through the influence of Graeco-Roman legal theory on Christianity (chap. 4, esp. 138).

64. I take this phrase from Arthur C. Danto's *The Philosophical Disenfranchisement of Art* (New York: Columbia University Press, 1986).
65. E. N. Tigerstedt, "The Poet as Creator: Origins of a Metaphor," *Comparative Literature Studies* 5 (1968), 465–6.
66. Tigerstedt attributes the first articulation of this view to the Neoplatonist Cristoforo Landino, a follower of Marsilio Ficino. As Tigerstedt has pointed out, this was a different claim from the idea that the poet was possessed of divine furor. This idea, which comes from Plato and Cicero, need not imply a positive view of the poet (460). Also, the notion that the poet produces by divine inspiration is different from the claim that the poet produces by art (474). See also Pico della Mirandola's "Oration on the Dignity of Man," in which he describes man as the "maker and moulder of himself," "sui ipsius...plastes et fictor"; quoted by Ernst Cassirer, "Giovanni Pico della Mirandola: A Study in Renaissance Ideas (Part II)," *Journal of the History of Ideas* 3 (1942), 320 and 333.
67. Tigerstedt, "The Poet as Creator," 464, 469.
68. See Martin Kemp, "From 'Mimesis' to 'Fantasia': The Quattrocento Vocabulary of Creation, Inspiration, and Genius in the Visual Arts," *Viator* 8 (1977): 347–98. According to Kemp, the conception of the artist as quasi-divine creator emerged relatively late in quattrocento Renaissance art theory. Alberti compared the artist to God but qualified the comparison with an "as if" (393). In his early writings Leonardo da Vinci (1452–1519) argued—unusually for his time (397)—that the science of painting was a "semblance of the divine mind" and the artist was "master and god of all the things he wishes to generate." In his later work, Kemp has shown, Leonardo continued to emphasize man's divine powers of invention but he was also more concerned with "the scientific foundation and rational control of [artistic] invention" than he had been, and the verb he used most often to describe this process was not "creare" but "fare"—to make—"the standard verb of production and, as such, the one used almost invariably in contracts" between painter and patron (381, 397).
69. Tigerstedt, "The Poet as Creator," argues that Landino was probably influenced by Ficino's account of man's power to invent new arts and techniques as similar to God's creative power (471).

70. Ibid., 456. *Marvels and Commonplaces*, chap. 3. Also important here was the influence of the image of the divine demiurge or craftsman in Plato's *Timaeus*, whose creation is not ex nihilo and does not involve divine inspiration. See Robert M. Durling, *The Figure of the Poet in Renaissance Epic* (Cambridge: Harvard University Press, 1965), who argues that this notion of the craftsman was particularly influential on Ariosto (130–1).

71. Philip Sidney, *A Defence of Poetry*, ed. J. A. Van Dorsten (Oxford: Oxford University Press, 1973), 24–5.

72. On Bacon's emphasis of making and doing over knowing, see *The New Organon*, ed. Lisa Jardine and Michael Silverthorne (Cambridge and New York: Cambridge University Press, 2000), book 1, Aphorism 3: "Human knowledge and human power come to the same thing, because ignorance of cause frustrates effect. For Nature is conquered only by obedience; and that which in thought is a cause, is like a rule in practice" (33); and book 2, Aphorism 4: "what is most useful in operating is truest in knowing" (104). On Vico's importance to this tradition, including his notion that "verum et factum convertuntur," see Amos Funkenstein, *Theology and the Scientific Imagination from the Middle Ages to the Seventeenth Century* (Princeton: Princeton University Press, 1986), 279–90.

73. See Antonio Pérez-Ramos, *Francis Bacon's Idea of Science and the Maker's Knowledge Tradition* (Oxford: Clarendon Press, 1988), 55 on Plato, *Republic* 600a; and 56 on a passage in Proclus's commentary on Euclid's *Elements*, which "was to be repeated almost verbatim by Cusa, Mersenne, Hobbes, Vico and Kant in modern times" (56). See 55 on the creator God as knower/maker. Medieval writers also conceive of their work as artisanal. See, for example, book 1 of Lydgate's *Fall of Princes*. But according to Andrew Galloway, "they never call themselves 'poets,'" and "they rarely claim to be producing anything beyond artisanal products, with the exception of dream visions." See Galloway, "Imagining the Literary in Medieval English," in *Imagining Medieval English*, ed. Tim William Machan (Cambridge: Cambridge University Press, 2016), 218.

74. Funkenstein, *Theology and the Scientific Imagination*, 12.

75. Pamela H. Smith, *The Body of the Artisan: Art and Experience in the Scientific Revolution* (Chicago: University of Chicago Press, 2004), 21, quoting Paolo Rossi, *Philosophy, Technology, and the Arts* (New York: Harper & Row, 1970); Panofsky, *Artist, Scientist, Genius* (New York: Metropolitan Museum of Art, 1953); Paul Oskar Kristeller, "The Modern System of the Arts," in *Renaissance Thought II: Papers on Humanism and the Arts* (New York: Harper

& Row, 1961), 163–227. Kristeller discusses the emancipation in sixteenth-century Italy of painting, sculpture, and architecture from the craft guilds and their elevation to higher status, thereby anticipating the eighteenth-century notion of fine arts (182–3). On this elevation of the status of mechanical arts, including painting, sculpture, and architecture, and of the human faculties of discretion and practical judgment that produced such arts, see also Pamela O. Long, *Openness, Secrecy, Authorship: Technical Arts and the Culture of Knowledge from Antiquity to the Renaissance* (Baltimore: Johns Hopkins University Press, 2001); Long, *Artisan/Practitioners and the Rise of the New Sciences 1400–1600* (Corvallis, OR: Oregon State University Press, 2011); and David Summers, *The Judgment of Sense: Renaissance Naturalism and the Rise of Aesthetics* (Cambridge: Cambridge University Press, 1987).

76. Smith, *Body of the Artisan*, 10. Ghiberti himself argued that Giotto was the inventor or discoverer of the "*dottrina* of art which had lain buried for six hundred years." Here he was borrowing the scientific and rhetorical vocabulary of invention to make claims of intellectual seriousness for the artist. As Martin Kemp has argued, invention in this sense "could be used in close conjunction with the term *dottrina* (or *doctrina* [meaning true knowledge, 388]), which was at the very heart of Renaissance artists' claims to intellectual respectability." See Kemp, "From 'Mimesis' to 'Fantasia,'" 349. Kemp quotes Ghiberti on Giotto, 349.

77. Smith, *Body of the Artisan*, 22. See also *Rossi, Philosophy, Technology and the Arts*, who argues for their mutual influence (15, 23).

78. Philip Sidney, *Defence*, 24. Sidney may have been influenced by Julius Caesar Scaliger, quoted in Hathaway, *Marvels and Commonplaces*, 92: "But the poet makes another nature and other outcomes for men's acts, and finally in the same way makes himself another God, as it were. The other sciences are as it were users of what the maker of them all produced; but poetry, when it so splendidly gives the appearances of the things that are and of those that are not, seems not to narrate the events, as others, like the historians, do, but as a God to produce them." See also George Puttenham, *The Arte of English Poesie*, II.3, cited in Hathaway, 97.

79. Here again we see the rhetorical influence on the idea of poetry as an art. In the *Nicomachean Ethics*, Aristotle includes art among the intellectual virtues, but insists that production (poiesis) is separate from action (1140a). In the *Poetics*, Aristotle qualifies his own distinction in the realm of poetry by defining poetry (poiesis) as the "imitation of an action."

In Sidney and other Renaissance defenses of poetry, the distinction between poiesis and action, or at the very least, the active life, is often blurred, insofar as poiesis is a vehicle of prudence or practical reasoning. On this last point, see my *Rhetoric, Prudence, and Skepticism in the Renaissance*, especially chap. 1.

80. Funkenstein, *Theology and the Scientific Imagination*, 297. On the new "ergetic" ideal of knowing by doing or making, see especially pp. 290–345. The causes for this shift are many. Pérez-Ramos argues that "the ancient and medieval notion of human art as mere imitation of Nature began to be challenged as a result of new technological developments for which no genuine natural analogue could be found" (*Francis Bacon*, 291). Funkenstein has traced the sources of maker's knowledge to medieval nominalism and the early modern secularization of theology, by which he means the practice of theology by laymen but also what happens to theological explanations in light of the new science (10).

81. See Jerome Schneewind, *The Invention of Autonomy: A History of Modern Moral Philosophy* (Cambridge: Cambridge University Press, 1998). This, as Schneewind points out, is not the same as saying that the concern with moral autonomy was a secularizing project. "Indeed, if I were forced to identify something or other as 'the Enlightenment project' for morality, I should say it was the effort to limit God's control over earthly life, while keeping him essential to morality" (8). See also Ethan Shagan, *The Birth of Modern Belief*, on the emphasis on sovereign judgment in the early modern period.

82. See Mary Carruthers, *The Craft of Thought: Meditation, Rhetoric, and the Making of Images, 400–1200* (Cambridge: Cambridge University Press, 1998) on the medieval understanding of invention. Carruthers stresses that invention was not simply concerned with the rote reproduction of existing arguments. Medieval arts of memory, which were a precondition of invention, "are useful not as devices for reproduction alone (rote), but as collecting and re-collecting mechanisms with which to compose the designs of one's own learning" (20).

83. Mary Carruthers, *The Experience of Beauty in the Middle Ages* (Oxford: Oxford University Press, 2013), 14.

84. There are immediate precedents for this trouble in Counter-Reformation Italy. On the vexed relation between Aristotelian ideas of making, and Counter-Reformation ideas of religious belief, see Baxter Hathaway, *Marvels and Commonplaces*. Hathaway charts the debate about the

representation of pagan gods in Christian epic as raising particular questions about verisimilitude and believability, and also posing the danger that the reader might believe in false gods. But poetic representation also presented the danger that Christianity might itself appear to be invented. On the vexed status of belief in Tasso and Ariosto, see Robert Durling, *The Figure of the Poet in Renaissance Epic* (Cambridge: Harvard University Press, 1965), 167; Margaret W. Ferguson, *Trials of Desire: Renaissance Defenses of Poetry* (New Haven and London: Yale University Press, 1983), 58–65; Albert Ascoli, *Ariosto's Bitter Harmony: Crisis and Evasion in the Italian Renaissance* (Princeton: Princeton University Press, 1987), esp. 284–304; and Ascoli, "Faith as Cover-up: Ariosto's *Orlando Furioso*, Canto 21, and Machiavellian Ethics," *I Tatti Studies in the Italian Renaissance* 8 (1999): 135–70.

85. There were, of course, also social and economic reasons for the new attitudes towards rhetorical faith and promise keeping, which in turn affected attitudes towards religious belief. While these social and economic changes are well beyond the scope of these lectures to canvas, I have discussed some of these developments and the extensive secondary literature on these issues in my *Wayward Contracts: The Crisis of Political Obligation in England, 1640–1674* (Princeton: Princeton University Press, 2004). For early important work on the social implications of rhetorical faith in early modern England, see Lorna Hutson, *The Usurer's Daughter*, and Craig Muldrew, *The Economy of Obligation: The Culture of Credit and Early Modern Social Relations* (London: Palgrave Macmillan, 1998), a work much indebted to Hutson. For the changing legal culture of economic contracts that affected thinking about promises and keeping faith, see David Harris Sacks, "The Promise and the Contract in Early Modern England: Slade's Case in Perspective," in *Rhetoric and Law in Early Modern Europe*, ed. Victoria Kahn and Lorna Hutson (New Haven: Yale University Press, 2001), 28–53; and Christopher Hill, "Covenant Theology and the Concept of 'A Public Person,'" in *The Collected Essays of Christopher Hill*, 3 vols. (Amherst, MA: University of Massachusetts Press, 1986), 3: 300–24. Some scholars of covenant theology, including Hill, believe that the religious covenant came to be understood on the analogy of an economic contract between man and God. This suggests another way of thinking about belief as a made thing, the artifact of a contract.

86. Sidney, *Defence*, 75.
87. There is a longstanding controversy about Shakespeare's beliefs in the secondary literature on Shakespeare's plays. For the view that Shakespeare uses rather than espouses beliefs in his drama, see George Santayana, "The Absence of Religion in Shakespeare," *Interpretations of Poetry and Religion* (New York: Charles Scribner's Sons, 1900), 147–65; and T. S. Eliot, "Shakespeare and the Stoicism of Seneca," in *Selected Essays, 1917–32* (New York: Harcourt, Brace, and Company, 1932), 107–20. On Shakespeare's representation of religion, see also David Scott Kastan, *A Will to Believe: Shakespeare and Religion* (Oxford: Oxford University Press, 2014). For an argument that Shakespeare's plays defend an irenic Erasmian Christianity, see Jeffrey Knapp, *Shakespeare's Tribe: Church, Nation, and Theater in Renaissance England* (Chicago: University of Chicago Press, 2002).
88. Jonson, *Discoveries*, in *The Complete Poems*, ed. George Parfitt (London: Penguin, 1996), 378.
89. See Ethan Shagan, *The Birth of Modern Belief* (Princeton: Princeton University Press, 2018), especially chap. 7 on Mandeville.

Lecture 2

1. Martin Butler, "The Condition of the Theaters in 1642," in Jane Milling and Peter Thomson, eds. *The Cambridge History of British Theater, vol 1: Origins to 1660* (Cambridge: Cambridge University Press, 2004), 439–57.
2. For the criticism of the classics, see *Leviathan*, ed. Richard Tuck (Cambridge: Cambridge University Press, 1996), chap. 21, p. 150 (subsequent references are to chapter first, then page). References to *EW* are to *The English Works of Thomas Hobbes of Malmesbury*, ed. Sir William Molesworth, 11 vols. (London: Bohn, 1839–45). Hobbes, of course, was not the first to claim to be charting a new course for politics: see Machiavelli, preface to Book 1 of *The Discourses*.
3. J. W. N. Watkins, *Hobbes's System of Ideas* (New York: Barnes and Noble, 1965) 28; Aubrey, *Brief Lives*, ed. O. L. Dick (London: Secker and Warburg, 1950), 150. Recently, Timothy Raylor has encouraged us to be skeptical of Aubrey's account of Hobbes on Euclid. See n17 below.
4. See Leopold Damrosch, "Hobbes as Reformation Theologian," *Journal of the History of Ideas* 40 (1979): 339–53.
5. *Leviathan*, "Review and Conclusion," 491.
6. *Leviathan*, "Review and Conclusion," 483.

7. This is the argument of Quentin Skinner, *Reason and Rhetoric in the Philosophy of Hobbes* (Cambridge: Cambridge University Press, 1996). For an argument that Skinner and others fundamentally misconstrue this sentence as expressing Hobbes's own views, see Karl Schuhmann, "Skinner's Hobbes," *British Journal of the History of Philosophy* 6 (1998): 115–25. However, the next quotation in the passage (and my paragraph) definitely expresses Hobbes's view.
8. See Hobbes, *Leviathan*, 3.20 and 15.110; Victoria Kahn, *Rhetoric, Prudence, and Skepticism in the Renaissance* (Ithaca: Cornell University Press, 1985), chap. 6; Tom Sorell, "Hobbes's UnAristotelian Political Rhetoric," *Philosophy and Rhetoric* 23 (1990), 98–9; and Hoekstra, "The End of Philosophy (The Case of Hobbes)," *Proceedings of the Aristotelian Society* 106 (2006): 23–60.
9. Also relevant here are Hobbes's remarks about how the philosopher as well as the poet needs imagination to arrive at the truth. See Baxter Hathaway, *Marvels and Commonplaces: Renaissance Literary Criticism* (New York: Random House, 1968), 107. As Hathaway notes, in the Preface to *Gondibert*, Hobbes defends the imagination in ways reminiscent of George Puttenham's or Philip Sidney's emphasis on the poet as maker: "But so far forth as the fancy of man has traced the ways of true philosophy, so far it has produced many marvelous effects to the benefit of mankind. All that is defensible in building, or marvelous in engines and instruments of motion, whatsoever commodity men receive from the observations of the heavens, from the description of the earth, from the account of time, from walking on the seas, and whatsoever distinguisheth the civility of Europe from the barbarity of the American savages, is the workmanship of fancy, but guided by the precepts of true philosophy" (qtd. 107).
10. There is an extensive secondary literature on the relationship between Hobbes's early interest in rhetoric and his later work. Those who emphasize continuity—and the centrality of rhetoric to Hobbes's political science—include myself in *Rhetoric, Prudence, and Skepticism in the Renaissance*; Victoria Silver, "Hobbes on Rhetoric" in *The Cambridge Companion to Hobbes*, ed. Tom Sorell (Cambridge: Cambridge University Press, 1996), 329–45; Bryan Garsten, *Saving Persuasion: A Defense of Rhetoric and Judgment* (Cambridge: Harvard University Press, 2006); Ioannis D. Evrigenis, *Images of Anarchy: The Rhetoric and Science of Hobbes's State of Nature* (Cambridge: Cambridge University Press, 2014). Tom Sorell and Jeffrey

Barnouw argue for Hobbes's incorporation of rhetorical techniques of argument into his conception of logic. See Sorell, "Hobbes's UnArisotelian Rhetoric"; and Barnouw, "Persuasion in Hobbes's *Leviathan*," *Hobbes Studies* 1 (1988): 3–25. In *Philosophy, Rhetoric, and Thomas Hobbes* (Oxford: Oxford University Press, 2018), Timothy Raylor argues for continuity in Hobbes's critical attitude towards humanist rhetoric: "Hobbes's objection to the humanist ideal of the eloquent *vir civilis* both preceded his turn to the scientific demonstration of political precepts and continued to preoccupy him throughout his life" (92). But Raylor rightly points out that Hobbes was consistently interested in developing his own perspicuous rhetorical style and mode of argument. Quentin Skinner argues for a break with and then return to rhetoric in *Reason and Rhetoric in the Philosophy of Hobbes*. In his review of Skinner, Karl Schuhmann insists that Hobbes's antipathy to rhetoric and desire to put science on a logical foundation was unchanging; see "Skinner's Hobbes."

11. Raylor chastises others for treating rhetoric in *Leviathan* in terms of elocution, but his conception of rhetoric in Hobbes's works is still one of lucid diction, illustration, or ornamentation.
12. See Jeffrey Barnouw, "Persuasion in Hobbes's *Leviathan*," 24. Barnouw is discussing parts 3 and 4 of *Leviathan*, but I believe his point applies to parts 1 and 2 as well.
13. For a related argument, see Ioannis Evrigenis, *Images of Anarchy*.
14. This is the argument of Kinch Hoekstra in "Hobbes's Thucydides," in *The Oxford Handbook to Hobbes*, ed. A. P. Martinich and Kinch Hoekstra (Oxford: Oxford University Press, 2016), 547–74. On "contexture of narration," see Hobbes's address "To the Readers" of his translation of Thucydides, in *EW*, 8:viii.
15. Aubrey, *Brief Lives*, 150.
16. *EW*, 7:184.
17. Here it's worth pausing to note, with Timothy Raylor, that the anecdote recounted by Aubrey is rhetorically effective but implausible. Hobbes would most likely have encountered Euclid earlier, whether at Oxford or when he assisted the mathematician William Senior in surveying the Cavendish estates in 1610. See Raylor, *Hobbes*, 127.
18. See Silver, "Hobbes on Rhetoric," esp. 338–9. For a similar argument about how to understand Hobbes's borrowing from Euclid, see also D. W. Hanson, "The Meaning of 'Demonstration' in Hobbes's Science," *History of Political Thought* 11 (1990): 587–626.

19. Hobbes, *EW*, 1:7. I discuss this passage in *Rhetoric, Prudence, and Skepticism*, 156. See also Hoekstra, "The End of Philosophy," 28.
20. On Hobbes's interest in Aristotle's *Rhetoric*, see Raylor, *Hobbes*, chap. 4, esp. 127, 141–38, and 154. On the cross-referencing to Aristotle's *Poetics*, see 179. Raylor shows that Skinner's argument about Hobbes's turn away from rhetoric is implausible. He also demonstrates that the rhetoric that Hobbes was interested in was Aristotle's, not Cicero's. But his main point is that rhetoric, for Hobbes, was incompatible with logical argument.
21. See Hobbes, *De Cive: The English Version*, ed. Howard Warrender (Oxford: Clarendon Press, 1983), 10.11, p. 137, and *The Elements of Law: Human Nature and De Corpore Politico*, ed. J. C. A. Gaskin (Oxford: Oxford University Press, 1994), 2.27.14, p. 171.
22. Hobbes, *De Cive*, 12.12, p. 154.
23. Something similar seems to be a work in the chart of sciences in chapter 9 of *Leviathan*, where Hobbes characterizes rhetoric, poetry, and logic as species of "knowledge of consequences of speech": "In Magnifying, Vilifying, etc. POETRY; ii) In Persuading, RHETORIQUE; iii) In Reasoning, LOGIQUE; iv) In Contracting, The Science of JUST and UNJUST." If, on the one hand, the division maintains the separation between persuasion and reason, it also locates all three disciplines under a single rubric of science as the knowledge of the consequences of words. Skinner also notes Hobbes's more positive view of rhetoric in chapter 9 of *Leviathan* in *Reason and Rhetoric*, 356–7.
24. See Aristotle, *Rhetoric*, W. Rhys Roberts trans., in *The Works of Aristotle*, ed. W. D. Ross, vol. 11. (Oxford: Clarendon Press, 1924), 1.1.14 (1355b); Hobbes's Digest translates this passage in Aristotle as "faciendam fidem" (Raylor, *Hobbes*, 165).
25. Thomas Hobbes, *A Briefe of the Art of Rhetorique*, in *The Rhetorics of Thomas Hobbes and Bernard Lamy*, ed. John T. Harwood (Carbondale: Southern Illinois University Press, 1986), 1.2, p. 40; see also 1.3: "the end of *Rhetorique* is victory; which consists in having gotten *beleefe*"; and Hobbes, *The Elements of Law* 2.8.12.
26. Hobbes, *Leviathan*, 3.21 and 3.23.
27. Hobbes, *Leviathan*, 4.24–5; cf. 4.34 on method as involving the definition of words. Raylor, *Hobbes*, 220–30, and Skinner, *Reason and Rhetoric*, 257–308, also note Hobbes's antipathy to the humanist rhetorical notion of invention, but neither comments on Hobbes's practical redefinition of invention as *solertia*.

28. Hobbes, *Leviathan*, 4.24.
29. Ibid., 5.35–6.
30. Hobbes's emphasis on the autonomy of invention also gives a new life to metaphor, making it more rather than less central to the project of *Leviathan*. For, while Hobbes famously censures "Metaphor, Tropes, and other Rhetoricall figures" for their deviation from the literal sense and their obstruction of logical reasoning (5.35), he also makes it clear that abstract thinking depends on precisely this kind of deviation from the literal sense. Describing the role of language in translating perceptions into concepts, Hobbes writes that "the generall use of Speech, is to transferre our Mentall Discourse into Verbal; or the Trayne of our Thoughts, into a Trayne of Words" (4.25). In describing the conventionalism of language in terms of the "transference" of mental discourse into verbal, Hobbes borrows from the etymology of metaphor (from the Greek "to transport or carry over"), and implicitly suggests the metaphorical relationship of all language to reality. I provide a fuller account of Hobbes's Euclidean approach to language in "Hobbes and the Science of Metaphor," in *Scientific Statesmanship, Governance and the History of Political Philosophy*, ed. Kyriakos N. Demetriou and Antis Loizides (New York and London: Routledge, 2015), 85–100.
31. Hobbes, Introduction to *Leviathan*, 9–10.
32. In his "Life of Thucydides," Hobbes divides elocution into narration and style, and describes how Thucydides often sets out the "grounds and motives" of action "narratively" (*EW*, 8:xxi). He also insists on the importance of enargeia: "Digressions for instructions' cause, and other such open conveyance of precepts (which is the philosopher's part), he never useth; as having so clearly set before men's eyes the ways and events of good and evil counsels, that the narration itself doth secretly instruct the reader, and more effectually than can possibly be done by precept" (xxii). For a good recent analysis of the way Hobbes's account of the state of nature evolves from his earlier work to *Leviathan*, see Evrigenis, *Images of Anarchy*. Evrigenis also argues that the antithesis between science and rhetoric has been overemphasized in the secondary literature on Hobbes, with many critics taking Hobbes's reliance on Euclid and his professed antipathy to rhetoric at face value. He notes as well that Hobbes breaks down the distinction between epic poetry and political theory in his *Answer to Gondibert*.

33. Rita Copeland, "The History of Rhetoric and the Longue Durée," *JEGP* 106 (2007), 186. See Cicero, *De inventione*, trans. H. M. Hubbell, Loeb Classical Library (Cambridge: Harvard University Press, 1949) 1.19.27: "Argument is an imaginary case, which still might have happened"; and *Ad Herennium*, trans. Harry Caplan, Loeb Classical Library (Cambridge: Harvard University Press, 1954), 1.13. As Copeland points out, Cicero himself gives us such an argumentum in his account of the origins of rhetoric in a pre-civil state. See *De inventione*, 1.1.2–1.2.2. But Hobbes does not only echo Cicero's account, he also revises it: we move from the state of nature to the state, with no intervening concept of society. There is no social contract that could challenge the authority of the political contract.
34. See Quintilian, *Institutio oratoria*, trans. H. E. Butler, 4 vols. (Cambridge: Harvard University Press, 1979–86), 5.10.95–6.
35. Kathy Eden, *Poetic and Legal Fiction in the Aristotelian Tradition* (Princeton: Princeton University Press, 1986), 47–8.
36. This is just what we should expect from Hobbes's attention to rhetorical invention in the *Briefe* and his attention to the argumentative force of narration in Thucydides: "The narration itself doth secretly instruct the reader, and more effectually than can possibly be done by precept" (*EW*, 8:xxii). On this last point, see Hoekstra, "Thucydides"; Ioannis Evrigenis, *Images of Anarchy*, 25–43; and Raylor, *Hobbes*, chap. 3.
37. I've made this argument at greater length in *Wayward Contracts: The Crisis of Political Obligation in England, 1640–74* (Princeton: Princeton University Press, 2004), chap. 6.
38. This eclipse of society is important. Hobbes does not want individual subjects to be able to claim autonomy from the sovereign by virtue of a pre-existing social contract. Society is, in Hobbes's argument, an effect of the political contract, not a prior state.
39. On consent as an act of the imagination, see Douglass, "The Body Politic 'is a fictitious body': Hobbes on Imagination and Fiction," *Hobbes Studies* 27 (2004): 126–47.
40. See Andrea Wilson Nightingale, *Spectacles of Truth in Classical Philosophy: Theoria in its Cultural Context* (2004).
41. Tuck, Introduction to *Leviathan*, xxxvi, note 50. See also Skinner, *Reason and Rhetoric*, who argues that Hobbes's theory of representation actually begins even earlier, in chap. 1 of *Leviathan*.
42. Hobbes, *Leviathan*, 16.114.

43. Ibid., 16.111. There is considerable debate in the secondary literature about what Hobbes means by person. See among others Quentin Skinner, "Hobbes and the Purely Artificial Person of the State," *Journal of Political Philosophy* 7 (1999): 1–29; David Runciman, "What Kind of Person is Hobbes's State? A Reply to Skinner," *Journal of Political Philosophy* 8 (2000): 26–78; A. P. Martinich, "Authorization and Representation in Hobbes's *Leviathan*," in A. P. Martinich and Kinch Hoekstra, eds., *The Oxford Handbook of Hobbes* (Oxford: Oxford University Press, 2016), 315–38; Philippe Crignon, "Representation and the Person of the State," *Hobbes Studies* 31 (2018): 48–74, as well as the works cited in nn46 and 51 below. In "The Two Faces of Personhood: Hobbes, Corporate Agency, and the Personality of the State," *European Journal of Political Theory* (forthcoming; DOI: 10.1177/1474885117731941), Sean Fleming persuasively argues that we need to attend to the two complementary facets of Hobbes's notion of person, as representative and represented (*Leviathan*, chaps. 16 and 42), and that Hobbes's notion of the state as an artificial person should be understood to suggest that the state is best understood as a fictional character.
44. See Philippe Crignon, "Representation and the Person of the State," 56–7. Crignon also notes that, while the corporation was not conceived of as having its own will, the sovereign is fully capable of willing (63).
45. In addition to the passage he cites, Hobbes could have learned this lesson from the comparisons of rhetoric to the theater in Cicero, *De oratore*, trans. E. W. Sutton and H. Rackham, Loeb Classical Library (Cambridge: Harvard University Press, 1948), 2.49.193; and Quintilian, *Institutio oratoria*, 11.3.2–11.3.6. See my discussion of these passages in lecture 1.
46. I have analyzed chapter 16 and Hobbes's indebtedness to rhetorical and theatrical senses of representation in greater detail in my *Rhetoric, Prudence, and Skepticism in the Renaissance*, 167–71. For an analysis of Hobbes on representation that is essentially compatible with my own, see Mónica Brito Vieira, *The Elements of Representation in Hobbes* (Leiden: Brill, 2009); and Vieira, "Performative Imaginaries: Pitkin versus Hobbes on Political Representation," in *Reclaiming Representation: Contemporary Advances in the Theory of Political Representation*, ed. Vieira (New York: Routledge, 2017), 25–49, esp. 44. On the importance of fiction to Hobbes, beginning with his discussion of the state as a "fictitious body" in the *Elements of Law*, 2.21.4, p. 120, see also Douglass, "The Body Politic."

47. For the claim that the artificial person is a mere simile, see Raylor, *Hobbes*, 262.
48. Philip Pettit, *Made with Words: Hobbes on Language, Mind, and Politics* (Princeton: Princeton University Press, 2008).
49. In *Reason and Rhetoric*, Quentin Skinner describes parts 3 and 4 of *Leviathan* as the confirmatio of the arguments put forward in the first half of the book, and a refutatio of his enemies' arguments (384). In *Hobbes*, Timothy Raylor argues that they are not merely a confirmatio, but the application of Hobbes's argument to a new context, albeit one that is not susceptible of philosophical argument. Raylor thus concedes the greater "rhetoricity" of these books but does not see them as impinging on the logical arguments of parts 1 and 2 (265–6). Both approaches make the second half of *Leviathan* inessential to the logical argument for obedience.
50. In addition to Damrosch, "Hobbes as Reformation Theologian," see Jonathan Sheehan, "Thomas Hobbes, D.D.: Theology, Orthodoxy, and History," *The Journal of Modern History* 88 (2016): 249–74.
51. See Arash Abizadeh, "Hobbes's Conventionalist Theology, the Trinity, and God as an Artificial Person by Fiction," *Historical Journal* 60 (2017): 915–41, esp. 915 and 926 on how *Leviathan* chap. 16 discusses representation of the true God of Christianity by fiction. As Hobbes writes in chapter 16, "There are few things, that are uncapable of being represented by Fiction." This extends even to God: "The true God may be Personated. As he was, first by *Moses*; . . . Secondly, by the Son of man, his own son, our Blessed Saviour *Jesus Christ* . . . . And thirdly, by the Holy Ghost." The implication, which Hobbes will develop in parts 3 and 4 of *Leviathan*, is that God may also be personated by the sovereign or even, given our ignorance of God's essential nature, that he can only be represented by the sovereign. Something of this slippage between God and the sovereign is already evident in the frontispiece and the Introduction to *Leviathan*. Here, the image of the sovereign is accompanied by an epigraph from the book of Job concerning God's awe-inspiring power: "non est potestas super terram quae comparetur ei"—there is no power to be compared to Him. Despite the claim that God is incomparable, the effect is implicitly to compare the sovereign as mortal God to God himself.
52. Hobbes, *Elements*, 1.5.7, p. 37.
53. The *Oxford English Dictionary* tracks Hobbes's definitions. Its first definition of faith is "The fulfilment of a trust or promise, and related senses." The

second definition is "Inducement to belief or trust," where belief encompasses the crediting of some ordinary event or of Christ's miracles. The fifth meaning is "belief in or acceptance of the doctrines of religion."

54. In the *Elements*, this work begins in the very next chapter, "Of Knowledge, Opinion and Belief." For belief here is reduced to a kind of opinion, in contrast to knowledge of the truth. And conscience itself is defined as "the opinion of evidence" (1.6.8, p. 42).

55. Here Hobbes is playing with a long Christian tradition of reflecting on the difference between believing and believing in. For theologians such as Augustine, believing in referred to the specific belief in God or Christ, as opposed to simply believing X or believing that, the kind of belief we have about ordinary, historical events. For Augustine and others, believing in is equated with saving faith, whereas ordinary believing is termed historical faith. But Hobbes collapses this distinction. I am indebted to Ethan Shagan for helping me see this point.

56. Cf *Leviathan*, 42.356: "the Power to make the Scriptures (which are the Rules of Christian Faith) Laws." Hobbes makes the same point in his analysis of the Decalogue. "There is no doubt but they were made Laws by God himselfe: But because a Law obliges not, nor is Law to any, but to them that acknowledge it to be the act of the Soveraign; how could the people of Israel that were forbidden to approach the Mountain to hear what God said to Moses, be obliged to obedience to all those laws which Moses propounded to them?" Hobbes answers that those commandments that were based on the law of nature were acknowledged by all mankind to be God's laws. But those commandments that were "peculiar to the Israelites" were obligatory only because the Israelites had chosen Moses as their leader. These commandments "became Lawes, [only] by vertue of the same promise of obedience to Moses" (42.357). Scripture is not canonical because it is the word of God; instead, Scripture is "*made* Canonicall by Moses the Civill Soveraign" (42.358, my emphasis).

57. See also *Leviathan*, 44.422–3 and 45.451 on the Eucharist; and 35.286 on converting the sacrament into something like an oath or sign of allegiance.

58. As Leo Strauss noted in *"Hobbes's Critique of Religion" and Related Writings*, trans. and ed. Gabriel Bartlett and Svetozar Minkov (Chicago: University of Chicago Press, 2011), the critique of miracles is at the center of Hobbes's critique of religion, and our protection against the abuse of miracles is "man's capacity for art," as evidenced in the construction of the commonwealth (111–13).

59. See also *Leviathan*, 45.446: images of God are mere representations of our fancies; there can be no similitude of the true God; 45.448: there can be no image of God.
60. See Cicero, *De partitione oratoriae*, 9.31; *Brutus*, 50.187; *De officiis*, 2.9.33; Quintilian, *Institutio oratoria*, 5.8.1. Aristotle defines rhetoric as "the faculty of observing in any given case the available means of persuasion" (*Rhetoric* 1.2, 1355b). As we've seen, in his *Briefe* of Aristotle's *Rhetoric*, Hobbes defines rhetoric as "that Faculty, by which wee understand what will serve our turne, concerning any subject, to winne beliefe in the hearer." On this divergence from Aristotle, see Evrigenis, *Images of Anarchy*, 54.
61. See *Leviathan*, 41.335: "The Kingdome hee claimed was to bee in another world: He taught all men to obey in the mean time them that sate in Moses seat: He allowed them to give Caesar his tribute, and refused to take upon himselfe to be a Judg. How then could his words, or actions bee seditious, or tend to the overthrow of their then Civill Government?"
62. See *Leviathan*, 44.419–20, where Hobbes compares the Pope's claim to speak for Christ to a similar claim "in particular Common-wealths by Assemblies of the Pastors of the place, (when the Scripture gives it to none but to Civill Soveraigns)."
63. See also *Leviathan*, 44.419–20 on this error about the kingdom of God.
64. Barnouw, "Persuasion in Hobbes's *Leviathan*," 24.
65. See Anthony Ashley Cooper, the third Earl of Shaftesbury, *Characteristics of Men, Manners, Opinions, Times*, 3 vols. (1711; Indianapolis: Liberty Fund, 2001). For Shaftesbury, civil government and society were natural rather than "a kind of Invention, and Creature of Art" (1:70). True self-interest was perfectly and naturally compatible with the common good because it is in our self-interest to follow nature and give way to common affections (1:76). Shaftesbury also conceived of his essays explicitly as a response to Hobbes. Against Hobbes's "cool philosophy," Shaftesbury celebrated the rhetorical power of literature to educate the heart and moderate the passions (1:85, 91, 157). He adopted the dialogue form precisely because it was sociable and anti-systematic, and the soliloquy because it offered a "dramatick Method" of self-inspection (1:99, 103, 106, 122). He defended disinterestedness, but as a prelude to judgment in the political realm (2:17, 65, 68). In "Concerning Virtue or Merit," he argued that we have a natural sense of right and wrong that is independent of religion; at the same time, he insisted that virtue, to be complete, requires piety and belief in God (2:25, 44).

66. On disinterestedness, see ibid., 1: 62–4, 92, 139, 175, 221–2. On the importance of Shaftesbury for the emergent notion of aesthetic disinterestedness, see Jerome Stolnitz, "On the Origins of 'Aesthetic Disinterestedness,'" *Journal of Aesthetics and Art Criticism* 20 (1961): 131–43. For the further intellectual history of this concept, see the important articles by M. H. Abrams, "Art-as-Such: The Sociology of Modern Aesthetics," and "From Addison to Kant: Modern Aesthetics and Exemplary Art," in *Doing Things with Texts*, ed. Michael Fischer (New York: W. W. Norton, 1989), 135–58, 158–87.

67. Howard Caygill, *Art of Judgement* (Oxford: Blackwell, 1989), 8.

68. Ibid., 13: "What is inconceivable to Aquinas ... is the constitution of truth by the human intellect alone. Such as view of truth was subsequently proposed by his nominalist critics, who defined truth as the agreement of individuals created by God with universals established by man. The freedom of the human intellect to create its own universals and perform acts of judgement according to them was central to Renaissance humanism, which transformed Aquinas's objective proportion into a subjective proportion constituted by human activity. The humanists inverted Aquinas's priority of speculative over practical philosophy and dissolved the objective order of proportionality into subjectivity. What is with Aquinas a residual category of little intrinsic interest—human artifice measuring its own products—had within a century and a half become central to human understanding" (13). Human artifice measuring its own products is an apt description of *Leviathan*, as well as an apt description of what I have been calling maker's knowledge. But according to Caygill, such knowledge (which seemed to be relatively unproblematic in the earlier Italian Renaissance) produces a crisis of judgment in *Leviathan*. This crisis appears when Hobbes turns to the problem of constructing the commonwealth out of the state of nature—the problem, that is, of unifying discrete individuals into a single person, or to put it in Kantian language, unifying a manifold under a concept or universal.

69. Jürgen Habermas, *The Philosophical Discourse of Modernity*, trans. Frederick G. Lawrence (Cambridge: MIT Press, 1987), 7, 8, and 106–30. It is surprising that Habermas doesn't mention Kant in this context. As we will see in the fourth lecture, Kant also saw the aesthetic judgment as a way of grounding his philosophical project. In Kant's philosophy, aesthetics is one response to the crisis of epistemological legitimation described by Habermas. Luc Ferry has also advanced a positive view of

the contribution of aesthetics to modernity. In Ferry's view, aesthetics is "the field par excellence in which the problems brought about by the subjectivization of the world characteristic of modern times can be observed in a chemically pure state." Ferry mentions Hobbes only in passing, but his view of Kant helps explain why Hobbes's suspension of belief might have been important for later thinking about aesthetics. Hobbes performed for political theory what Kant would later perform for philosophy, the marginalization of God as inessential to human maker's knowledge, that is, the world that we ourselves construct. See Luc Ferry, *Homo Aestheticus: The Invention of Taste in the Democratic Age*, trans. Robert de Loaiza (Chicago: University of Chicago Press, 1993), 3; and on Kant, 77–113.

70. See my *Rhetoric, Prudence, and Skepticism in the Renaissance*, chap. 6; and *Wayward Contracts*, chap. 6.

71. As Richard Rorty argues in *Philosophy and Social Hope* (London: Penguin, 1999), "the relativity of descriptions to purposes is the pragmatist's principal argument for his antirepresentational view of knowledge—the view that inquiry aims at utility for us rather than an accurate account of how things are in themselves" (xxvi).

72. On Peirce, see ibid., xxiv. Of course, Hobbes's views are not identical with Rorty's. Among other differences, Hobbes holds on to a notion of truth, even if such truth may need to be compromised in the sphere of politics. See Kinch Hoekstra, "The End of Philosophy."

73. Here it is helpful to remember Leo Strauss's argument about the difference between Hobbes's conception of art and the traditional conception of art as the imitation of nature. Given Hobbes's view that nature itself can't be known (since knowledge for Hobbes is knowledge not of empirical facts but rather of logical consequences), art itself can no longer be understood as the imitation of nature but must instead be equated with sovereign invention. Strauss discusses sovereign invention in *"Hobbes's Critique of Religion,"* 113. For a related argument about the importance of sovereign judgment in Hobbes, see Ethan Shagan, *The Birth of Modern Belief* (Princeton: Princeton University Press, 2018), 268–70.

74. There is also a second version of the difference pragmatism makes to thinking about literature and literariness, if we think about these terms historically. If, for the pragmatist, morality and religious belief are not a matter of "the transcultural moral law," but instead "the outgrowth of the historical development of a particular society," then the same must be

true of literature and literariness. The idea that we're talking about the same thing across the centuries is a product of the conversation we want to have with writers in earlier times. But this conversation reveals that literariness or the essence of literature has, historically, been a matter of considerable dispute. As I suggested in the first lecture, this dispute is one of the things we mean by literariness.

Lecture 3

1. On Milton's education in and views of rhetoric, see Donald Lemen Clark, *John Milton at St. Paul's School* (New York: Columbia University Press, 1948); and Thomas Festa, *The End of Learning: Milton and Education* (London: Routledge, 2006). On his rhetorical exercises at Cambridge, see Donald Lemen Clark, "Milton's Rhetorical Exercises," *Quarterly Journal of Speech* 46 (1960): 297–301. Milton praises the study of rhetoric in his *Of Education*, and defends the humanistic ideal of the poet in the preface to part 2 of *The Reason of Church Government*. Studies of Milton's rhetoric in his controversial prose works and his poetry are legion. See, among others, J. B. Broadbent, "Milton's Rhetoric," *Modern Philology* 56 (1959): 224–42; Stanley E. Fish, *Surprised by Sin: The Reader in "Paradise Lost"* (New York: St. Martin's Press, 1967); and *How Milton Works* (Cambridge: Harvard University Press, 2001); Thomas O. Sloane, *Donne, Milton, and the End of Humanist Rhetoric* (Berkeley: University of California Press, 1985); Lana Cable, *Carnal Rhetoric: Milton's Iconoclasm and the Poetics of Desire* (Durham and London: Duke University Press, 1995); William Pallister, *Between Worlds: The Rhetorical Universe of "Paradise Lost"* (Toronto: University of Toronto Press, 2008); and Daniel Shore, *Milton and the Art of Rhetoric* (Cambridge: Cambridge University Press, 2012).
2. Hobbes, Epistle dedicatory to *De corpore*, in *The English Works of Thomas Hobbes*, ed. William Molesworth, 11 vols. (London: Bohn, 1839), 1: xviii–ix.
3. Milton was not the first to represent God speaking in poetry; for earlier examples, see Watson Kirkconnell, *The Celestial Cycle: The Theme of Paradise Lost in World Literature with Translations of the Major Analogues* (Toronto: University of Toronto Press, 1952); and Tobias Gregory, *From Many Gods to One: Divine Action in Renaissance Epic* (Chicago: University of Chicago Press, 2006). I quote *Paradise Lost* from John Milton, *Complete Poems and Major Prose*, ed. Merritt Y. Hughes (Indianapolis: Bobbs-Merrill, 1984) and abbreviate as *PL*.

4. On Deucalion and Pyrrha, see David Quint, *Inside "Paradise Lost"* (Princeton: Princeton University Press, 2014), 241–2.
5. On Milton's understanding of the close relationship, perhaps even identity, of faith and belief, see the remarks to his *De Doctrina Christiana*, ed. and trans. John K. Hale and J. Donald Cullington, in *The Complete Works of John Milton*, ed. Thomas N. Corns and Gordon Campbell (Oxford: Oxford University Press, 2012), vol. 8, part 1, pp. 4–5: "Verùm cùm aeternae salutis viam non nisi propriae cuiusque fidei Deus aperuerit, postuletque hoc à nobis, ut qui salvus esse vult, pro se quisque credat, statui divinis in rebus, non aliorum niti vel fide vel iudicio, sed quid credendum in religione est, id fide non aliund[e] quam divinitus accepta, et quod mearum erat partium non omisso, ex ipsa Dei scriptura quam diligentissime perlecta atque perpensa, unumquodque habere mihimet ipsi, meaque ipsius opera exploratum atque cognitum." ["God has revealed the way of eternal salvation only to the individual faith of each man, and demands of us that any man who wishes to be saved should work out his beliefs for himself. So I made up my mind to puzzle out a religious creed for myself by my own exertions, and to acquaint myself with it thoroughly. In this the only authority I accepted was God's self-revelation, and accordingly I read and pondered the Holy Scriptures themselves with all possible diligence, never sparing myself in any way."] See also book 1, chap. 20, pp. 582–3, where the rhetorical dimension of faith is clear: "Effectum regenerationis alterum est **Salvifica fides**. Eas est **dono Dei ingenita nobis plena persuasio, qua, propter ipsam promittentis Dei authoritatem, credimus, ea omnia esse nostra, quae Deus nobis in Christo promisit; gratiam praesertim vitae aeternae**." ["The other effect of regeneration is SAVING FAITH. This means THE FIRM PERSUASION IMPLANTED IN US BY THE GIFT OF GOD, BY VIRTUE OF WHICH WE BELIEVE, ON THE AUTHORITY OF GOD'S PROMISE, THAT ALL THOSE THINGS WHICH GOD HAS PROMISED US IN CHRIST ARE OURS, AND ESPECIALLY THE GRACE OF ETERNAL LIFE."] Hereafter I will cite the English text of *On Christian Doctrine* from *Complete Prose Works of John Milton*, gen. ed. Don M. Wolfe, 8 vols. (New Haven: Yale University Press, 1953–82), vol. 6. *Christian Doctrine* will be cited by book, chapter, and page in the Yale edition. All other references to Milton's prose works are to this edition, cited as *CPW*.

6. John Carey, "A Work in praise of terrorism? September 11 and *Samson Agonistes*," *Times Literary Supplement*, 6 September 2002, 16.
7. Gordon Campbell, "The Mortalist Heresy in Paradise Lost," *Milton Studies* 13 (1979): 33–6.
8. *Areopagitica*, in *CPW*, 2:544. A little later Milton referred to such religion as "ready made" and the pastor as a "factor" or business agent "To whose care and credit he may commit the whole managing of his religious affairs."
9. I've made this argument more fully in *Machiavellian Rhetoric: From the Counter-Reformation to Milton* (Princeton: Princeton University Press, 1994), 173–9.
10. Milton, *Eikonoklastes* in *CPW*, 3:366.
11. Milton, *On Christian Doctrine*, book 1, chap. 2, p. 133; "assent to this truth" is the Hughes translation (*Complete Poems and Major Prose*, 905). See also Hobbes, *Leviathan*, ed. Richard Tuck (Cambridge: Cambridge University Press, 1996), chap. 3, page 23.
12. See Milton, *On Christian Doctrine*, book 1, chap. 30, 582.
13. Ibid., 1.27, 536; see also 1.30, 583–4. For the Latin text, see *De Doctrina Christiana*, 714.
14. Milton, *On Christian Doctrine*, 1.30, 589; for the Latin text, see *De Doctrina Christiana*, 810. Elsewhere Milton seems to be trying to develop a single vocabulary of work that will encompass both poetry and belief. For example, later in *Christine Doctrine* he explains that "no work of ours can be good except through faith. Faith, then, is the form of good works, because the definition of *form* is *that through which a thing is what it is*" (book 2, chap. 1, 639). In the *Art of Logic*, Milton then links the form through which a thing is what it is with art, understood as technē, which depends on both deliberation and the will (*Art of Logic* in *CPW*, 8:232). And in *Of Education*, he defines this idea of art as an organon, a set of rules for investigation and demonstration. He goes on to explain that art so conceived encompasses not only logic but also poetry, adding that by poetry, he doesn't mean prosody, but "That sublime art" found in "*Aristotles Poetics*, in *Horace*," and in others, which "teaches what the laws are of a true *Epic* poem, what of a *Dramatic*, what of a *Lyric*, what decorum is, which is the grand master peece to observe. This would make them soon perceive...what Religious, what glorious and magnificent use might be made of Poetry, both in divine and human things" (*CPW*, 2:404-6).

15. In William Empson's powerful reading, Milton in book 3 is grappling with the orthodox Protestant conception of the deity and wants us to grapple with it as well. Thus he deliberately forces us to confront the "repulsive theology" of an omniscient, omnipotent God who allows Adam and Eve to fall when he could have prevented it, and then has the bad taste to complain about it. For Empson, the best that could be said of Milton was that at least he was uncomfortable with his beliefs: "He is struggling to make his God appear less wicked [as he tells us when he says he will 'justify the ways of God to men']... and does succeed in making him noticeably less wicked than the traditional Christian [God]; though, after all his efforts, owing to his loyalty to the sacred text and the penetration with which he makes its story real to us, his modern critics still feel, in a puzzled way, that there is something badly wrong about it all." See *Milton's God* (London: Chatto and Windus, 1965), 11, and 146 on "God's thorough unscrupulousness... [and] bad temper." Empson's view is extreme and perhaps not convincing to all readers, but he is right about one thing: faith for Milton was not something to be taken for granted. It was a challenge, and it demanded that the believer grapple with difficult and, at times, repugnant truths.

16. On the relationship between the rule of charity and equitable interpretation, see Kathy Eden, *Poetic and Legal Fiction in the Aristotelian Tradition* (Princeton: Princeton University Press, 1986); and Eden, *Hermeneutics and the Rhetorical Tradition: Chapters in the Ancient Legacy and its Humanist Reception* (New Haven: Yale University Press, 1997), esp. 41–63. I have discussed Milton's interest in charitable interpretation, especially in the Divorce Tracts, in my *Wayward Contracts: The Crisis of Political Obligation in England, 1640–74* (Princeton: Princeton University Press, 2004), chap. 8.

17. On these repetitions (the rhetorical figures of conduplicatio and polyptoton), see Pallister, *Between Worlds*: "The reduplicated word patterns scattered throughout God's speech have been leading up to the fulfillment of Christian destiny that is contained in the climactic reduplication, echoing St Paul (1 Corinthians 15:28), of God's being 'All in All.'... Conduplicatio, along with its cousin polyptoton, may be thought of as the master rhetorical scheme in heaven, since its rhythms anticipate and lay stylistic foundation for the state of God's completeness, and the completeness of all things in God" (131–2). Pallister is discussing God's speech at 3.294–302, but his comments apply to God's earlier rhetoric as well.

18. See also *Paradise Lost*, 10.1081–96 on prayer and repentance.

19. Malcolm Mackenzie Ross, *Poetry and Dogma* (1954; New York: Octagon Books, 1969), 19. This argument is seconded by Debora Shuger, *Habits of Thought in the English Renaissance* (Berkeley: University of California Press, 1990), 37–41 and 67–8.
20. Ross, *Poetry and Dogma*, 68.
21. Ibid., 183.
22. Ibid., 184.
23. See Barbara Kiefer Lewalski, *Protestant Poetics and the Seventeenth-Century Religious Lyric* (Princeton: Princeton University Press, 1979), and Brian Cummings, *The Literary Culture of the Reformation: Grammar and Grace* (Oxford: Oxford University Press, 2002). In a slightly more provocative vein, Gordon Teskey has suggested that the Protestant doctrine of *sola fide* produced the modern aesthetic concept of literature: "the peculiar sense of the literary as constituting an autonomous world, one that might be related to ours through various ingenious operations, such as allegory, but that is wholly distinct nevertheless, was something new in the long Tudor century, even if many elements that went into it existed before. Kant's famous definition of the aesthetic as purposiveness without purpose—'Zweckmässigkeit ohne Zweck'—is a modern idea that has its origin here, in London, in the second half of the sixteenth century. For what are Protestant good works, since they have no salvific force, but an aesthetic activity, performed for their beauty? They are not done in the hope that they will prove a sign of God's grace but rather to provide an aesthetic escape from the terrible regime of that grace." See Gordon Teskey, "Literature," in *Cultural Reformations: Medieval and Renaissance in Literary History*, ed. Brian Cummings and James Simpson (Oxford: Oxford University Press, 2010), 388.
24. See, among others, Stanley Fish, *Self-Consuming Artifacts: The Experience of Seventeenth-Century Literature* (Berkeley and Los Angeles: University of California Press, 1972); Michael O'Connell, *The Idolatrous Eye: Iconoclasm and Theater in Early-Modern England* (Oxford: Oxford University Press, 2000); Barbara Lewalski, "Milton and Idolatry," *Studies in English Literature* 43 (2003): 213–32; James Simpson, *Under the Hammer: Iconoclasm in the Anglo-American Tradition* (Oxford: Oxford University Press, 2011).
25. See Gabriel Josipovici, *The Book of God: A Response to the Bible* (New Haven: Yale University Press, 1988), 24.
26. On the hypothesis of motive as essential to the construction of character in Renaissance drama, see Lorna Hutson, *The Invention of Suspicion: Law and*

Mimesis in Shakespeare and Renaissance Drama (Oxford: Oxford University Press, 2007).

27. Regina Schwartz, "John Milton," in *The Oxford Encyclopedia of the Bible and the Arts*, ed. Timothy Beal (Oxford: Oxford University Press, 2015), 2: 98.
28. See, among others, David Loewenstein, *Milton and the Drama of History* (Cambridge: Cambridge University Press, 1990); and Loewenstein, *Representing Revolution in Milton and His Contemporaries: Religion, Politics, and Polemics in Radical Puritanism* (Cambridge: Cambridge University Press, 2001). It should be clear here that I agree with those who argue for a composition date in the late 1650s or 1660s.
29. See, among others, Joseph Wittreich, *Interpreting "Samson Agonistes"* (Princeton: Princeton University Press, 1986); and Wittreich, *Shifting Contexts: Reinterpreting "Samson Agonistes"* (Pittsburgh: Duquesne University Press, 2002).
30. See Marshall Grossman, "Poetry and Belief in *Paradise Regained, to which is added, Samson Agonistes*," *Studies in Philology* 110 (2013), 399–400 for the argument that we read *Samson Agonistes* through eyes of Jesus, but—in contrast to the reading I propose here—Grossman sees Samson as a failure, as a negative example of enthusiasm.
31. As my colleague James Turner has reminded me, Milton is faithful to Jesus's historical context and to the fact that he would have read the Hebrew Bible not in book form but in a scroll. See Acts 17:11; John 5:39; and Dayton Haskin, *Milton's Burden of Interpretation* (Philadelphia: University of Pennsylvania Press, 1994), 154. Haskin's argument that *Paradise Regain'd* and *Samson Agonistes* are about the process of composing Scripture through interpretation is entirely consistent with my argument here, as is the argument of Sanford Budick in "Milton and the Scene of Interpretation," in *Midrash and Literature*, ed. Geoffrey H. Hartman and Sanford Budick (New Haven and London: Yale University Press, 1986), 195–212.
32. Here, and in the following paragraphs, I draw on my article "Job's Complaint in *Paradise Regained*," *English Literary History* 76 (2009): 625–60.
33. Here we can contrast the narrator's reading of Jesus' baptism to that of Hobbes in *Leviathan*. After arguing that there can be no such thing as an incorporeal spirit, Hobbes writes, "Our Saviour, immediately after the Holy Ghost descended upon him in the form of a Dove, is said by St. *Matthew* (Chapt.4.1.) to have been *led up by the Spirit into the Wilderness*... Whereby it is evident, that by *Spirit* there, is meant the Holy Ghost. This

cannot be interpreted for a Possession: For Christ, and the Holy Ghost, are but one and the same substance..." (45.443). He goes on to say Jesus's being carried up to a high mountain from which he saw the kingdoms of the world must be interpreted as "a Vision." Hobbes is concerned to interpret the Dove as a mere symbol and to demystify the Holy Spirit as being like "any other Corporeall Spirit, by which [the] body is naturally moved." He wants to get rid of the literariness of the Bible, to vaporize the Dove, and to translate the Holy Spirit into his materialist psychology: the Holy Ghost and Christ are the same substance. By contrast, Milton preserves the poetry, while making a distinction between Satan's refusal to interpret ("what e'er it meant") and the narrator's careful preservation of both letter and spirit.

34. See, among others, Barbara Lewalski, *Milton's Brief Epic* (Providence, R.I.: Brown University Press, 1966); Mary Ann Radzinowicz, *Toward "Samson Agonistes"* (Princeton: Princeton University Press, 1978), 251–62; and Victoria Silver, *Imperfect Sense: The Predicament of Milton's Irony* (Princeton: Princeton University Press, 2001), 26–44.

35. Silver, *Imperfect Sense*, argues that Milton's characteristic mode of proceeding is ironic, in both his poetry and prose. But she traces this irony to the Lutheran idea of the hidden God, which dictates that every human effort to conceptualize the divine must of necessity stand in an indirect relation to what cannot be revealed. In my view, Milton is not a Lutheran but an Arminian. While he concedes that God accommodates himself figuratively to human understanding, his emphasis on labor and the renewed will show that the ironic relation of every interpretation to the literal text does not implicate Lutheran theology.

36. In *Milton's Burden of Interpretation*, Dayton Haskin argues that in *Paradise Regain'd* and *Samson Agonistes*, Milton is exploring the way canonical Scripture is created out of a process of interpretation. As Haskin recognizes, the argument works the other way as well: in showing how Scripture is constructed, Milton also dismantles the independent authority of Scripture and gives greater authority to the individual reader who may also be, as in the case of Milton, a writer. See Haskin, 119.

37. Harold Fisch, "Milton and the Heresies," in his *Jerusalem and Albion: The Hebraic Factor in Seventeenth-Century Literature* (London: Routledge & Kegan Paul, 1964), 153, commenting on *Paradise Regain'd*.

38. See Anthony Low, "Milton, *Paradise Regained*, and Georgic," *PMLA* 98 (1983): 152–69, and Low, *The Georgic Revolution* (Princeton: Princeton

University Press, 1985), 322–53. See also the chapter on *Paradise Regain'd* in Louis L. Martz, *The Paradise Within* (New Haven: Yale University Press, 1964), as well as Martz, "*Paradise Regained*: Georgic Form, Georgic Style," *Milton Studies* 42 (2003): 7–25.

39. Philip Sidney described Job as an example of biblical poetry in his *Defence of Poetry*. The Junius-Tremellius Protestant Latin version of the Bible named Job as one of the poetic parts of Scripture. Both were drawing on a long tradition of commentary extending at least as far back as Jerome, who argued that the central chapters of Job were written in hexameter verse.
40. Robert Alter, *Canon and Creativity: Modern Writing and the Authority of Scripture* (New Haven: Yale University Press, 2000), 21–62.
41. For a very different reading of the significance of labor in *Samson Agonistes*, see Richard Halpern, *Eclipse of Action: Tragedy and Political Economy* (Chicago: University of Chicago Press, 2017).
42. I have developed this interpretation of Samson's encounters in "Aesthetics as Critique: Tragedy and Trauerspiel in *Samson Agonistes*," in *Reading Renaissance Ethics*, ed. Marshall Grossman (New York: Routledge, 2007), 104–27. In *Toward "Samson Agonistes,"* Mary Ann Radzinowicz also argues for the growth of Samson's understanding through dialectical exchanges with his interlocutors.
43. This, I think, is why, in addition to quoting Aristotle's definition of tragedy as the imitation of an action in the epigraph to *Samson Agonistes*, Milton glosses this definition in terms of the imitation of the *passions* in the prefatory note to the poem. Samson's labor of interpretation involves interpreting and transcending his own initial passionate response to his enslaved condition. See my "Aesthetics as Critique." This gloss on Aristotle also invites us to think about the relationship between Samson's passions and Christ's Passion, as does Milton's reference to Gregory Nazianzen's poem *Christ Suffering* a few lines later. On Milton's vexed relationship to the Passion, see John Rogers, "Milton's Circumcision," in *Milton and the Grounds of Contention*, ed. Mark R. Kelley, Michael Lieb, and John T. Shawcross (Pittsburgh: Duquesne University Press, 2003), 188–213; and Rogers' lecture 24 on *Samson Agonistes* for Yale Open Courses (https://oyc.yale.edu/english/engl-220/lecture-24).
44. Milton, "Of that sort of Dramatic Poem which is call'd Tragedy," prefatory note to *Samson Agonistes* (Hughes ed., 550).

45. See Aristotle, *Poetics*, 1451b on the poet as a "maker of plots"; and Paul Ricoeur, "Mimesis and Representation," *Annals of Scholarship* 2 (1981): 15–32. I return to Ricoeur in the last lecture.
46. See Lecture 1, n25 above.
47. The phrase "rousing motions" makes emotion into a principle of motion or action. On this transformation, see Erich Auerbach, "*Passio* as Passion," in *Time, History, and Literature: Selected Essays of Erich Auerbach*, ed. James I. Porter, trans. Jane O. Newman (Princeton: Princeton University Press, 2016), 165–87. Auerbach discusses the history of the idea that *passio* may become active through the force of *motus animi* (emotion or, literally, the movement of the soul).
48. Ricoeur argues that "for Aristotle *mimesis* only takes place within the area of human action, or production, or *poiesis*.... Accordingly, for Aristotle, there is *mimesis* only where there is *poiesis*. On the other hand, far from producing a weakened image of preexisting things, *mimesis* brings about an augmentation of meaning in the field of action, which is its privileged field. It does not equate itself with something already given. Rather, it produces what it imitates, if we continue to translate *mimesis* by 'imitation'" ("Mimesis and Representation," 16).
49. See ibid., 29. Here I agree with Dayton Haskin that *Paradise Regain'd* "demonstrates that a commitment to 'the Bible only' not only does not preclude producing one's own work but requires and inspires it" (162).
50. In *Milton's Burden of Interpretation*, Haskin argues that for Milton interpretation cannot be understood "on the model of supplementation" (146). I think, by contrast, that if Milton's interpretations are not to be mere subjective fantasies, there needs to be some sense in which Scripture is not simply the product of his imagination. Even Haskin acknowledges that Milton did not simply leave Scripture behind in favor of "an inward light. Rather, he continued to interpret the biblical texts, allowing that they have at least the priority of existing before though not apart from interpretive activity" (182).
51. John Milton, *On Christian Doctrine*, book 1, chap. 30, 589.
52. "On Paradise Lost," pp. 209–10 in Milton, *Complete Poems*, ed. Hughes. Marvell's diction here is odd and strangely Miltonic: ruin as an English verb derives from the Latin noun "ruina," meaning not only ruin but destruction or downfall. In English it means to ruin, reduce to ruins, to damage, to destroy, to invalidate. But there is no example in the Oxford English Dictionary of "ruin to." Here, it seems, Marvell wants us to

understand that ruin to fable and old song means something like reduce or even demystify.
53. See Grossman, "Poetry and Belief," 382–401, esp. 384, 391.
54. T. S. Eliot, "A Note on Poetry and Belief," in *The Complete Prose of T. S. Eliot: The Critical Edition: Literature, Politics, Belief, 1927–1929*, ed. Francis Dickey, Jennifer Formichelli, and Ronald Suchard (Baltimore: Johns Hopkins University Press, 2015), 19.
55. Here I'm in agreement with those who argue that the genre of tragedy captures the paradoxes of Christian theology: in the lapidary formulation of Edward W. Tayler, *Samson Agonistes* is a Christian tragedy because "Samson guided solely by God is not 'tragic,' as Samson guided solely by himself is not 'Christian.'" See Tayler, *Milton's Poetry: Its Development in Time* (Pittsburgh: Duquesne University Press, 1979), 121.
56. See Milton, *On Christian Doctrine*, book 1, chap. 6, 287–8, cited in Haskin, 121: "Let us assume that, appropriately enough, when God wants us to understand and thus believe in a particular doctrine as a primary point of faith, he teaches it to us not obscurely or confusedly, but simply and clearly, in plain words. Let us also take it for granted that, in religion, we should beware above all of exposing ourselves to the charge which Christ brought against the Samaritans in John iv.22: *you worship something you do not know.*"
57. Philip Sidney, *A Defence of Poetry*, ed. J. A. Van Dorsten (Oxford: Oxford University Press, 1973), 53.
58. I take the notion of "aboutness" from the philosopher of art Arthur C. Danto, *The Transfiguration of the Commonplace* (Cambridge: Harvard University Press, 1981). For Danto, imitation acquires the status of "art when it does not merely resemble something, like a mirror image, but is about what it resembles, like an impersonation." Danto goes on to clarify that imitation does not always imply resemblance to an *existing* object. Imitation does not refer by way of "extension"; it is instead what in semantics is called "an intensional concept," that is, it is about meanings rather than the things designated (68). Imitations are accordingly "vehicles of meaning" (70–1). By contrast, Milton's and Hobbes's versions of aboutness are about more than style or a way of seeing, which does not fully capture the robust sense of making or construction at the heart of their work.
59. Samuel Johnson, "Life of Milton," in *Milton, 1732–1801: The Critical Heritage*, ed. John T. Shawcross (London and Boston: Routledge, 1972), 304.
60. Ibid., 305.

Lecture 4

1. See Nicholas von Maltzahn, "The War in Heaven and the Miltonic Sublime," in *A Nation Transformed: England after the Restoration* (Cambridge: Cambridge University Press, 2001), 154–79, esp. 158–60 and 165. Von Maltzahn discusses Dryden and Addison, among others.
2. Richard Rorty, "Philosophy as a Transitional Genre," in *Philosophy as Cultural Politics*, vol. 4 of *Philosophical Papers* (Cambridge: Cambridge University Press, 2007), 91; see G. W. F. Hegel, *Philosophy of Right*, trans. Knox (Oxford: Oxford University Press, 1967), 12–13 for this gray on gray. As I've argued throughout these lectures, this challenge is a perennial feature of the history of Western culture. As Rorty goes on to argue, Nietzsche was also responding to the crisis of philosophy after Hegel.
3. At least some early Russian formalists did aim to transform society. See Lecture 1, n11.
4. Ian Hacking, *The Social Construction of What?* (Cambridge: Harvard University Press, 1999), and Onora O'Neill, *Kant's Constructions of Reason* (Cambridge: Cambridge University Press, 1989), cited by Hacking. For an earlier discussion of the importance of fiction in Kant, see Hans Vaihinger, *The Philosophy of "As If,"* trans. C. K. Ogden (New York: Barnes & Noble, 1968), esp. 151–3, 271–318. Vaihinger, however, devotes only two pages to the *Critique of Judgment* (307–8).
5. See Arthur Danto on Kant's also needing to explain his awe before the starry sky above and moral law within (*The Abuse of Beauty: Aesthetics and the Concept of Art* [Chicago: Open Court, 2003], 156).
6. See Immanuel Kant, *Critique of the Power of Judgment* (*CJ*), trans. Paul Guyer and Eric Matthews (Cambridge: Cambridge University Press, 2001), § 40, and Hannah Arendt, *Lectures on Kant's Political Philosophy*, ed. Ronald Beiner (Chicago: University of Chicago Press, 1989), 65.
7. See Kant, *CJ*: "Now this happens by one holding his judgment up not so much to the actual as to the merely possible judgments of others, and putting himself into the position of everyone else, merely by abstracting from the limitations that contingently attach to our own judging...and attending solely to the formal peculiarities of his representation or representational state" (§ 40, p. 174).
8. See *CJ*, § 40, p. 173 (emphasis in the original).

9. See *CJ*, § 3, p. 91, note; and § 41, p. 176, on the "interest in that which has already pleased for itself and without respect to any sort of interest"; as well as § 42.
10. It's worth noting that, in addition to the argument from disinterestedness, Kant also makes a different kind of argument for the ethical import of certain kinds of literature, notably poetry (§ 49, p. 193). He argues that poetry is preeminent in producing "aesthetic ideas," which he defines as "a representation of the imagination that occasions much thinking, though without it being possible for any determinate thought, i.e., concept, to be adequate to it" (§ 49, p. 192). In the same section, Kant also argues that aesthetic ideas amount to a presentation of rational ideas. Here he seems to suggest aesthetic ideas can serve as a bridge to rational ideas and, in so doing, educate us about our supersensible vocation and our capacity for virtue. Elsewhere, Kant argues that aesthetic experience cultivates moral feeling (see §§ 42, 44) or is a symbol of morality (§ 59). In all these ways, he recovers a rhetorical and pedagogical dimension for literature that he elsewhere denies.
11. See also *CJ*, § 22, p. 124 on the uncertain status of common sense, which Kant here suggests might simply be "a demand of reason." "As it were" as a confession of failure functions differently from the as if of aesthetic judgment, which we experience not as a fictional claim but as a real one.
12. This involves a transvaluation of the Aristotelian view of the autonomy of art. In its difference from the real world, art becomes radically free to represent the possible or hypothetical.
13. See Paul de Man, "Phenomenality and Materiality in Kant," in *The Textual Sublime*, ed. Hugh J. Silverman and Gary E. Aylesworth (Albany: State University of New York Press, 1990), 87–108, esp. 107; and Terry Eagleton, *The Ideology of the Aesthetic* (Oxford: Blackwell, 1990).
14. Despite Kant's effort to distinguish the realm of cognition, in which subjects have objective knowledge of the world, from the subjective realm of aesthetic judgment, many readers have thought that the *Critique of Judgment* actually dramatizes the crisis of this distinction by making the harmony of our faculties in cognition depend on the hypothesis—the "as it were"—of aesthetic judgment. In so doing, Kant could be said to dismantle the aesthetic as a separate realm of experience that undergirds critical philosophy, and to make the features of aesthetic judgment characteristic of all judgment. See, among others, Luc Ferry, *Homo Aestheticus: The Invention of Taste in the Democratic Age*, trans. Robert de

Loaiza (Chicago and London: University of Chicago Press, 1993); Andrew Bowie, *From Romanticism to Critical Theory: The Philosophy of German Literary Theory* (London and New York: Routledge, 1997), 56–61; and Anthony J. Cascardi, *Consequences of Enlightenment* (Cambridge: Cambridge University Press, 1999), 83–5. Gianni Vattimo argues that the incipient breakdown between science and aesthetics in Kant is characteristic of modernity in general. See "The Structure of Artistic Revolutions," in *The End of Modernity: Nihilism and Hermeneutics in Post-modern Culture*, trans. Jon R. Synder (Cambridge, England: Polity Press, 1988), 90–109.

15. The *Critique of Judgment* was owned by Kierkegaard and appears in the auction catalogue of his books after his death, along with Kant's *Critique of Pure Reason* and an edition of minor treatises. See Ronald M. Green, "Kant: A Debt both Obscure and Enormous," in *Kierkegaard and his Contemporaries, Tome 1: Philosophy*, ed. Jon Stewart (Aldershot, England: Ashgate, 2007), 179. Critics who have discussed Kierkegaard's engagement with Kant have focused on the latter's ethical writings, not the *Critique of Judgment*. See, e.g., Ronald M. Green, *Kierkegaard and Kant: The Hidden Debt* (Albany: State University of New York Press, 1992); Philip L. Quinn, *Selves in Discord and Resolve: Kierkegaard's Moral-Religious Psychology from Either/Or to Sickness unto Death* (New York: Routledge, 1996), and the articles by Green and Quinn in *The Cambridge Companion to Kierkegaard*, ed. Alastair Hannay and Gordon D. Marino (Cambridge: Cambridge University Press, 1998). As far as I have been able to determine, Kierkegaard never directly cites the *Critique of Judgment*, but his position on aesthetics indirectly engages with Kant. In "Kierkegaard's Contribution to the Danish Discussion of 'Irony,'" K. Brian Söderquist argues that debates about Romantic irony in Denmark during Kierkegaard's life were responding in part to Kant's circumscription of the realm of knowledge. For Kierkegaard's contemporary Eggert Tryde, "the way romantic ironists deal with Kantian restrictions of the knowledge of God leads to 'an indeterminate foundation of life' which is ultimately unsatisfying for those who experience 'a deeper feeling for truth'" (*Kierkegaard and His Contemporaries: The Culture of Golden Age Denmark* [Berlin: De Gruyter, 2003], 90). Kierkegaard's own remarks about Kant in *The Concept of Irony* in *Kierkegaard's Writings, II*, ed. Howard V. Hong and Edna H. Hong (Princeton, 1989), 272–5, support this view.

16. See *The Concept of Irony*, 275. The aesthete, then, has a concept of self-fashioning or "living poetically" (280) but it is, in Kierkegaard's eyes, very far from the positive engagement with the world implied by Renaissance notions of poiesis. And this in turn means that "a poetic construction of life cannot bring about a reconciliation with actuality." See Söderquist, "Kierkegaard's Contribution," 103.
17. Here it's important to note that Kierkegaard distinguishes between three spheres of existence: the aesthetic, the ethical, and the religious. The aesthetic sphere is characterized by immediacy or the paradoxical and self-defeating search for immediacy. The aesthete, for example, might be a seducer, consumed by the particulars of sensuous or artistic existence, but unable to experience immediacy precisely because it is his explicit, self-conscious goal or plan to do so. The ethical man is governed by universal categories of good and evil, and commitment to family and the state. He may be a married man, or a tax collector, or both. Insofar as the ethical man lives by universals, he also draws near to the philosopher. The highest sphere is the religious life, which Kierkegaard divides into types A and B. A is the knight of infinite resignation, who sacrifices his interest in this world for his belief in the next. B is the knight of faith, who—like Job and Abraham—both resigns his interest in this world and believes that everything will be given back to him. He looks like a tax collector and may even be one. But, in contrast to these figures of bourgeois respectability, the knight of faith does not confuse his commitment with ethics; instead, he understands it as a leap of faith. The knight of faith thus inhabits the world, but he does so ironically. This is not the irony of the aesthete who is concerned with the ways in which the world falls short of his ideas. It is instead the irony of the believer for whom our ideas must always fall short of the divine. To put it another way, it is the irony of the believer for whom the true message of Christianity must always remain absurd.
18. Kierkegaard, *Repetition*, in *Kierkegaard's Writings*, VI, ed. and trans. Howard V. Hong and Edna H. Hong (Princeton: Princeton University Press, 1983), 228. Kierkegaard's perception of the similarities between the aesthete and knight of faith helps explain his antipathy to the systematic theology of the Danish Church.
19. *The Concept of Irony*, 297; quoted by Söderquist, 104. This account of poetry sounds very much like Adorno, whose own notion of the aesthetic was influenced by Kierkegaard. See Peter E. Gordon, *Adorno and Existence*

(Cambridge: Harvard University Press, 2016). I return to this point below.
20. Quoted by Ronald M. Green, "'Developing' *Fear and Trembling*," in *The Cambridge Companion to Kierkegaard*, epigraph.
21. See *Fear and Trembling* in *Kierkegaard's Writings*, VI, ed. and trans. Howard V. Hong and Edna H. Hong (Princeton: Princeton University Press, 1983), on the difference between the knight of infinite resignation and the knight of faith. The former "are ballet dancers and have elevation. They make the upward movement and come down again, and this, too, is not an unhappy diversion and is not unlovely to see. But every time they come down, they are unable to assume the posture immediately, they waver for a moment, and this wavering shows that they are aliens in the world" (41).
22. The points of similarity between Kierkegaard and Nietzsche are numerous, despite Kierkegaard's faith and Nietzsche's assertion of the death of God. Both cultivate highly literary modes of writing as a way of undermining the claims of philosophy; both adopt a variety of personae; for both, irony is a pervasive rhetorical mode; both distance themselves from Kant's account of the disinterestedness of aesthetic pleasure.
23. See Kierkegaard, *Repetition*, 227. See 226 on the battle between the exception and the universal.
24. On Kierkegaard and Kant's categorical imperative, see George Schrader, "Kant and Kierkegaard on Duty and Inclination," in *Kierkegaard: A Collection of Critical Essays*, ed. Josiah Thompson (Garden City, NY: Anchor Books, 1972), 324–41; and Ronald M. Green, "Deciphering *Fear and Trembling*'s Secret Message," *Religious Studies* 22 (1986), 103.
25. See *The Concept of Irony* on the "poetic element" or "poetic temperament" in Plato (105, 122); see also pp. 96–109, esp. 101n on the relationship between the mythical and the poetical in Plato's dialogues. See also Kierkegaard's comment on his own *Either/Or* in his *Journal*: "There was a youth, richly gifted as an Alcibiades. He went astray in this world. In his distress he looked about for a Socrates, but among his contemporaries he found him not. Then he begged the gods to transform him into one...." Quoted in Walter Lowrie's Introduction to *Either/Or* (Oxford: Oxford University Press, 1944), vol. 2, xv.

26. Quoted in Louis Mackey, *Kierkegaard: A Kind of Poet* (Philadelphia: University of Pennsylvania Press, 1971), 270.
27. See Kierkegaard, "My Activity as a Writer," in Kierkegaard, *The Point of View for My Work as an Author and related Writings*, trans. Walter Lowrie, ed. Benjamin Nelson (New York: Harper Torchbooks, 1962), 151, emphasis in the original.
28. Kierkegaard, *Concluding Unscientific Postscript*, trans. David F. Swenson and Walter Lowrie (Princeton: Princeton University Press, 1968), 232–3; quoted in Mackey, 271. In *The Point of View*, Kierkegaard refers to some of his pseudonymous works as "the aesthetic works" because they adopt poetic strategies of irony and indirectness. For this reason, it is tempting to say that Kierkegaard the writer inhabits the aesthetic realm, but I think this would be only partially correct. Kierkegaard sees the aesthetic as a means of engaging the reader and precipitating a commitment to the religious life. It is for these reasons that Kierkegaard refers to his pseudonymous publications as "my literary work," "the whole literary activity" or simply "literature" (73, 92, 141).
29. See Mackey, *Kierkegaard*, 285–96. On Lessing, see also *Concluding Unscientific Postscript*, 67–113.
30. Kant had interpreted Abraham's intention to sacrifice Isaac as an example of murder, thereby subordinating the example of Abraham to, and judging him in relation to, the ethical imperative. Hegel had conversely seen Abraham as an instance of "an abstract and alienated relationship to God," of slavish obedience to divine commandments, and an inability to love, not least of all his son. The quotation is from James I. Porter, "Old Testament Realism in the Writings of Erich Auerbach," in *Jews and the Ends of Theory*, ed. Shai Ginsburg and Jonathan Boyarin (New York: Fordham University Press, 2018), 215n23. Hegel discusses Abraham in "The Spirit of Christianity and its Fate," in G. W. F. Hegel, *On Christianity: Early Theological Writings*, trans. T. M. Knox (Gloucester, Mass.: Peter Smith, 1970), 182–9. On the Jews' "slavish obedience to the laws," see also "The Positivity of the Christian Religion," in *On Christianity*, 69, and 178. Kant discusses Abraham in *Religion within the Limits of Reason Alone*, trans. Theodore M. Greene and Hoyt H. Hudson (New York: Harper and Row, 1960), 175. Kant's argument against religiously motivated actions that run counter to the ethical law interestingly echoes Hobbes. He imagines an inquisitor who condemns a heretic to death on the basis of a past divine injunction:

"After all, the revelation has reached the inquisitor only through men and has been interpreted by men, and even did it appear to have come to him from God Himself (like the command delivered to Abraham to slaughter his own son like a sheep) it is at least possible that in this instance a mistake has prevailed.... Hence it is unconscientious to follow such a faith with the possibility that perhaps what it commands or permits may be wrong, i.e. with the danger of disobedience to a human duty which is certain in and of itself" (175). Johannes criticizes Hegel directly in *Fear and Trembling*, 55 and 68 ("Problema I" and "Problema II"), and Kant indirectly, especially in "Problema II." On Kierkegaard's dialogue with Kant in *Fear and Trembling*, see Ronald M. Green, "'Developing' *Fear and Trembling*," 270; Green, *Kierkegaard and Kant*; and Schrader, "Kant and Kierkegaard on Duty and Inclination."

31. For these vignettes, see Kierkegaard, *Fear and Trembling*, 12–14.
32. *Fear and Trembling*, 34.
33. In "Kierkegaard's Lyric of Faith: A Look at *Fear and Trembling*," *Rice Institute Pamphlet* 47 (1960), 45, Louis Mackey reads this description as inadequate. Cf. Alastair Hannay, who reads this portrait as only superficially antithetical to the example of Abraham. See his Introduction to *Fear and Trembling*, trans. Hannay (London: Penguin, 1986), 20.
34. *Fear and Trembling*, trans. Hong and Hong, 39.
35. This means that for Kierkegaard, the *relationship* between the aesthetic and the religious is also one of repetition. The man of faith is an exception who repeats the aesthetic category of the exception "forward" or in a different key. Repetition is, at least for Kierkegaard, the theological equivalent of Romantic irony. Friedrich Schlegel famously opined that "There is so much poetry and yet there is nothing more rare than a poem!" It's hard to believe Kierkegaard wasn't thinking of this when he argued that, in contemporary Denmark, there is Christianity but no Christians. See Schlegel, Critical Fragment #4 in *Philosophical Fragments*, trans. Peter Firchow (Minneapolis: University of Minnesota Press, 1991), 1.
36. Stanley Cavell, "Kierkegaard's 'On Authority and Revelation,'" in *Kierkegaard: A Collection of Critical Essays*, ed. Josiah Thompson, 388–91. Cavell first upholds the distinction between the aesthetic and the religious, noting that for Kierkegaard there is a difference between speaking metaphorically and speaking religiously: "To understand a metaphor you must be able to interpret it; to understand an utterance religiously you have to be able to share its perspective." For Kierkegaard,

Cavell notes, there is a distinction between the truly religious person and those aesthetes "who translate the real terrors of the religious life into sublime spectacles of suffering with which to beguile their hours of spiritual leisure." In an important caveat, Cavell writes, "I do not insist that for us art has become religion... but that the activity of modern art, both in production and reception, is to be understood in categories which are, or were, religious" (389). For Cavell, in the end, there does not seem to be very much of a difference between interpreting an utterance and sharing its perspective; between "categories which are, or were, religious" and metaphors (384). It's arguable that this is what the young man does at the end of *Repetition*; see Arne Melberg, "Repetition (in the Kierkegaardian Sense of the Term)," *Diacritics* 20 (1990): 71–87, who reads the young man's sublime rhetoric as suggesting he has misinterpreted repetition in aesthetic categories.

37. See Arthur C. Danto, *The Transfiguration of the Commonplace* (Cambridge: Harvard University Press, 1981), and Lecture 3, n58 above.
38. Paul Ricoeur, "Mimesis and Representation," in *Annals of Scholarship* 2 (1982): 29–30.
39. Ibid., 17.
40. This is what Rorty meant, I think, when he defended the literariness of the post-metaphysical age.
41. Kierkegaard, *Point of View*, 35.
42. See Mark Sanders and Nancy Ruttenburg, "J. M. Coetzee and his Doubles," *Journal of Literary Studies* 25 (2009), 1, quoting Coetzee, *Diary of a Bad Year*, 151.
43. Lennard Davis, *Factual Fictions: The Origins of the English Novel* (New York: Columbia University Press, 1983).
44. Catherine Gallagher, "The Rise of Fictionality," in *The Novel, vol. 1: History, Geography, and Culture*, ed. Franco Moretti (Princeton: Princeton University Press, 2006), 338, quoting the *OED*, and 340. See also William Nelson, *Fact or Fiction: The Dilemma of the Renaissance Storyteller* (Cambridge: Harvard University Press, 1973), 112–13, who asserts a similar distinction between Renaissance and eighteenth-century ideas of fiction.
45. For a critique of the notion that Renaissance fiction should be equated with the marvelous, see, for example, Baxter Hathaway, *Marvels and Commonplace: Renaissance Literary Criticism* (New York: Random House, 1968), chap. 2, "Realism and the Marvelous" (43–87). I note that in *Nobody's Story: The Vanishing Acts of Women Writers in the Marketplace*,

1670–1820 (Berkeley: University of California Press, 1994), Gallagher connects the Renaissance idea of fiction to the heroic rather than the marvelous; see xvi, n7.

46. J. M. Coetzee, *Elizabeth Costello* (New York: Viking, 2003), 120–1.
47. *Elizabeth Costello*, 122.
48. *Elizabeth Costello*, 122–3.
49. Quoted in Richard Sheppard, "Kafka, Kierkegaard and the K.'s: Theology, Psychology and Fiction," *Literature and Theology* 5 (1991), 279.
50. This point is made by Leena Eilttä in "Art as Religious Commitment: Kafka's Debt to Kierkegaardian Ideas and their Impact on his Late Stories," *German Life and Letters* 53 (2000): 499–510. There is a whole mini-industry exploring Kafka's relationship to Kierkegaard in the secondary literature on Kafka. See, among others, Brian F. M. Edwards, "Kafka and Kierkegaard: A Reassessment," in *German Life and Letters* 20 (1967): 218–25; Reed Merrill, "'Infinite Absolute Negativity': Irony in Socrates, Kierkegaard and Kafka," *Comparative Literature Studies* 16 (1979): 222–36; Claude David, "Die Geschichte Abrahams: Zu Kafkas Auseinandersetzung mit Kierkegaard," in *Bild und Gedanke* (Munich: Fink, 1980), 79–90; and Hideo Nakazawa, "Zu Kafkas und Brods Kierkegaard-Deutung," *Doitsu Bungaku* 79 (1987): 128–35.
51. Eilttä, "Art as Religious Commitment," 510.
52. See Mikhail Bakhtin, *Problems of Dostoevsky's Poetics*, trans. Caryl Emerson (Minneapolis: University of Minnesota Press, 1984), on the Menippean "dialogue of the threshold" (116). According to Bakhtin, Menippean satire also accorded great importance to the underworld, which Elizabeth will as well in this chapter. Pages 116–17 in Bakhtin read as a description of *Elizabeth Costello*.
53. Coetzee, *Elizabeth Costello*, 194, 200, 207–8.
54. Ibid., 211.
55. Elizabeth then doesn't appear to accept Erich Auerbach's distinction between reading Homer and reading the Bible: one can believe in Homer after all, if not exactly in the way Auerbach discusses belief in the biblical text. See Auerbach, *Mimesis: The Representation of Reality in Western Literature*, trans. Willard R. Trask (1946; Princeton: Princeton University Press, 2003), chap. 1.
56. Coetzee may be confusing this episode with the one where Odysseus escapes by hiding under Polyphemus's favorite ram in book 9 of the

Odyssey. Note also that, in the underworld, Homer only refers to "sheep," not a single favorite ram. I owe these comments to Leslie Kurke.

57. See Dostoevsky, *Brothers Karamazov*, trans. Richard Pevear and Larissa Volokhonsky (New York: Farrar, Strauss & Giroux, 1990), book 5, chap. 3, where Ivan declares to Alyosha "I love the sticky little leaves as they open in spring, I love the blue sky" (230). For "sticky blood," see Dostoevsky, *Crime and Punishment*, trans. Richard Pevear and Larissa Volokhonsky (New York: Knopf, 1992), book 1, chap. 5, p. 59. For Coetzee's interest in Dostoevsky, see his *The Master of St. Petersburg* (New York: Penguin, 1995). Both of these intertextual allusions deserve further exploration, just as the passage deserves to be compared with Raskolnikov's dream of the mare being beaten, or to the attention to Holbein's "Christ" in *The Idiot*.

58. It may be that Coetzee, like Adorno, is here signaling thematically his desire to break through "the illusion of a constitutive subjectivity." (See Gordon, *Adorno and Existence*, 82.) Against the privileging of the subject by philosophical idealism, Adorno insists on the lack of fit between the concept and the external world. But for Adorno this critique cannot simply take place on a thematic level; it must also be registered in the form of the work—and ultimately in the consciousness of the reading subject. As he writes in *Aesthetic Theory*, "art can only be reconciled with its existence by exposing its own semblance" (*Aesthetic Theory*, trans. Robert Hullot-Kentor [Minneapolis: University of Minnesota Press, 1997], 250). One of the ways Coetzee does this is to foreground the literariness of his own work.

59. I was alerted to the relevance of the Caravaggio painting to Kierkegaard by J. M. Bernstein, "Remembering Isaac: On the Impossibility and Immorality of Faith," *The Insistence of Art: Aesthetic Philosophy after Early Modernity*, ed. Paul A. Kottman (New York: Fordham University Press, 2017), 257–88. A detail of the painting also appears on the cover of the Penguin edition of *Fear and Trembling*, ed. and trans. Alastair Hannay.

60. Henrik Skov Nielsen, "Free Indirect Discourse as Inventive Discourse," forthcoming.

61. Coetzee, *Elizabeth Costello*, 224.

62. I am indebted to Dora Zhang for helping me think through these points. For a different interpretation of ethical readings of *Elizabeth Costello*, see Dorothy J. Hale, *The Novel and the New Ethics*, forthcoming from Stanford University Press.

63. Josipovici also discusses Coetzee's relation to Beckett. See "Kierkegaard and the Novel," in *Kierkegaard: A Critical Reader*, ed. Jonathan Rée and Jane Chamberlain (Oxford: Blackwell, 1998), 116.
64. Hugo von Hofmannsthal, *The Lord Chandos Letter and Other Writings*, trans. Joel Rotenberg (New York: New York Review Books, 2005), 123, 125.
65. Ibid., 127–8.
66. Samuel Taylor Coleridge, *Biographia Literaria*, ed. George Watson (London: Dent, 1971), chap. 14, p. 169.

List of Works Cited

Abizadeh, Arash. "Hobbes's Conventionalist Theology, the Trinity, and God as an Artificial Person by Fiction." *The Historical Journal* 60 (2017): 915–41.

Abrams, M. H. *Doing Things with Texts: Essays in Criticism and Critical Theory*. Edited by Michael Fischer. New York: W. W. Norton, 1989.

Abrams, M. H. *The Mirror and the Lamp: Romantic Theory and the Critical Tradition*. Oxford: Oxford University Press, 1971.

Adorno, Theodor W. *Aesthetic Theory*. Translated by Robert Hullot-Kentor. Minneapolis: University of Minnesota Press, 1997.

Alter, Robert. *Canon and Creativity: Modern Writing and the Authority of Scripture*. New Haven: Yale University Press, 2000.

Altieri, Charles. *Reckoning with the Imagination: Wittgenstein and the Aesthetics of Literary Experience*. Ithaca: Cornell University Press, 2015.

Altman, Joel B. *The Improbability of Othello: Rhetorical Anthropology and Shakespearean Selfhood*. Chicago: The University of Chicago Press, 2010.

Altman, Joel B. *The Tudor Play of Mind: Rhetorical Inquiry and the Development of Elizabethan Drama*. Berkeley, Los Angeles, London: University of California Press, 1978.

Angier, Tom. "Aristotle on Work." *Revue internationale de philosophie* 4 (2016): 435–49.

Arendt, Hannah. *Lectures on Kant's Political Philosophy*. Edited by Ronald Beiner. Chicago: University of Chicago Press, 1989.

Arendt, Hannah. *The Human Condition*. Chicago: University of Chicago Press, 1958.

Aristotle. *Aristotle's "Poetics."* Edited and translated by James Hutton. New York: W. W. Norton, 1982.

Aristotle. *Rhetorica*. Translated by W. Rhys Roberts. *The Works of Aristotle*, edited by W. D. Ross, vol. 11. Oxford: Clarendon Press, 1924.

Ascoli, Albert Russell. *Ariosto's Bitter Harmony: Crisis and Evasion in the Italian Renaissance*. Princeton: Princeton University Press, 1987.

Ascoli, Albert Russell. "Faith as Cover-up: Ariosto's *Orlando Furioso*, Canto 21, and Machiavellian Ethics." *I Tatti Studies in the Italian Renaissance* 8 (1999): 135–70.

Attridge, Derek. *The Singularity of Literature*. New York: Routledge, 2004.
Aubrey, John. *Aubrey's Brief Lives*. Edited by O. L. Dick. London: Secker and Warburg, 1950.
Auden, W. H. *Collected Poems*. New York: Vintage, 1991.
Auerbach, Erich. *Mimesis: The Representation of Reality in Western Literature*. Translated by Willard R. Trask. 1946. Princeton: Princeton University Press, 2003.
Auerbach, Erich. "Passio as passion." In *Time, History, and Literature*, edited by James I. Porter, translated by Jane O. Newman, 165–87. Princeton: Princeton University Press, 2014.
Auerbach, Erich. "*Camilla* and the Rebirth of the Sublime." In *Literary Language and its Public*, translated by Ralph Mannheim, 183–224. New York: Pantheon, 1965.
Augustine. *On the Trinity*. Translated by Stephen McKenna. Washington, D. C.: Catholic University of America Press, 1962.
Bacon, Francis. *The New Organon*. Edited by Lisa Jardine and Michael Silverthorne. Cambridge and New York: Cambridge University Press, 2000.
Bakhtin, Mikhail. *Problems of Dostoevsky's Poetics*. Translated by Caryl Emerson. Minneapolis: University of Minnesota Press, 1984.
Baldwin, Charles Sears. "St. Augustine and the Rhetoric of Cicero." *Proceedings of the Classical Association* 22 (1925): 24–46.
Barfield, Owen. "Poetic Diction and Legal Fiction." In *Essays Presented to Charles Williams*, edited by C. S. Lewis, 106–27. Oxford: Oxford University Press, 1947.
Barnouw, Jeffrey. "Persuasion in Hobbes's *Leviathan*." *Hobbes Studies* 1 (1988): 3–25.
Berger, Harry. *Second World and Green World: Studies in Renaissance Fiction-Making*. Edited by John Patrick Lynch. Berkeley and Los Angeles: University of California Press, 1990.
Bernstein, J. M. "Remembering Isaac: On the Impossibility and Immorality of Faith." In *The Insistence of Art: Aesthetic Philosophy after Early Modernity*, edited by Paul A. Kottman, 257–88. New York: Fordham University Press, 2017.
Boutcher, Warren. "Literature." In *Palgrave Advances in Renaissance Historiography*, 210–40. Houndsmills, England: Palgrave Macmillan, 2005.
Bowie, Andrew. *From Romanticism to Critical Theory: The Philosophy of German Literary Theory*. London and New York: Routledge, 1997.

Boyle, Marjorie O'Rourke. *Rhetoric and Reform: Erasmus' Civil Dispute with Luther*. Cambridge: Harvard University Press, 1983.

Boyle, Marjorie O'Rourke. "Augustine in the Garden of Zeus: Love, Lust, and Language." *Harvard Theological Review* 83 (1990): 117–39.

Broadbent, John B. "Milton's Rhetoric." *Modern Philology* 56 (1959): 224–42.

Buber, Martin. *Two Types of Faith*. London: Routledge, 1951.

Budick, Sanford. "Milton and the Scene of Interpretation: From Typology toward Midrash." In *Midrash and Literature*, edited by Sanford Budick and Geoffrey H. Hartman, 195–212. New Haven and London: Yale University Press, 1986.

Bultman, Rudolph. "Pisteuo, Etc." In *Theological Dictionary of the New Testament*, edited by Gerhard Kittel, translated by Geoffrey W. Bromily. Grand Rapids, Michigan: Eerdmans, 1964.

Burke, Kenneth. *A Rhetoric of Motives*. Berkeley and Los Angeles: University of California Press, 1969.

Butler, Martin. "The Condition of the Theatres in 1642." In *The Cambridge History of British Theatre, Vol. 1: Origins to 1660*, edited by Jane Milling and Peter Thomson, 439–57. Cambridge: Cambridge University Press, 2004.

Cable, Lana. *Carnal Rhetoric: Milton's Iconoclasm and the Poetics of Desire*. Durham and London: Duke University Press, 1995.

Campbell, Gordon. "The Mortalist Heresy in *Paradise Lost*." *Milton Quarterly* 13 (1979): 33–6.

Camporeale, Salvatore. *Christianity, Latinity, and Culture: Two Studies on Lorenzo Valla*. Edited by Patrick Baker and Christopher S. Celenza. Leiden: Brill, 2013.

Camporeale, Salvatore. "*Institutio Oratoria*, Lib. I, Cap. 6.3 e le variazioni su tema di Lorenzo Valla: sermo e interpretatio." *Rhetorica: A Journal of the History of Rhetoric* 13 (1995): 285–300.

Camporeale, Salvatore. *Lorenzo Valla: Umanesimo e teologia*. Florence: Nella sede dell'instituto, 1972.

Camporeale, Salvatore. *Lorenzo Valla: Umanesimo, riforma e controriforma: studi e testi*. Rome: Storia e letteratura, 2002.

Camporeale, Salvatore. "Renaissance Humanism and the Origins of Humanist Theology." In *Humanity and Divinity in Renaissance and Reformation: Essays in Honor of Charles Trinkaus*, edited by John W. O'Malley, 101–24. Leiden: Brill, 1993.

Camporeale, Salvatore. "Umanesimo e teologia tra '400 e '500." In *Problemi di storia della chiesa nei secoli XV–XVII*, 137–64. Naples: Edizioni Dehoniane, 1979.

Carey, John. "A Work in Praise of Terrorism? September 11 and *Samson Agonistes*." *Times Literary Supplement*, September 6, 2002.

Carruthers, Mary. *The Craft of Thought: Meditation, Rhetoric, and the Making of Images, 400–1200*. Cambridge: Cambridge University Press, 1998.

Carruthers, Mary. *The Experience of Beauty in the Middle Ages*. Oxford: Oxford University Press, 2013.

Cascardi, Anthony J. *Consequences of Enlightenment*. Cambridge: Cambridge University Press, 1999.

Cassirer, Ernst. "Giovanni Pico della Mirandola: A Study in the History of Renaissance Ideas (Part II)." *Journal of the History of Ideas* 3 (1942): 319–46.

Cave, Terence. *Recognitions: A Study in Poetics*. Oxford: Oxford University Press, 1998.

Cave, Terence. *The Cornucopian Text: Problems of Writing in the French Renaissance*. Oxford: Oxford University Press, 1979.

Cavell, Stanley. "Kierkegaard's 'On Authority and Revelation.'" In *Kierkegaard: A Collection of Critical Essays*, edited by Josiah Thompson. Garden City, NY: Anchor Books, 1972.

Caygill, Howard. *Art of Judgement*. Oxford: Blackwell, 1989.

Cicero, Marcus Tullius. *Ad Herennium*. Translated by Harry Caplan. Loeb Classical Library 403. Cambridge: Harvard University Press, 1954.

Cicero, Marcus Tullius. *De inventione*. Translated by H. M. Hubbell. Loeb Classical Library 386. Cambridge: Harvard University Press, 1979.

Cicero, Marcus Tullius. *De oratore*. Translated by E. W. Sutton and H. Rackham. Loeb Classical Library 348. Cambridge: Harvard University Press, 1949.

Clark, Donald Lemen. *John Milton at St. Paul's School*. New York: Columbia University Press, 1948.

Clark, Donald Lemen. "Milton's Rhetorical Exercises." *Quarterly Journal of Speech* 46 (1960): 297–301.

Coetzee, J. M. *Elizabeth Costello*. New York: Viking, 2003.

Coetzee, J. M. *The Master of St. Petersburg*. New York: Penguin, 1995.

Cohen, Walter. *A History of European Literature: The West and the World from Antiquity to the Present*. Oxford: Oxford University Press, 2017.

Coleridge, Samuel Taylor. *Biographia Literaria; or, Biographical Sketches of My Literary Life and Opinions*. Edited by George Watson. London: Dent, 1971.

Cooper, Anthony Ashley. *Characteristics of Men, Manners, Opinions, Times. 1711*. 3 vols. Indianapolis: Liberty Fund, 2001.

Copeland, Rita. "The History of Rhetoric and the Longue Durée: Ciceronian Myth and Its Medieval Afterlives." *The Journal of English and Germanic Philology* 106 (2007): 176–202.

Crignon, Philippe. "Representation and the Person of the State." *Hobbes Studies* 31 (2018): 48–74.

Culler, Jonathan. *Structuralist Poetics: Structuralism, Linguistics, and the Study of Literature*. Ithaca: Cornell University Press, 1975.

Culler, Jonathan. *The Literary in Theory*. Stanford: Stanford University Press, 2006.

Cummings, Brian. *The Literary Culture of the Reformation: Grammar and Grace*. Oxford: Oxford University Press, 2002.

Damrosch, Leopold. "Hobbes as Reformation Theologian: Implications of the Free-Will Controversy." *Journal of the History of Ideas* 40 (1979): 339–52.

Danto, Arthur C. *The Abuse of Beauty: Aesthetics and the Concept of Art*. Chicago: Open Court, 2003.

Danto, Arthur C. *The Philosophical Disenfranchisement of Art*. New York: Columbia University Press, 1986.

Danto, Arthur C. *The Transfiguration of the Commonplace: A Philosophy of Art*. Cambridge: Harvard University Press, 1981.

David, Claude. "Die Geschichte Abrahams. Zu Kafkas Auseinandersetzung mit Kierkegaard." In *Bild und Gedanke. Festschrift für Gerhart Baumann*, edited by Günter Schnitzler, 79–90. Munich: Fink, 1980.

Davis, Lennard. *Factual Fictions: The Origins of the English Novel*. New York: Columbia University Press, 1983.

de Man, Paul. *Aesthetic Ideology*. Edited by Andrzej Warminski. Minneapolis: University of Minnesota Press, 1996.

de Man, Paul. *Allegories of Reading*. New Haven: Yale University Press, 1979.

de Man, Paul. "Phenomenality and Materiality in Kant." In *The Textual Sublime: Deconstruction and Its Differences*, edited by Hugh J. Silverman and Gary E. Aylesworth, 87–108. Albany: State University of New York Press, 1990.

Derrida, Jacques. *Marges de la Philosophie*. Paris: Editions Minuit, 1972.

Derrida, Jacques. *Dissémination*. Paris: Seuil, 1972.

Dostoevsky, Fyodor. *Crime and Punishment*. Translated by Richard Pevear and Larissa Volokhonsky. New York: Knopf, 1992.

Dostoevsky, Fyodor. *The Brothers Karamazov*. Translated by Richard Pevear and Larissa Volokhonsky. New York Farrar, Strauss & Giroux, 1990.

Douglass, Robin. "The Body Politic 'is a fictitious body': Hobbes on Imagination and Fiction." *Hobbes Studies* 27 (2014): 126–47.
Durling, Robert M. *The Figure of the Poet in Renaissance Epic*. Cambridge: Harvard University Press, 1965.
Eagleton, Terry. *The Ideology of the Aesthetic*. Oxford: Blackwell, 1990.
Eden, Kathy. *Friends Hold All Things in Common: Tradition, Intellectual Property, and the Adages of Erasmus*. New Haven: Yale University Press, 2001.
Eden, Kathy. *Hermeneutics and the Rhetorical Tradition: Chapters in the Ancient Legacy and Its Humanist Reception*. New Haven: Yale University Press, 1997.
Eden, Kathy. *Poetic and Legal Fiction in the Aristotelian Tradition*. Princeton: Princeton University Press, 1986.
Edwards, Brian F. M. "Kafka and Kierkegaard: A Reassessment." *German Life and Letters* 20 (1967): 218–25.
Eilttä, Leena. "Art as Religious Commitment: Kafka's Debt to Kierkegaardian Ideas and Their Impact on His Late Stories." *German Life and Letters* 53 (2000): 499–510.
Eliot, T. S. "A Note on Poetry and Belief." In *The Complete Prose of T.S. Eliot: The Critical Edition: Literature, Politics, Belief, 1927–1929*, edited by Frances Dickey, Jennifer Formichelli, and Ronald Schuchard, 18–21. Baltimore: Johns Hopkins University Press, 2015.
Eliot, T. S. "Shakespeare and the Stoicism of Seneca." In *Selected Essays, 1917–32*, 107–20. New York: Harcourt, Brace, and Company, 1932.
Empson, William. *Milton's God*. London: Chatto and Windus, 1965.
Enterline, Lynn. *Shakespeare's Schoolroom: Rhetoric, Discipline, Emotion*. Philadelphia: University of Pennsylvania Press, 2011.
Evrigenis, Ioannis D. *Images of Anarchy: The Rhetoric and Science in Hobbes's State of Nature*. Cambridge: Cambridge University Press, 2014.
"faith, n. and int." *OED Online*. March 2019. Oxford University Press.
Ferguson, Margaret W. *Trials of Desire: Renaissance Defenses of Poetry*. New Haven and London: Yale University Press, 1983.
Ferry, Luc. *Homo Aestheticus: The Invention of Taste in the Democratic Age*. Translated by Robert de Loaiza. Chicago: University of Chicago Press, 1993.
Festa, Thomas. *The End of Learning: Milton and Education*. London: Routledge, 2006.
Fisch, Harold. *Jerusalem and Albion: The Hebraic Factor in Seventeenth-Century Literature*. London: Routledge & Kegan Paul, 1964.

Fish, Stanley. *How Milton Works*. Cambridge: Harvard University Press, 2001.

Fish, Stanley. *Self-Consuming Artifacts: The Experience of Seventeenth-Century Literature*. Berkeley and Los Angeles: University of California Press, 1972.

Fish, Stanley. *Surprised by Sin: The Reader in "Paradise Lost."* New York: St. Martin's Press, 1967.

Fleming, Sean. Forthcoming. "The Two Faces of Personhood: Hobbes, Corporate Agency, and the Personality of the State." *European Journal of Political Theory*.

Forrest, Ian. *Trustworthy Men: How Inequality and Faith Made the Medieval Church*. Princeton: Princeton University Press, 2018.

Fraenkel, Eduard. "Zur Geschichte des Wortes Fides." *Rheinisches Museum* 71 (1916): 187–99.

Freyburger, Gérard. *Fides: étude sémantique et religieuse depuis les origines jusqu'à l'époque Augustéenne*. 2nd ed. Paris: Société d'Édition Les Belles Lettres, 2009.

Funkenstein, Amos. *Theology and the Scientific Imagination: From the Middle Ages to the Seventeenth Century*. Princeton: Princeton University Press, 1986.

Gallagher, Catherine. *Nobody's Story: The Vanishing Acts of Women Writers in the Marketplace, 1670–1820*. Berkeley: University of California Press, 1994.

Gallagher, Catherine. "The Rise of Fictionality." In *The Novel. Volume 1: History, Geography, and Culture*, edited by Franco Moretti, 336–63. Princeton: Princeton University Press, 2006.

Galloway, Andrew. "Imagining the Literary in Medieval English." In *Imagining Medieval English: Language Structures and Theories, 500–1500*, edited by Tim William Machan, 210–38. Cambridge: Cambridge University Press, 2016.

Garsten, Bryan. *Saving Persuasion: A Defense of Rhetoric and Judgment*. Cambridge: Harvard University Press, 2009.

Gordon, Peter E. *Adorno and Existence*. Cambridge: Harvard University Press, 2016.

Grafton, Anthony, and Lisa Jardine. *From Humanism to the Humanities: Education and the Liberal Arts in Fifteenth- and Sixteenth-Century Europe*. Cambridge: Harvard University Press, 1986.

Green, Ronald M. "Deciphering *Fear and Trembling*'s Secret Message." *Religious Studies* 22 (1986): 95–111.

Green, Ronald M. "'Developing' *Fear and Trembling*." In *The Cambridge Companion to Kierkegaard*, edited by Alastair Hannay and Gordon D. Marino, 257–81. Cambridge: Cambridge University Press, 1998.

Green, Ronald M. "Kant: A Debt Both Obscure and Enormous." In *Kierkegaard and His Contemporaries, Tome 1: Philosophy*, edited by Jon Stewart, 179–210. Aldershot, England: Ashgate, 2007.

Green, Ronald M. *Kierkegaard and Kant: The Hidden Debt.* Albany: State University of New York Press, 1992.

Greene, Thomas M. *The Light in Troy: Imitation and Discovery in Renaissance Poetry.* New Haven: Yale University Press, 1982.

Gregory, Tobias. *From Many Gods to One: Divine Action in Renaissance Epic.* Chicago: University of Chicago Press, 2006.

Grossman, Marshall. "Poetry and Belief in *Paradise Regained, to which is added, Samson Agonistes*." *Studies in Philology* 110 (2013): 382–401.

Habermas, Jürgen. *The Philosophical Discourse of Modernity: Twelve Lectures.* Translated by Frederick G. Lawrence. Cambridge: MIT Press, 1987.

Hacking, Ian. *The Social Construction of What?* Cambridge: Harvard University Press, 1999.

Hagendahl, Harald. *Augustine and the Latin Classics.* 2 vols. Göteborg: Göteborg University Press, 1967.

Halpern, Richard. *Eclipse of Action: Tragedy and Political Economy.* Chicago: University of Chicago Press, 2017.

Halpern, Richard. *The Poetics of Primitive Accumulation: English Renaissance Culture and the Genealogy of Capital.* Ithaca: Cornell University Press, 1991.

Hannay, Alastair, and Gordon D. Marino, eds. *The Cambridge Companion to Kierkegaard.* Cambridge: Cambridge University Press, 1998.

Hanson, D. W. "The Meaning of Demonstration in Hobbes' Science." *History of Political Thought* 11 (1990): 587–626.

Haskin, Dayton. *Milton's Burden of Interpretation.* Philadelphia: University of Pennsylvania Press, 1994.

Hathaway, Baxter. *Marvels and Commonplace: Renaissance Literary Criticism.* New York: Random House, 1968.

Hegel, G. W. F. *On Christianity: Early Theological Writings.* Translated by T. M. Knox. Gloucester, Mass.: Peter Smith, 1970.

Hegel, G. W. F. *Philosophy of Right.* Translated by T. M. Knox. Oxford: Oxford University Press, 1967.

Hill, Christopher. *The Collected Essays of Christopher Hill.* 3 vols. Amherst, MA: University of Massachusetts Press, 1986.

Hobbes, Thomas. *A Briefe of the Art of Rhetorique*. In *The Rhetorics of Thomas Hobbes and Bernard Lamy*, edited by John T. Harwood. Carbondale: Southern Illinois University Press, 1986.

Hobbes, Thomas. *De Cive: The English Version*. Edited by Howard Warrender. Oxford: Clarendon Press, 1983.

Hobbes, Thomas. *Leviathan*. Edited by Richard Tuck. Revised Edition. Cambridge: Cambridge University Press, 1996.

Hobbes, Thomas. *The Elements of Law Natural and Politic. Part I: Human Nature; Part II: De Corpore Politico*. Edited by J. C. A. Gaskin. Oxford: Oxford University Press, 1994.

Hobbes, Thomas. *The English Works of Thomas Hobbes of Malmesbury*. Edited by Sir William Molesworth. 11 vols. London: Bohn, 1839.

Hoekstra, Kinch. "Hobbes's Thucydides." In *The Oxford Handbook of Hobbes*, edited by A. P. Martinich and Kinch Hoekstra, 547–74. Oxford: Oxford University Press, 2016.

Hoekstra, Kinch. "The End of Philosophy (The Case of Hobbes)." *Proceedings of the Aristotelian Society* 106 (2006): 23–60.

Hofmannsthal, Hugo von. *The Lord Chandos Letter and Other Writings*. Translated by Joel Rotenberg. New York: New York Review Books, 2005.

Hume, David. *Principal Writings on Religion: Including Dialogues Concerning Natural Religion and The Natural History of Religion*. Edited by J. C. A. Gaskin. Oxford: Oxford University Press, 2008.

Hutson, Lorna. *Circumstantial Shakespeare*. Oxford Wells Shakespeare Lectures. Oxford: Oxford University Press, 2015.

Hutson, Lorna. "Civility and Virility in Ben Jonson." *Representations* 78 (2002): 1–27.

Hutson, Lorna. *The Invention of Suspicion: Law and Mimesis in Shakespeare and Renaissance Drama*. Oxford: Oxford University Press, 2007.

Hutson, Lorna. *The Usurer's Daughter: Male Friendship and Fictions of Women in Sixteenth-Century England*. London and New York: Routledge, 1994.

Jakobson, Roman. *Selected Writings, Vol. 3: Poetry of Grammar and Grammar of Poetry*. The Hague: Mouton, 1981.

Jauss, Hans Robert. "Poiesis." Translated by Michael Shaw. *Critical Inquiry* 8 (1982): 591–608.

Johnson, Samuel. "Life of Milton." In *Milton, 1732–1801: The Critical Heritage, Vol. 2*, edited by John T. Shawcross, 290–310. London and Boston: Routledge, 1972.

Johnson, W. R. "Isocrates Flowering: The Rhetoric of Augustine." *Philosophy & Rhetoric* 9 (1976): 217–31.

Jonson, Ben. *The Complete Poems*. Edited by George Parfitt. London: Penguin, 1996.

Josipovici, Gabriel. "Kierkegaard and the Novel." In *Kierkegaard: A Critical Reader*, edited by Jonathan Rée and Jane Chamberlain, 114–28. Oxford: Blackwell, 1998.

Josipovici, Gabriel. *The Book of God: A Response to the Bible*. New Haven: Yale University Press, 1988.

Joughin, John J., and Simon Malpas, eds. *The New Aestheticism*. Manchester: Manchester University Press, 2003.

Kahn, Victoria. "Aesthetics as Critique: Tragedy and Trauerspiel in *Samson Agonistes*." In *Reading Renaissance Ethics*, edited by Marshall Grossman, 104–27. New York: Routledge, 2007.

Kahn, Victoria. "Hobbes and the Science of Metaphor." In *Scientific Statesmanship, Governance and the History of Political Philosophy*, edited by Kyriakos N. Demetriou and Antis Loizides, 85–100. New York and London: Routledge, 2015.

Kahn, Victoria. "Job's Complaint in *Paradise Regained*." *English Literary History* 76 (2009): 625–60.

Kahn, Victoria. *Machiavellian Rhetoric: From the Counter-Reformation to Milton*. Princeton: Princeton University Press, 1994.

Kahn, Victoria. *Rhetoric, Prudence, and Skepticism in the Renaissance*. Ithaca: Cornell University Press, 1985.

Kahn, Victoria. "The Passions and the Interests in Early Modern Europe: The Case of *Il Pastor fido*." In *Reading the Early Modern Passions*, edited by Gail Kern Paster, Katherine Rowe, and Mary Floyd-Wilson, 217–39. Philadelphia: University of Pennsylvania Press, 2004.

Kahn, Victoria. *Wayward Contracts: The Crisis of Political Obligation in England, 1640–1674*. Princeton: Princeton University Press, 2004.

Kant, Immanuel. *Critique of the Power of Judgment*. Translated by Paul Guyer and Eric Matthews. Cambridge: Cambridge University Press, 2001.

Kant, Immanuel. *Religion within the Limits of Reason Alone*. Translated by Theodore M. Greene and Hoyt H. Hudson. New York: Harper and Row, 1960.

Kastan, David Scott. *A Will to Believe: Shakespeare and Religion*. Oxford: Oxford University Press, 2014.

Kemp, Martin. "From 'Mimesis' to 'Fantasia': The Quattrocento Vocabulary of Creation, Inspiration and Genius in the Visual Arts." *Viator* 8 (1977): 347–98.

Kennedy, George A. *A New History of Classical Rhetoric*. Princeton: Princeton University Press, 1994.

Kennedy, George A. *Classical Rhetoric and Its Christian and Secular Traditions from Ancient to Modern Times*. Durham: University of North Carolina Press, 1980.

Kennedy, George A. *Greek Rhetoric under Christian Emperors*. Princeton: Princeton University Press, 1983.

Kierkegaard, Søren. *Concluding Unscientific Postscript*. Translated by David F. Swenson and Walter Lowrie. Princeton: Princeton University Press, 1968.

Kierkegaard, Søren. *Either/Or*. Translated by Walter Lowrie. 2 vols. Oxford: Oxford University Press, 1944.

Kierkegaard, Søren. *Fear and Trembling*. Edited and translated by Alastair Hannay. London: Penguin, 1986.

Kierkegaard, Søren. *Fear and Trembling; Repetition*. Edited and translated by Howard V. Hong and Edna H. Hong. Kierkegaard's Writings, VI. Princeton: Princeton University Press, 1983.

Kierkegaard, Søren. *The Concept of Irony: With Continual Reference to Socrates*. Edited and translated by Howard V. Hong and Edna H. Hong. Kierkegaard's Writings, II. Princeton: Princeton University Press, 1989.

Kierkegaard, Søren. *The Point of View for My Work as an Author and Related Writings*. Edited by Benjamin Nelson. Translated by Walter Lowrie. New York: Harper Torchbooks, 1962.

Kinneavy, James L. *Greek Rhetorical Origins of Christian Faith: An Inquiry*. New York: Oxford University Press, 1987.

Kirkconnell, Watson. *The Celestial Cycle: The Theme of Paradise Lost in World Literature with Translations of the Major Analogues*. Toronto: University of Toronto Press, 1952.

Knapp, Jeffrey. *Shakespeare's Tribe: Church, Nation, and Theater in Renaissance England*. Chicago: University of Chicago Press, 2002.

Knight, Kelvin. *Aristotelian Philosophy: Ethics and Politics from Aristotle to MacIntyre* Cambridge: Cambridge University Press, 2007.

Kristeller, Paul Oskar. *Renaissance Thought II: Papers on Humanism and the Arts*. New York: Harper & Row, 1961.

Lacoue-Labarthe, Philippe. "Diderot: Paradox and Mimesis." In *Typographies: Mimesis, Philosophy, and Politics*, edited by Christopher Fynsk, 248-66. Cambridge: Harvard University Press, 1989.

Lewalski, Barbara Kiefer. "Milton and Idolatry." *Studies in English Literature* 43 (2003): 213–32.

Lewalski, Barbara Kiefer. *Milton's Brief Epic: The Genre, Meaning, and Art of Paradise Regained*. Providence, R.I.: Brown University Press, 1966.

Lewalski, Barbara Kiefer. *Protestant Poetics and the Seventeenth-Century Religious Lyric*. Princeton: Princeton University Press, 1979.

Lienhard, Joseph T. "A Note on the Meaning of Pistis in Aristotle's Rhetoric." *The American Journal of Philology* 87 (1966): 446–54.

Loewenstein, David. *Milton and the Drama of History*. Cambridge: Cambridge University Press, 1990.

Loewenstein, David. *Representing Revolution in Milton and His Contemporaries: Religion, Politics, and Polemics in Radical Puritanism*. Cambridge: Cambridge University Press, 2001.

Long, Pamela O. *Artisan/Practitioners and the Rise of the New Sciences 1400–1600*. Corvallis, OR: Oregon State University Press, 2011.

Long, Pamela O. *Openness, Secrecy, Authorship: Technical Arts and the Culture of Knowledge from Antiquity to the Renaissance*. Baltimore: Johns Hopkins University Press, 2001.

Low, Anthony. "Milton, *Paradise Regained*, and Georgic." *PMLA* 98 (1983): 152–69.

Low, Anthony. *The Georgic Revolution*. Princeton: Princeton University Press, 1985.

Mackey, Louis. *Kierkegaard: A Kind of Poet*. Philadelphia: University of Pennsylvania Press, 1971.

Mackey, Louis. "Kierkegaard's Lyric of Faith: A Look at *Fear and Trembling*." *Rice Institute Pamphlet* 47 (1960): 30–47.

Marino, Adrian. *The Biography of "the Idea of Literature" from Antiquity to the Baroque*. Translated by Virgil Stanciu and Charles M. Carlton. SUNY Press, 1996.

Markell, Patricia. "Arendt's Work: On the Architecture of *The Human Condition*." *College Literature* 38 (2011): 15–44.

Marrou, Henri-Irénée. *Saint Augustin et la fin de la culture antique*. 4th ed. Paris: Brocard, 1958.

Martinich, A. P. "Authorization and Representation in Hobbes's Leviathan." In *The Oxford Handbook of Hobbes*, edited by A. P. Martinich and Kinch Hoekstra, 315–38. Oxford: Oxford University Press, 2016.

Martz, Louis L. "Paradise Regained: Georgic Form, Georgic Style." *Milton Studies* 42 (2003): 7–25.

Martz, Louis L. *The Paradise Within: Studies in Vaughan, Traherne, and Milton*. New Haven: Yale University Press, 1964.

Melberg, Arne. "Repetition (in the Kierkegaardian Sense of the Term)." *Diacritics* 20 (1990): 71–87.

Merrill, Reed. "'Infinite Absolute Negativity': Irony in Socrates, Kierkegaard and Kafka." *Comparative Literature Studies* 16 (1979): 222–36.

Milton, John. *Complete Poems and Major Prose*. Edited by Merritt Y. Hughes. Indianapolis: Bobbs-Merrill, 1984.

Milton, John. *De Doctrina Christiana*. Edited by John K. Hale and J. Donald Cullington. Vol. 8 (2 parts) in *The Complete Works of John Milton*, edited by Thomas N. Corns and Gordon Campbell. Oxford: Oxford University Press, 2012.

Milton, John. *Complete Prose Works of John Milton*, 8 vols. Edited by Don M. Wolfe. New Haven: Yale University Press, 1953–82.

Morgan, Teresa. *Roman Faith and Christian Faith: "Pistis" and "Fides" in the Early Roman Empire and Early Churches*. Oxford: Oxford University Press, 2015.

Muldrew, Craig. *The Economy of Obligation: The Culture of Credit and Early Modern Social Relations*. London: Palgrave Macmillan, 1998.

Nakazawa, Hideo. "Zu Kafkas und Brods Kierkegaard-Deutung." *Doitsu Bungaku* 79 (1987): 128–35.

Nederman, Cary J. "Men at Work: Poesis, Politics and Labor in Aristotle and Some Aristotelians." *Analyse & Kritik* 30 (2008): 17–31.

Nelson, William. *Fact or Fiction: The Dilemma of the Renaissance Storyteller*. Cambridge: Harvard University Press, 1973.

Nielsen, Henrik Skov. Forthcoming. "Free Indirect Discourse as Inventive Discourse."

Nightingale, Andrea Wilson. *Spectacles of Truth in Classical Greek Philosophy: Theoria in Its Cultural Context*. Cambridge: Cambridge University Press, 2004.

O'Neill, Onora. *Constructions of Reason: Explorations of Kant's Practical Philosophy*. Cambridge: Cambridge University Press, 1989.

Ong, Walter J. "Latin Language Study as a Renaissance Puberty Rite." *Studies in Philology* 56 (1959): 103–24.

Pallister, William. *Between Worlds: The Rhetorical Universe of "Paradise Lost."* Toronto: University of Toronto Press, 2008.

Panofsky, Erwin. *Artist, Scientist, Genius: Notes on the "Renaissance-Dämmerung."* New York: Metropolitan Museum of Art, 1953.

Pérez-Ramos, Antonio. *Francis Bacon's Idea of Science and the Maker's Knowledge Tradition*. Oxford: Clarendon Press, 1988.

Pettit, Philip. *Made with Words: Hobbes on Language, Mind, and Politics.* Princeton: Princeton University Press, 2008.

Pigman, G. W. "Versions of Imitation in the Renaissance." *Renaissance Quarterly* 33 (1980): 1–32.

Plato. *Timaeus, Critias, Cleitophon, Menexenus, Epistles.* Translated by R. G. Bury. Loeb Classical Library 234. Cambridge: Harvard University Press, 1975.

Porter, James I. "Old Testament Realism in the Writings of Erich Auerbach." In *Jews and the Ends of Theory*, edited by Shai Ginsburg, Martin Land, and Jonathan Boyarin, 187–224. New York: Fordham University Press, 2018.

Prendergast, Christopher. *The Order of Mimesis: Balzac, Stendhal, Nerval, Flaubert.* Cambridge: Cambridge University Press, 1986.

Quinn, Philip L. *Selves in Discord and Resolve: Kierkegaard's Moral-Religious Psychology from Either/Or to Sickness unto Death.* New York: Routledge, 1996.

Quint, David. *Inside Paradise Lost: Reading the Designs of Milton's Epic.* Princeton: Princeton University Press, 2014.

Quintilian. *Institutio oratoria.* Translated by H. E. Butler. 4 vols. Loeb Classical Library. Cambridge: Harvard University Press, 1979–86.

Radzinowicz, Mary Ann. *Toward "Samson Agonistes": The Growth of Milton's Mind.* Princeton: Princeton University Press, 1978.

Rancière, Jacques. *Disagreement: Politics and Philosophy.* Translated by Julie Rose. Minneapolis: University of Minnesota Press, 1999.

Rancière, Jacques. *The Politics of Aesthetics: The Distribution of the Sensible.* Translated by Gabriel Rockhill. New York: Continuum, 2004.

Raylor, Timothy. *Philosophy, Rhetoric, and Thomas Hobbes.* Oxford: Oxford University Press, 2018.

Ricoeur, Paul. "Mimesis and Representation." *Annals of Scholarship* 2 (1981): 15–32.

Rogers, John. "Milton's Circumcision." In *Milton and the Grounds of Contention*, edited by Mark R. Kelley, Michael Lieb, and John T. Shawcross, 188–213. Pittsburgh: Duquesne University Press, 2003.

Rorty, Richard. *Philosophy and Social Hope.* London: Penguin, 1999.

Rorty, Richard. "Philosophy as a Transitional Genre." In *Philosophy as Cultural Politics: Philosophical Papers*, Vol. 4, 89–104. Cambridge University Press, 2007.

Ross, Malcolm Mackenzie. *Poetry & Dogma: The Transfiguration of Eucharistic Symbols in Seventeenth Century English Poetry.* New York: Octagon Books, 1954.

Rossi, Paolo. *Philosophy, Technology, and the Arts in the Early Modern Era.* Edited by Benjamin Nelson. Translated by Salvator Attanasio. New York: Harper & Row, 1970.

Runciman, David. "What Kind of Person Is Hobbes's State? A Reply to Skinner." *Journal of Political Philosophy* 8 (2000): 268–78.

Sacks, David Harris. "The Promise and the Contract in Early Modern England: Slade's Case in Perspective." In *Rhetoric and Law in Early Modern Europe*, edited by Victoria Kahn and Lorna Hutson, 28–53. New Haven: Yale University Press, 2001.

Sanders, Mark, and Nancy Ruttenburg. "J. M. Coetzee and His Doubles." *Journal of Literary Studies* 25 (2009): 1–6.

Santayana, George. "The Absence of Religion in Shakespeare." In *Interpretations of Poetry and Religion*, 147–65. New York: Charles Scribner's Sons, 1900.

Saussy, Haun. "Exquisite Cadavers Stitched from Fresh Nightmares: Of Memes, Hives, and Selfish Genes." In *Comparative Literature in an Age of Globalization*, 3–42. Baltimore: Johns Hopkins University Press, 1995.

Scarry, Elaine. *The Body in Pain: The Making and Unmaking of the World.* New York, NY: Oxford University Press, 1987.

Schlegel, Friedrich. *Philosophical Fragments.* Translated by Peter Firchow. Minneapolis: University of Minnesota Press, 1991.

Schneewind, Jerome. *The Invention of Autonomy: A History of Modern Moral Philosophy.* Cambridge: Cambridge University Press, 1998.

Schoeck, R. J. "Rhetoric and Law in Sixteenth-Century England." *Studies in Philology* 50 (1953): 110–27.

Schrader, George. "Kant and Kierkegaard on Duty and Inclination." In *Kierkegaard: A Collection of Critical Essays*, edited by Josiah Thompson, 324–41. Garden City, NY: Anchor Books, 1972.

Schuhmann, Karl. "Skinner's Hobbes." *British Journal for the History of Philosophy* 6 (1998): 115–25.

Schwartz, Regina. "John Milton." In *The Oxford Encyclopedia of the Bible and the Arts*, edited by Timothy Beal, 2: 97–101. Oxford: Oxford University Press, 2015.

Shagan, Ethan. *The Birth of Modern Belief: Faith and Judgment from the Middle Ages to the Enlightenment.* Princeton: Princeton University Press, 2018.

Sheehan, Jonathan. "Thomas Hobbes, DD: Theology, Orthodoxy, and History." *The Journal of Modern History* 88 (2016): 249–74.

Sheppard, Richard. "Kafka, Kierkegaard and the K.'s: Theology, Psychology and Fiction." *Literature and Theology* 5 (1991): 277–96.

Shklovsky, Victor. "Art as Technique." In *Russian Formalist Criticism: Four Essays*, edited by Lee T. Lemon and Marion J. Reis, 3–24. Lincoln: University of Nebraska Press, 1965.

Shore, Daniel. *Milton and the Art of Rhetoric*. Cambridge: Cambridge University Press, 2012.

Shuger, Debora K. *Habits of Thought in the English Renaissance: Religion, Politics, and the Dominant Culture*. Berkeley: University of California Press, 1990.

Sidney, Philip. *A Defence of Poetry*. Edited by J. A. Van Dorsten. Oxford: Oxford University Press, 1973.

Silver, Victoria. "Hobbes on Rhetoric." In *The Cambridge Companion to Hobbes*, edited by Tom Sorell, 329–45. Cambridge: Cambridge University Press, 1996.

Silver, Victoria. *Imperfect Sense: The Predicament of Milton's Irony*. Princeton: Princeton University Press, 2001.

Simpson, James. *Under the Hammer: Iconoclasm in the Anglo-American Tradition*. Oxford: Oxford University Press, 2011.

Skinner, Quentin. "Hobbes and the Purely Artificial Person of the State." *Journal of Political Philosophy* 7 (1999): 1–29.

Skinner, Quentin. *Reason and Rhetoric in the Philosophy of Hobbes*. Cambridge: Cambridge University Press, 1996.

Sloane, Thomas O. *Donne, Milton, and the End of Humanist Rhetoric*. Berkeley: University of California Press, 1985.

Smith, Pamela H. *The Body of the Artisan: Art and Experience in the Scientific Revolution*. Chicago: University of Chicago Press, 2004.

Söderquist, K. Brian. "Kierkegaard's Contribution to the Danish Discussion of 'Irony.'" In *Kierkegaard and His Contemporaries The Culture of Golden Age Denmark*, edited by Jon Stewart, 78–105. Berlin: De Gruyter, 2003.

Sorell, Tom. "Hobbes's UnAristotelian Political Rhetoric." *Philosophy & Rhetoric* 23 (1990): 96–108.

Stolnitz, Jerome. "On the Origins of 'Aesthetic Disinterestedness'." *The Journal of Aesthetics and Art Criticism* 20 (1961): 131–43.

Strauss, Leo. *"Hobbes's Critique of Religion" and Related Writings*. Translated and edited by Gabriel Bartlett and Svetozar Minkov. Chicago: University of Chicago Press, 2011.

Summers, David. *The Judgment of Sense: Renaissance Naturalism and the Rise of Aesthetics*. Cambridge: Cambridge University Press, 1987.

Taminiaux, Jacques. "Poiesis and Praxis in Fundamental Ontology." *Research in Phenomenology* 17 (1987): 137–69.

Teskey, Gordon. "Literature." In *Cultural Reformations: Medieval and Renaissance in Literary History*, edited by Brian Cummings and James Simpson, 379–95. Oxford: Oxford University Press, 2010.

Tétard, Maurice. *Augustin et Cicéron*. 2 vols. Paris: Etudes Augustiniennes, 1958.

Tigerstedt, E. N. "The Poet as Creator: Origins of a Metaphor." *Comparative Literature Studies* 5 (1968): 455–88.

Tihanov, Galin. "The Politics of Estrangement: The Case of the Early Shklovsky." *Poetics Today* 26 (2005): 665–96.

Trimpi, Wesley. *Muses of One Mind: The Literary Analysis of Experience and Its Continuity*. Princeton: Princeton University Press, 1983.

Tynyanov, Yury. "The Literary Fact." In *Modern Genre Theory*, edited by David Duff, 29–49. New York: Longman Publishing Group, 2000.

Vaihinger, Hans. *The Philosophy of "As If"*. Translated by C. K. Ogden. New York: Barnes & Noble, 1968.

Vattimo, Gianni. "The Structure of Artistic Revolutions." In *The End of Modernity: Nihilism and Hermeneutics in Postmodern Culture*, translated by Jon R. Synder, 90–109. Cambridge, England: Polity Press, 1988.

Vieira, Mónica Brito. "Performative Imaginaries: Pitkin versus Hobbes on Political Representation." In *Reclaiming Representation: Contemporary Advances in the Theory of Political Representation*, edited by Mónica Brito Vieira, 25–49. New York: Routledge, 2017.

Vieira, Mónica Brito. *The Elements of Representation in Hobbes: Aesthetics, Theatre, Law, and Theology in the Construction of Hobbes's Theory of the State*. Leiden: Brill, 2009.

von Maltzahn, Nicholas. "The War in Heaven and the Miltonic Sublime." In *A Nation Transformed: England after the Restoration*, edited by Alan Houston and Steven Pincus, 154–79. Cambridge: Cambridge University Press, 2001.

Watkins, John W. N. *Hobbes's System of Ideas: A Study in the Political Significance of Philosophical Theories*. New York: Barnes and Noble, 1965.

Weinberg, Bernard. *A History of Literary Criticism in the Italian Renaissance*. 2 vols. University of Chicago Press, 1961.

Wellek, René. *Discriminations: Further Concepts of Criticism*. New Haven: Yale University Press, 1970.

Wellek, René, and Austin Warren. *Theory of Literature*. New York: Harcourt, Brace, and Company, 1942.

Wellek, René, and Stephen G. Nichols. "The Crisis of Comparative Literature." In *Concepts of Criticism*, 282–96. New Haven: Yale University Press, 1973.

Williams, Raymond. *Keywords: A Vocabulary of Culture and Society*. Revised ed. Oxford: Oxford University Press, 1985.

Wittreich, Joseph. *Interpreting "Samson Agonistes."* Princeton: Princeton University Press, 1986.

Wittreich, Joseph. *Shifting Contexts: Reinterpreting "Samson Agonistes"*. Pittsburgh: Duquesne University Press, 2002.

Index

For the benefit of digital users, indexed terms that span two pages (e.g., 52–53) may, on occasion, appear on only one of those pages.

Abizadeh, Arash 147n.51
Abraham and Isaac 105–8, 115–16
   Kant and Hegel on 167n.30
Abrams, M. H. 123n.4, 134nn.62–3
accommodation, doctrine of 67–8, 93–4
Adorno, Theodor W. 95–6, 165n.19, 171n.58
aesthetics 9, 56–9, 97–100, 156n.23,
   and ideology 99–100
   and religious experience 109
Adorno, Theodor
Alter, Robert 83
Altieri, Charles 9–10
Altman, Joel 21
Aristotle 3, 43
   Nicomachean Ethics 137n.79
   Physics 128n.24
   Poetics 11–15, 86–7, 104–5, 137n.79
   Renaissance reception of 22–4
   Rhetoric 14–15
Attridge, Derek 2–3, 9–10
Auerbach, Erich 13–14, 131n.44, 160n.47, 170n.55
Augustine, St. 17–19, 148n.55
   on *fides* 18–19
   on scriptural interpretation 68–9
autonomy 22–4, 47–8
   of invention 27, 41–2
   of literature 11, 83–4

Bacon, Francis 25, 118–20
Bakhtin, Mikhail 170n.52
Barnouw, Jeffrey 36–7, 56–7
belief, *see also* pistis
   and belief in 148n.55
   definitions of 3–4
   fides 16, 21, 27, 48–9, 129n.35, 130n.41; *see also* facere fidem
   fides quae creditur and *qua creditur*, 18–19
   fides distinguished from *pistis* 15–16, 130n.41

   and irony 108
   and maker's knowledge 27, 114–15
   private and public 51–4, 56
   and probable knowledge 3–4
   in the Reformation 28
   suspension of 54, 120–1
   as work of interpretation 79, 88–9
Benjamin, Walter 95–6
Bible, *see* scripture
Boyle, Marjorie O'Rourke 18
Brecht, Bertolt 95–6

Caravaggio, Michelangelo Merisi da 115–16
Carey, John 64
Carruthers, Mary 27
Cave, Terence 13–14, 129n.28
Cavell, Stanley 109
Caygill, Howard 58–9
Charles I, King of Great Britain and Ireland
   Eikon Basilike 65–7
Cicero 15–16, 145n.33, 149n.60
Coetzee, J. M.
   Elizabeth Costello 110–21
Coleridge, Samuel Taylor 1, 120–1
construction and constructionism 97–8, 134n.63; *see also* maker's knowledge
contract 43, 45–6, 49–50
   faith as 54–5, 61
Culler, Jonathan 124n.8, 125n.9
Cummings, Brian 76

Danto, Arthur 109–10, 135n.64, 161n.58
Davis, Lennard 111
de Man, Paul 7–8
Derrida, Jacques 127n.20
Dostoevsky, Fyodor 115–16

Eden, Kathy 21, 43, 127n.22, 129nn.31,34, 134n.63
Empson, William 69–70, 74–5

enthymeme, *see* proof (rhetoric)
epic (genre) 82, 144n.32
equity (law and rhetoric) 12, 43, 70–2, 77, 87–8, 127n.22
Evrigenis, Ioannis 142n.13, 144n.32, 145n.36, 149n.60

facere fidem 15–16, 21, 48–9, 53–4, 63, 143n.24
faith, *see also* belief
  analogy of faith 68
  historical versus saving 148n.55
  implicit 50, 65
Ferry, Luc 150n.69, 163n.14
fiction
  God as 48–9, 93–4
  Hobbes on 43, 47–8, 52–3
  and hypothesis 116–17
  and invention 90–1
  legal 43, 47
  political 56
  in the Renaissance 111–12
  religious 65
  Sidney on 90–1
fides, *see* belief
Fish, Stanley 64
Fleming, Sean 145–6n.43
Funkenstein, Amos 25–7

Gallagher, Catherine 111–12
Ghiberti, Lorenzo 25–6

Habermas, Jürgen 59
Haskin, Dayton 157n.31, 158n.36, 160n.50
Hobbes, Thomas
  A Briefe of the Art of Rhetorique 39–41, 149n.60
  De Cive 39–40, 62–3
  Elements of Law 49–50, 143nn.21, 25
  on faith 49–50, 53–5
  and geometry 37–9
  De Homine 38–9
  Leviathan
    figurative language in 45, 144n.30
    as literature 34–5, 59–61
    and *Samson Agonistes* 92
    suspension of belief in 54
  Preface to Thucydides 37–8, 144–5n.32, 145n.36
  prefiguration of aesthetics 56–9
  on representation and personation 47–8
  relation to rhetoric 35–41, 43
Hoekstra, Kinch 142n.14, 145n.36
Hofmannsthal, Hugo von 118–20
Homer 13–14, 115–17
humanism, *see* studia humanitatis
Hutson, Lorna 21–2, 127n.21
Hutton, James 13–14

imitation, *see also* mimesis
  in humanist pedagogy 20–1
invention (also *inventio*) 15–16, 20–2, 27, 40–2, 60, 90–1, 137n.76
  in *Paradise Regain'd* 79–80
irony 100, 103, 108–9, 165n.17

Jakobson, Roman 5–7, 109–10
Job, Book of 79–81
Johnson, Samuel 87–8, 93–4
Jonson, Ben 21–2, 29–30
Josipovici, Gabriel 118

Kafka, Franz 113–14
Kant, Immanuel 9–10, 25–6, 58, 97–100, 123n.7, 150n.69, 156n.23
  constructionism 97–8
  Critique of Judgment 98–100
  Critique of Pure Reason 97–8
  and Kierkegaard 100, 167n.30
Kennedy, George 17–19
Kierkegaard, Søren 100–5
  The Concept of Irony 165nn.16,19
  Concluding Unscientific Postscript 104
  Either/Or 166n.25
  Fear and Trembling 100–1, 105–8
  and Hegel 101, 167n.30
  and Kant 100–3
  The Point of View for My Work as an Author 104, 107, 110
  repetition (concept) 107–9
  Repetition 168n.36
  three spheres of existence 165n.17
Kinneavy, James 130n.41, 132nn.50–1

letters (*litterae humaniores*)
  and imaginative literature 19–20
Lewalski, Barbara 76
literariness 3–4
  and estrangement 120, 124n.8

Index

modern 4–11, 95–6, 109–10, 116–17
  of *Paradise Regain'd* and *Samson Agonistes* 91–3
  and social critique 95–6
  and pragmatism 60–1
  Reformation 28–32
  Renaissance 19–28
  secular 29–30
  and self-reflexivity 11, 60, 109–10
Lyotard, Jean-François 9

maker's knowledge 25–7, 114–15, 120, 150nn.68–9
  Hobbes and 37–41
  Kant and 97–8
  and religious belief 48–9
Mandeville, Bernard 30–1
Marvell, Andrew
  "On Paradise Lost" 62–3, 160n.52
Milton, John
  Art of Logic 154n.14
  and rhetoric 152n.1
  On Christian Doctrine 67–9, 88–9, 153n.5, 161n.56
  Of Education 154n.14
  on faith and belief 65, 93–4, 153n.5
  on interpretation 67–9, 77–89
  on *opera fidei* (works of faith) 68–9, 74
  Paradise Lost 62–3, 69–75
    figures of speech 71–2, 76, 155n.17
    as pastoral 82
  Paradise Regain'd 78–84
    and epic 82
    figurative language in 79
    style 91–2
  Samson Agonistes 78, 84–92
    style 91–2
mimesis 7, 11–12, 86–8, 109–10, 120, 127n.20
Morgan, Teresa 130n.41

Pallister, William 155n.17
Passion of Christ 18, 90, 159n.43
passions, the 11–12, 14, 16–18, 36–7, 45, 86–7
Peirce, Charles Sanders 60
Pérez-Ramos, Antonio 136n.73, 138n.80
Pettit, Philip 48–9

Pico della Mirandola, Giovanni 135n.66
pistis 11–12, 14–18, 127n.23, 130n.41; *see also* belief
Plato
  critique of rhetoric 11–12
  The Republic 3, 127n.23
  Timaeus 127n.23, 136n.70
poiesis 3–4, 43, 86–8
  and aesthetic self-fashioning 165n.16
  Aristotle on 12–14
  and divine creation 24, 42
  versus labor and action 12, 87, 137n.79
pragmatism (philosophy) 60–1
Prendergast, Christopher 13–14
probable knowledge 3–4, 11–12; *see also* proof (rhetoric)
proof (rhetoric) 14–16, 40–1; *see also* pistis
  enthymematic 14, 39

Quintilian 16–17, 146n.45, 149n.60
  on *argumentum* 43
  Renaissance reception 19

Rancière, Jacques 9
Raylor, Timothy 36–7, 39, 142n.17, 143n.20, 145n.36, 147n.49
Reformation, the
  and English literature 2–3, 28, 75–7
  and figurative language 76
  and scriptural interpretation 68–9
Rembrandt van Rijn 106*f*
rhetoric 8, 14–19
  and civic virtue 15
  definitions of 16, 149n.60
  and early Christianity 17–18, 132n.48
  forensic 21–2
  Hobbes and 35–41
  and maker's knowledge 40–1
  and the passions 16–17
  and poetics 11–19
  in Renaissance humanism 19
Ricoeur, Paul 109–10, 128n.24, 160n.48
Rorty, Richard 8–9, 60, 88–9, 96–7
Ross, Malcolm 75–6
Rossi, Paolo 25–6

Saussy, Haun 125n.9
Scarry, Elaine 123n.2
Schlegel, Friedrich 166n.25

Schneewind, Jerome 27
Schwartz, Regina 77
Scripture and scriptural
    interpretation 15–16, 52–3,
    57–8, 62, 67–9, 78–81, 88,
    148n.56, 153n.5
  Hobbes on 157n.33
  literary dimension of 2, 27, 76, 83
  and secular literature 88
secular, the 83–4, 88
self-fashioning 135n.66
Shaftesbury, Anthony Ashley Cooper,
    third Earl of 57–8
Shagan, Ethan 30–1, 151n.73
Shakespeare, William
  and belief 29–30
  Othello 21
Shklovsky, Victor 109–10, 123n.6,
    126n.11
Sidney, Philip 24–6, 28–9, 65–7,
    90–1

Silver, Victoria 142n.18, 158n.35
Skinner, Quentin 36–7, 141nn.7,10,
    145n.41, 147n.49
Strauss, Leo 58–9, 151n.73
studia humanitatis 19–20, 112–13

technē 15, 114–15, 154n.14
Teskey, Gordon 156n.23
Thucydides 37–8, 145n.36
Tigerstedt, E. N. 135n.66
tragedy 86–91

Valla, Lorenzo 132n.52
verisimilitude 3–4, 51, 129n.34
  production of 21–2
  Milton on 86–7
Vico, Giambattista 25
Virgil 82

Wellek, René 125n.9
  and Austin Warren 125n.10

The manufacturer's authorised representative in the EU for product safety is Oxford University Press España S.A. of el Parque Empresarial San Fernando de Henares, Avenida de Castilla, 2 – 28830 Madrid (www.oup.es/en or product.safety@oup.com). OUP España S.A. also acts as importer into Spain of products made by the manufacturer.

www.ingramcontent.com/pod-product-compliance
Lightning Source LLC
LaVergne TN
LVHW051911060526
838200LV00004B/85